SACRED
TRAVELS

275 PLACES TO

Find Joy, Seek Solace,
and Learn to Live
More Fully

MEERA LESTER

Aadamsmedia

AVON, MASSACHUSETTS

For my son, Joshua Solomon Lester,
and his sons, Mark Steven and Logan James.

Published by
Adams Media, a division of F+W Media, Inc.
57 Littlefield Street, Avon, MA 02322. U.S.A.
www.adamsmedia.com

ISBN 10: 1-4405-2489-0
ISBN 13: 978-1-4405-2489-9
eISBN 10: 1-4405-2545-5
eISBN 13: 978-1-4405-2545-2

Printed in the United States of America.

10 9 8 7 6 5 4 3 2 1

Library of Congress Cataloging-in-Publication Data
Lester, Meera.
Sacred travels / Meera Lester.
p. cm.
Includes index.
ISBN 978-1-4405-2489-9
1. Tourism—Religious aspects.
2. Sacred space. I. Title.
G156.5.R44L37 2011
910.4—dc22
2011010370

Scriptural passages from the Bible quoted in this book are taken from King James Holy Bible, Old and New Testaments; translated out of the original tongues: and with the former translations diligently compared and revised by His Majesty's special command. Appointed to be read in churches. Oxford University Press, Publication—no date. London; Oxford University Press, Publication—no date; Amen Corner, New York: 35 West 32nd Street.

This book is available at quantity discounts
for bulk purchases. For information, please
call 1-800-289-0963.

CONTENTS

ACKNOWLEDGMENTS

With utmost appreciation, I would like to thank my editor, Andrea Norville, for bringing me this project that connects so deeply with my heart and for holding the vision and demonstrating infinite patience, guidance, and skillful editing. I would also like to express my appreciation to everyone at Adams Media who worked so diligently to bring this project to fruition.

I also would like to thank Katerina Lorenzatos Makris for her valuable insights for this book and for accompanying me to Athens, her ancestral island of Kefalonia, Pátmos, and Turkey. And thanks to Carlos Carvajal for showing me churches in the Caribbean.

INTRODUCTION

*H*umans have long sought sacred places to express their faith, find meaning, gain guidance, receive healing, mourn a loss, and experience renewal. Such places are as varied as the people who visit them. Judeo-Christians, for example, might visit sacred sites in the Middle East, such as the Holy Sepulchre that covers the locations of Jesus's Crucifixion, entombment, and Resurrection and is currently watched over by clergy from the Greek Orthodox, Syrian, Ethiopian, Armenian Orthodox, Coptic, and Roman Catholic churches.

Followers of Buddha might yearn to circumambulate Mount Kailash or visit the holy sites the Buddha claimed as sacred. Muslims might find themselves drawn to the holy cities of Medina, Mecca, and Hebron. A pilgrimage to learn about the ancient mysteries of Machu Picchu in Peru, or the energy vortexes of Sedona, Arizona, or the sacred stones of Stonehenge in England might appeal more to New Age followers. Native Americans, Wiccans, and pagans might prefer to seek sacred spaces in nature, like Mount Shasta in Northern California or Crater Lake in the Cascade Mountains of Oregon.

Holy environments, which are often associated with mysterious energies or special powers, can serve as oases for an arid heart or lift a spiritually yearning soul closer to the Divine. In sacred places, you can perform penance for spiritual purification, engage in a rite of passage, light a devotional candle, venerate a saint, meditate or reflect on some symbolism or traditional practice, pay homage to your ancestors, or simply offer a heartfelt prayer.

This book is your guide to 275 sacred places throughout the world. These hallowed sites range from hidden grottoes, natural springs, red-colored cliffs, and ancient stone circles to vaulted-ceilinged cathedrals, massive megaliths, stone pyramids, intricately carved temples, and totems. There are even entire towns, mountain ranges, seemingly endless rivers, and ancient forests and Iron Age ring forts that are considered sacred to followers of certain religious traditions.

Although we have worked diligently to provide accurate travel information, such information is subject to change. Please note that some sites are located in countries that are undergoing or have experienced civil unrest and political turmoil and may be problematic for tourists. Visit the U.S. Department of State's site for international travel information and a list of specific countries with travel warnings or advisories at *http://travel .state.gov/*. In addition, some historical data are subject to change as new evidence and research become available, and some of the religious and spiritual information is subject to change as well as to interpretation. The scriptural passages and religious/spiritual doctrines quoted and referenced in this book may have been taken from various versions of those sacred texts and oral annals. All of the sources we explored in compiling this book indisputably confirm, however, that these 275 places are among the most fascinating and sacred sites in the world today.

Explore your spirituality. Visit one or more of the many sacred sites in the world to pay respect, meditate, reflect, perform a ritual, or follow the ancient cycle of prayer—that is, praise, worship, and listen. Then let inspiration guide you into action. Repeat the cycle, inspired by the sanctity of the holy places you visit.

CHAPTER 1

LOVE, COMPASSION, DEVOTION

A love for humanity came over me, and watered and fertilized the fields of my inner world, which had been lying fallow, and this love of humanity vented itself in a vast compassion.

—Georg Brandes (1842–1927),
Danish critic and scholar

1. Shrine of Rumi

KONYA, TURKEY

This is love: to fly toward a secret sky, to cause a hundred veils to fall each moment.
First to let go of life. Finally, to take a step without feet.
—Jalal al-Din Rumi (1207–1273), Persian poet and mystic

The Sufi poet Rumi was so absorbed with his love for the Divine that he danced through the streets of medieval Konya, praying and whirling in ecstasy. Today, in the heart of this conservative city located three hours (by car) south of Ankara, the turquoise dome of Rumi's mausoleum rises rapturously toward the heavens and its ornate interior pulsates with ethereal beauty while, over the city's din, the muezzin calls out *adhān* (call to prayer).

Whether you yearn to deepen your love for the Divine or to see Rumi's resting place, the Green Dome, now known as the Mevlâna Museum, is a sight to behold. The mausoleum's towering walls, adorned with enameled reliefs and Islamic script, encircle the gold-draped tomb of *Mevlâna* (Our Guide), as Rumi is called by the Whirling Dervish sect he inspired. An adjoining room displays ancient manuscripts, prayer beads, musical instruments, and other artifacts.

Soothe Your Spirit

Read Rumi's poetry and reflect on the twirling meditation that Rumi practiced to empty himself of ego in order to dwell on thoughts of the Divine. Feel your footsteps grow lighter as devotional love fills your heart.

A Deeper Look

Thousands of Muslims and non-Muslims visit the Green Dome annually, many on December 17, the anniversary of Rumi's death—his "wedding night with God." Islam followers place their foreheads on and kiss the silver step of Rumi's shrine.

2. Santiago de Compostela Cathedral (Shrine of Saint James)

SPAIN

. . . The Lord is full of compassion and mercy.
—Bible, James 5:11

fter the bones of the apostle James, one of three to witness Jesus's Transfiguration, were discovered in northwestern Spain, a chapel was built to safeguard the relics. Centuries later, Santiago de Compostela Cathedral was built on the site. This magnificent basilica, constructed in the style of the Latin cross, features soaring vaulted arches and a central window through which holy light seems to bathe visitors.

Catch a bus or taxi from either of two international airports, but get an early start as throngs of pilgrims soon fill this World Heritage Site. When entering through the cathedral's carved Pórtico de la Gloria, notice the carving of James on the central pillar; a groove has been worn in the stone where pilgrims have been touching it in prayer since the twelfth century.

Soothe Your Spirit

Place your fingers in the grooves of the Tree of Jesse on the central pillar topped with a statue of Saint James seated. Pray that your heart might be opened to Saint James's messages of love.

A Deeper Look

Santiago de Compostela, the third holiest city in Christendom (after Jerusalem and Rome), hosts a massive celebration each year on July 25, the feast day of James, Spain's patron saint.

3. Saint Peter's Basilica
(Blessed Sacrament Chapel)

ROME, ITALY

Darkness can only be scattered by light, hatred can only be conquered by love.
—Pope John Paul II (1920–2005)

When the late Pope John Paul II unexpectedly visited Saint Peter's Basilica—the world's largest church of Christian faith—he purportedly lamented to attendants that it had become more a museum than a church as there was no place reserved for prayers. The Holy Father apparently thought the basilica's Blessed Sacrament Chapel fit the bill, because he said Mass there and now signage states that the sanctuary is reserved exclusively for prayer.

The immense chapel features lustrous marble floors, gold-patterned walls, and glorious sacred art. Perhaps the most precious piece is the gilded bronze tabernacle by Bernini, in front of which the Blessed Sacrament is displayed for the "continuous adoration of the faithful." If you seek peaceful haven in a place where divine art calls the heart to prayer, come to the Blessed Sacrament Chapel. To avoid the crowds, rise early and catch a taxi or take the metro, especially if you want to attend the chapel's 8:30 A.M. Mass.

Soothe Your Spirit
Pray for inspiration about how to express greater selfless love as you reflect upon the meaning of the Blessed Sacrament (the body of Christ sacrificed for the sake of the world).

A Deeper Look
The Eucharist is often given in the Blessed Sacrament Chapel, which has been called the "heart and soul" of Saint Peter's Basilica and the most mystical of its eleven chapels.

4. Radhavallabh Temple

VRINDAVAN, UTTAR PRADESH, INDIA

I came for love-devotion; / seeing the world, I wept.
—Mirabai (1498–1596), Indian *bhakti* poetess/saint

*I*ncense wafts through the Radhavallabh Temple, where Hindu priests perform eight daily services honoring the flute-playing Lord Krishna and his eternal consort, Radha. Here, too, devotees of *bhakti* (loving devotion to the Divine as the means to salvation) offer prayers and brightly colored flowers at the altar of the god and goddess.

If you wish to intensify your spiritual love and devotion, go on a pilgrimage to the temple. Travel from Delhi to Vrindavan—childhood playground of Krishna and current home to hundreds of temples—by car, bus, or rail. Leave your shoes outside the door, and offer flowers or fruit before beginning your prayers and meditation.

Soothe Your Spirit

Tune in to the holy vibration of Lord Krishna, believed to be ever-present in the temple. If you hear the sound of Krishna's flute, it is a sign that your heart is open and the grace of the Lord is flowing through you.

A Deeper Look

Many Hindus live out their last years in Vrindavan on the belief that those who die there attain final transcendence in union with their Lord. The city acquired the moniker "City of Widows" because of the many widows who seek refuge there, including the legendary *bhakti* poet, saint, and widow Mirabai, who journeyed to Vrindavan ca. 1538 and composed hundreds of poems and songs of love for Krishna.

5. Basilique Sainte-Marie-Madeleine (Basilica Church of Saint Mary Magdalene)

VÉZELAY, FRANCE

I alone love the unseen in you. (Jesus talking to Mary Magdalene in Kahlil Gibran's *Jesus, the Son of Man*)
—Kahlil Gibran (1883–1931), Lebanese-born American artist, poet, and writer

When Saint Bernard of Clairvaux delivered his powerful sermon advocating the Second Crusade, he chose to speak at the Benedictine abbey now known as the Basilica Church of Saint Mary Magdalene. The Dominican church, a stunning example of French Burgundian Romanesque architecture, has been a favorite pilgrimage site since the Middle Ages.

If you want to show or be shown more compassion or to deepen your devotion to the Divine, visit the basilica to venerate Saint Mary Magdalene, whose name is often invoked by modern Christian women as an example of unconditional Divine love and unwavering devotion to Christ.

Soothe Your Spirit
Light a candle, and as you pray for the seeds of love and compassion to germinate and grow in your heart, feel the spirit of Mary Magdalene fill you with holy love.

A Deeper Look
The basilica's clerestory windows pierce the upper walls above the pews and are oriented so that at noon on the summer solstice the sunlight enters through the panes and illuminates precise locations, suggesting that the effect was intentional. The nave of the church is one of the longest in France—a few yards less than Notre Dame Cathedral in Paris.

6. Govind Devji Temple

JAIPUR, RAJASTHAN, INDIA

While God waits for his temple to be built of love, / men bring stones.
—Rabindranath Tagore (1861–1941), Indian writer and Nobel Laureate

At night, the light illuminating the graceful symmetry of the Govind Devji Temple, dedicated to the eternal lover Lord Krishna (affectionately called *Govind*), lends an air of shimmering otherworldliness to the shrine. Ringed by the craggy Aravalli Mountains, the City Palace complex in which the temple and surrounding Jai Niwas Gardens are situated was designed so the king could view the temple's sanctum from his private residence.

It is easy to get to Govind Devji Temple using local buses, taxis, or rickshaws. While the exterior is enchanting, inside the temple the fragrance of incense, thrum of Hindi chants, and voices lifted in sacred song will draw you inward, deepening your love for the Divine.

Soothe Your Spirit

Visit the temple at night, when the exterior façade is illuminated and awaiting devotees release a collective cry of exaltation as the doors open for evening worship. Open your heart to sacred love as you gaze upon the statue of Krishna when it is revealed for *darshan* (the beholding of a deity in image form) or during *aarti* (the ceremonial clockwise waving of sacred light, a ghee, or purified butter, lamp).

A Deeper Look

Located in the bustling metropolis of Jaipur—known as India's "Pink City" with nine districts symbolizing the sacred divisions of the universe—the Govind Devji Temple and Jai Niwas Gardens are popular destinations for tourists and the thousands of devotees of Krishna who visit each year.

7. The Western (Wailing) Wall

JERUSALEM, ISRAEL

He who has not seen the Temple of Herod, has never seen a beautiful building.
—Babylonian Talmud, Baba Batra, 4a; Shemot Rabba 36:1

Since the destruction of the Second Temple of Herod in A.D. 70, Jews have been coming to the only remnant of the temple—a section of stone wall that surrounded the complex—to lament and pray. The Western Wall, popularly known as the Wailing Wall, is the holiest Judaic site in the world, attracting more than eight million Jews and non-Jews annually. Today, the wall looks like God's message board, with notes containing prayers stuffed into the cracks.

If you wish to release your pain to God and open your heart to Divine love and compassion, visit Jerusalem to pray and reflect before the Wailing Wall. Go to the section designated for your gender (women and men pray in separate areas, according to Jewish Orthodox practice), and dress appropriately. Near the entrance, you can find head coverings for men and shawls and skirt coverings for women.

Soothe Your Spirit

Write your prayer on a slip of paper and tuck it into the sacred wall or take it home in a beautiful piece of Middle Eastern pottery that you designate as a prayer receptacle.

A Deeper Look

The site of the Western Wall has been sacred since the first Judaic temple of Jerusalem was built there five thousand years ago. Jews believe that God resides in the Western Wall and that praying there gives the supplicant the strongest earthly connection with the Divine.

8. Byodo-In Temple

OAHU, HAWAII, UNITED STATES

The essence of love and compassion is understanding.
—Thich Nhat Hanh (1926–), exiled Vietnamese Buddhist monk, scholar, poet, and peace activist

A stroll through the beautiful grounds of the Byodo-In Temple awakens the senses and inspires devotion. The lush tropical Japanese-style garden, the shimmering koi pond, and the three-ton brass peace bell are all sacred accouterments of the Buddhist temple that sits in the shadow of the vapor-enshrouded, jade-colored mountains. Inside the timeless temple, the nine-foot Lotus Buddha reposes in sublime bliss, seemingly absorbed yet ever-present for the whispered prayers of the faithful.

Whether you seek an oasis of peace and love or just need to tune out the world for a while, the Lotus Buddha of Byodo-In awaits. There is a small fee to enter the temple grounds, but getting there from downtown Honolulu is easy by bus (an hour and a half trip) or by rental car.

Remove your shoes before entering the temple and refrain from talking or taking flash pictures. For the best photos of the temple's exterior and garden, arrive in early morning when the sun is behind you.

Soothe Your Spirit
Light some incense, quiet your mind, and meditate on loving kindness, the practice of unconditional love for self, others, and the Divine.

A Deeper Look
Built in 1968 to honor Hawaii's first immigrant settlers, Byodo-In replicates a 950-year-old Buddhist temple in Kyoto, Japan. This nondenominational temple welcomes all people to worship, meditate, or simply enjoy the serene beauty of this sacred place.

9. Dakshineswar Kali Temple

DAKSHINESWAR, INDIA

Install my statue in a beautiful temple on the banks of the Ganges River and arrange for my worship there. Then I shall manifest myself in the image and accept worship at that place.
—Maha Kali as spoken in a dream to Rani Rashmoni (1793–1861), Indian philanthropist and founder of Dakshineswar Kali Temple

After taking charge of a temple dedicated to Maha Kali in 1856, the young Hindu priest Ramakrishna Paramahansa became so absorbed with love for Mother Kali that he would plunge deeply into ecstatic devotion and lose consciousness. This happened so often that he was relieved of his priestly duties but continued to live in the temple complex. The three-story Kali Temple, with its nine spires, is built in traditional Bengali style and surrounded by an enormous courtyard housing other smaller temples. The temple seems to rise from the nearby sacred Ganges as if it were a lotus with petals (instead of turrets) turned upward toward heaven.

If you would like to see where Ramakrishna lived, absorbed in ecstatic love for Divine Mother, visit Dakshineswar Kali Temple—preferably during the dry season (September to May). During holidays such as Diwali in October, the complex is packed with pilgrims. Travel from Calcutta by rental car, taxi, or local bus or rail service.

Soothe Your Spirit
Purchase a red flower to offer inside the temple, since red is Kali's favorite color. Then pray for blessings of love from the Mother of Infinite Love.

A Deeper Look
In addition to the Kali temple, the compound features twelve shrines to Shiva (Kali's companion) and a temple venerating Lord Krishna.

10. Chapel of the Holy Cross

SEDONA, ARIZONA, USA

That the church may come to life in the souls of men and be a living reality
—herein lies the whole message of this chapel.
—Marguerite Brunswig Staude (1899–1988), artist who designed and bequeathed
the Chapel of the Holy Cross

*L*ooking like a modern cross rising out of an ancient mesa, the Chapel of the Holy Cross is stunning in its simple but brilliant design, by Marguerite Brunswig Staude, a student of master architect/ designer Frank Lloyd Wright. A massive wall of glass—superimposed with a pale rose-colored cross stretching the full width of the chapel and thrusting 200 feet upward from the stone foundation to the roof—affords spectacular views of God's creation for miles around.

The chapel, built in 1956, sits on Coconino Forest land near the New Age mecca of Sedona, where many believe four energy vortexes exist, including one at the site of the Chapel of the Holy Cross. Visit this unique Roman Catholic chapel, which welcomes people of all faiths to infuse their souls with God's pure love.

Soothe Your Spirit
Let your prayer of love flow from your heart and across the breathtaking Verde Valley with its towering red-rock formations jutting into the azure sky.

A Deeper Look
Staude chose the chapel's site in part because of a red-rock formation visible to the east that looks like the Madonna and Child surrounded by rocks that are praying nuns to some visitors and suggestive of the three Wise Men to others.

11. Temples at Khajuraho

KHAJURAHO, MADHYA PRADESH, INDIA

The Plain is endless space expressed; / Vast is the sky above, / I only feel, against your breast, / Infinities of love.
—Laurence Hope (1865–1904), "Khan Zada's Song on the Hillside"

Central India's Chandela kings (the ninth to the twelfth centuries) built this compound of sacred temples in a forested area of Khajuraho. A few temples venerate Jain deities, but the majority honor Hindu deities—among them the gods Brahma, Vishnu, and Shiva and the goddess Devi Jagadambi. The stone shrines are richly embellished with carvings, many of them erotic scenes symbolizing the Divine male and female principles, a holy tribute to love and life.

Come to this spectacular World Heritage Site if you desire to deepen your Divine love and to balance your worldly life with your inner spiritual life. Take a flight from Delhi, Agra, or Jaipur to Khajuraho's airport, or travel by train through the scenic Vindhya Range to Jhansi or Satna (the nearest stations) and then take a bus or cab to the temple complex.

Soothe Your Spirit
Stroll through the temples, being fully present to thoughts and feelings evoked by the sacred images. Meditate and pray, inviting love and compassion into your soul.

A Deeper Look
The Temples at Khajuraho—built from yellow, pink, and buff sandstone between A.D. 950 and 1050—represent the highest level of achievement in medieval Indian architecture. About twenty of the eighty-five temples remain extant.

12. Yueh Hai Ching Temple (Temple of Love)

SINGAPORE

Kindness in giving creates love.

—Lao Tzu (600–531 B.C.), Chinese philosopher and father of Taoism

The Yueh Hai Ching Temple, unmistakable for its gabled roof and red entrance gate adorned with lanterns, was built in the 1820s, making it one of the city's oldest Taoist temples. Since its inception, sailors and traders have been praying at the shrine for safe passage and abundance. However, lovers also pray before the temple's statue of Yue Lao, the bearded elder matchmaker known as "The Man under the Moon" in Chinese mythology. His Divine power binds together the hearts of lovers with the red thread of marriage, ensuring the couple's happiness and positive relationships with family and friends.

If you appreciate the Taoist principles of balance or would like to ask for Yue Lao's blessings on you and your beloved, visit the Yueh Hai Ching Temple in Singapore. It is open from 6:00 A.M. to 6:00 P.M. daily. You can reach the temple, in the heart of the business district, by metro train, taxi, or rental car.

Soothe Your Spirit

Purchase a red string in the temple, light incense, place the string on Yue Lao, and pray for your heart's desire, for love and happiness, or for worldly/spiritual balance.

A Deeper Look

Yueh Hai Ching has two halls: one venerating Tian Hou (Heavenly Mother and goddess of the sea), the other Xuan Tian Shang Di (Heavenly Father). Coils of incense hang from red string at the entrance, symbolizing mortal marriage.

13. Temple of Aphrodite

GEYRE, TURKEY

One word frees us of all the weight and pain of life: that word is love.
—Sophocles (496–406 B.C.), Greek playwright and priest

*I*n the Aegean region of Turkey, about an hour and a half from the thermal springs of Pamukkale, sit the sprawling ruins of the ancient city of Aphrodisias, with a temple honoring Aphrodite, goddess of love, at its center. A marble statue of the goddess, recovered from the site, is now displayed in an outstanding museum there. Aphrodite appears in a long garment whose folds contain carved reliefs of the Three Graces with Aphrodite, three cupids with Aphrodite, and the sun god and moon goddess.

If meditating at a temple dating back centuries before Christ and honoring the goddess of love might help you to reconnect with Divine love, visit Aphrodite's Temple. Take a guided tour (the easiest route), or travel by bus or car from Denizli toward Nazilli on to Karacasu and Geyre. See the following website for more information: *www.turkeytravelplanner.com/go/Aegean/aphrodisias/trans.html.*

Soothe Your Spirit

Rub rose oil (the rose was believed sacred to Aphrodite) into the palm of your right hand, place your hand over your heart, and meditate on God's everlasting love or on your romantic love.

A Deeper Look

Considered a sacred site for six thousand years, Aphrodisias was founded in the third century B.C. and abandoned in the thirteenth century. The Temple of Aphrodite was converted into a Catholic basilica during the Byzantine era and destroyed in the twelfth century.

14. Convent of San Antonio de Padua (Saint Anthony of Padua)

IZAMAL, YUCATÁN, MEXICO

He prays best who does not know he is praying.
—Saint Anthony of Padua (1195–1231)

*T*his convent and cathedral dedicated to Saint Anthony of Padua (Lisbon), revered for his fierce love of God, sits atop the ruins of Pap-Hol Chac, a Mayan pyramid honoring Chac (god of rain). The convent's foundation is made of stones taken from the pyramid, toppled by conquistadors around 1549. The former monastery, built in a traditional fortress-like Franciscan style, features yellow stucco walls (replicated in many colonial buildings throughout town), sixteenth-century frescoes, and a statue of the Virgin of the Immaculate Conception, the patron saint of the Yucatán. A bronze statue of Pope John Paul II, who visited in 1993, keeps company in the courtyard with a Mayan sun stone.

If you believe Divine love can unite diverse ethnic and religious communities and would like to experience a place where that has manifested, visit Izamal. Located 42 miles east of Mérida, the capital of Yucatán, Izamal is accessible by bus or car.

Soothe Your Spirit

Attend Mass in the chapel or just contemplate as you stroll through the huge atrium (second only to Saint Peter's in Rome). Let the spiritual energy of this sanctuary ignite in your heart a fierce love of God.

A Deeper Look

Izamal was one of the oldest and most sacred Mayan cities. Today, the town is a harmonious blend of Mayan, colonial, and modern cultures and one of thirty-five *pueblos magicos* (magical villages) designated by Mexico's Ministry of Tourism.

15. Ellora Temple Caves

AURANGABAD, MAHARASHTRA, INDIA

Where love is, there God is also.
—Mohandas K. Gandhi (1869–1948), Indian political leader and father of India

*B*etween the sixth and tenth centuries A.D., Buddhist, Jain, and Hindu monks carved thirty-four sacred "caves" out of solid rock in west India's Charanandari Hills. Spectacular examples of Indian rock-cut architecture, these monasteries and temples are adorned with exquisite carvings, architectural details, sculptures, and paintings. The Buddhist caves (numbered 1–12) were created between 600 and 800, the Hindu caves (13–29) between 600 and 900, and the Jain caves (30–34) between 800 and 1000. This World Heritage Site represents a time and place when worshipers from three great religions coexisted peacefully and collaboratively.

If you believe that love and religious tolerance can bridge the differences dividing people, visit the Ellora Caves. The nearest domestic airport is in Chikalthana, about 7.5 miles from Aurangabad, which is also accessible by state bus and train from India's major cities. From Aurangabad, travel the 19 miles to Ellora by car, local bus, or auto rickshaw.

Soothe Your Spirit
After exploring the caves with a guide, offer a prayer of universal love to heal the world or of Divine love to fill your heart.

A Deeper Look
Although all of the temple caves are magnificent, the pièce de résistance is Kailasanatha (16), a massive, multistoried temple carved out of a single rock depicting Mt. Kailasa, the Himalayan home of Shiva, Hindu god of both sacred celibacy and spousal love.

16. Lake Orta

ORTA SAN GIULIO, PIEDMONT, ITALY

Orta, the Lord's watercolour, seems painted on silk, with the Sacro Monte towering above it . . . and facing it, the Isle of San Giulio, resembling Dante's airy purgatory, hesitant between water and the heavens.
—Piero Chiaro (1913–1986), Italian writer

Nestled between the Alps in Northern Italy, Lago d'Orta is the smallest but most peaceful and romantic of the region's glacial lakes, and Isola di San Giulio is the most beautiful and sacred of the region's islands. The magnificent Basilica di San Giulio rises from the center of the island. At the lake's edge is the picturesque town of Orta San Giulio, home to Santa Maria Assunta Church, consecrating the end of the plague in the fifteenth century, and Sacro Monte (Sacred Hills) d'Orta, featuring twenty chapels with life-size statues and frescoes devoted to Saint Francis of Assisi.

This enchanting place offers a serenely beautiful setting for a Catholic wedding or a spiritual retreat. From Milan, travel by rental car, taxi, or shuttle to Orta San Giulio.

Soothe Your Spirit
Take a ferry or water taxi to Isola di San Giulio and reflect on Divine love in the hilltop sanctuary housing the glass coffin of Saint Julius.

A Deeper Look
In the fourth century A.D., brothers Giulio and Giuliano erected ninety-nine chapels in the region. After driving an evil serpent off the island using only the sign of the cross, Giulio (patron saint of Novara) built his hundredth and last church on the site where the tenth-century Basilica di San Giulio stands today.

17. Prince Kuhio Park and Heiau (Temple)

PO'IPU, SOUTH KAUAI, HAWAIIAN ISLANDS, USA

Hawaii is not a state of mind, but a state of grace.
—Paul Theroux (1941–), American writer

The estate of Prince Jonah Kuhio Kalaniana'ole (1871–1922), last of the Hawaiian royalty and beloved for his tireless work on behalf of indigenous Hawaiians, is preserved in a three-acre park on the south shore of Kauai. Ruins of the royal home along with a fishpond and a *heiau* (temple) are preserved as a sacred site by the Hawaiian people in testament of their love for the "people's prince." The least populated and fourth largest of the Hawaiian Islands, Kauai is lush, peaceful, and mystical—and a popular honeymoon spot.

If you wish to infuse your heart with *aloha* or pray for compassion on behalf of indigenous people, visit Prince Kuhio Park. Go in March, when Hawaii celebrates the prince's birthday (March 26). Do not remove stones from the park; they are considered sacred.

Soothe Your Spirit
Offer flowers at the *heiau* and reflect on Divine love, brotherly love, or the love of your life as you walk around this holy site.

A Deeper Look
Native Hawaiian religious practices that include the hula, luaus, and leis were banned in the nineteenth century but today are protected by the Hawaiian constitution.

18. Swaminarayan Akshardham Temple

DELHI, INDIA

Still your mind in me, still yourself in me, and without a doubt you shall be united with me, Lord of Love, dwelling in your heart.
—Bhagavad Gita

The magnificent Akshardham Temple on the banks of the Yamuna River incorporates pink stone symbolizing *bhakti* (eternal love) with pure white marble symbolizing peace. Built in 2005, the world's largest Hindu temple is completely covered with ornate carvings and filled to the hilt with artwork. With its fantastic dioramas, IMAX theater, indoor boat ride, numerous exhibits, lighted musical fountain, 20,000 sculptures of statues and deities, and 60 acres of lawns and gardens, Swaminarayan Akshardham might best be described as a spiritual amusement park.

Visit this temple to seek knowledge about the great spiritual traditions of India, including *prema* (elevated love) and *bhakti* yoga (the path of love). Allow roughly four hours to see everything. Indira Gandhi International is the nearest airport; from there, taxis, metro trains, city buses, and auto rickshaws (bargain fare) make travel to the temple easy. No cameras, bags, backpacks, food, or water are allowed inside.

Soothe Your Spirit

Behold love for the Divine as you experience the temple and its offerings. Then during meditation, feel the depth and bliss of love in union with the Divine.

A Deeper Look

Thousands of volunteers and 7,000 sculptors worked to complete the temple in five years. With its sublime messages of spiritual love and national pride, Akshardham is a popular tourist attraction for Indians as well as spiritual seekers.

19. Wayfarers Chapel

RANCHO PALOS VERDES, CALIFORNIA, USA

The Divine of the Lord in heaven is love, for the reason that love is receptive of all things of heaven, such as peace, intelligence, wisdom and happiness.
—Emanuel Swedenborg (1688–1772), Swedish scientist, Christian mystic and theologian

The Wayfarers Chapel south of Los Angeles perches atop a hill overlooking the Pacific Ocean amid redwoods and roses. Designed by Lloyd Wright, eldest son of Frank Lloyd Wright, the chapel is a prime example of "organic architecture," whose key principle is that trees are architectural forms and the space within the forms is sacred. Erected in 1951 in the center of a redwood grove, the sanctuary sits on 3.5 landscaped acres featuring several gardens and a "hallelujah" tower that sailors have dubbed "God's Candle." This Swedenborgian church welcomes people of all faiths and has served as the setting for many Hollywood weddings, on screen and off.

If you and your beloved are ready to take your love to the next level, consider exchanging vows in this lovely glass-and-wood sanctuary where "nature and architecture unite to celebrate the presence of God."

Soothe Your Spirit
Take a drive with your beloved to the chapel and pray for spiritual guidance on where, when, and how to marry. Or sit in solitude before the stone altar framing the Pacific Ocean beyond, meditating on God's infinite love.

A Deeper Look
The Wayfarers Chapel is a memorial honoring Emanuel Swedenborg, the eighteenth-century scientist and theologian whose teachings inspired the Swedenborgian Church, a Christian denomination whose key tenets include that God is infinitely loving.

20. Basilica of Esquipulas (El Cristo Negro)

ESQUIPULAS, DEPARTMENT OF CHIQUIMULA, GUATEMALA

The distinctive mark of the Christian, today more than ever, must be love for the poor, the weak, the suffering.
—Pope John Paul II (1920–2005)

Perhaps the most revered pilgrimage site in Central America, the Basilica of Esquipulas enshrines the "Black Christ," a crucifix carved out of mahogany in 1594 and originally housed in a Mayan hut. Two miracles of healing, in the sixteenth and eighteenth centuries, are attributed to the icon. Today, however, it is revered as a "thanksgiving shrine" and a sacred symbol of hope and brotherly love. The faithful come a million strong each year—thousands for a midsummer processional (July 21–27), Easter Holy Week, and the Feast of El Cristo Negro (January 15)—to light candles and offer prayers of gratitude or for assistance for loved ones. After praying, worshipers walk backward out of the shrine so as not to turn their backs to Christ.

If you are inspired to give thanks for God's blessings or to offer prayers of compassion for the poor, visit Esquipulas. Drive or take a bus from Guatemala City, 80 miles west.

Soothe Your Spirit

Light a candle and pray for loved ones inside this simple church, where some say the energy of Divine love is palpable.

A Deeper Look

In 1996, Pope John Paul II made a pilgrimage to the basilica, where he prayed before El Cristo Negro for "millions of the poor in Latin America, crucified because of human injustice" and offered the Eucharist, which he described as "a moment of great spiritual intensity."

21. Glastonbury Abbey Ruins

GLASTONBURY, SOMERSET, ENGLAND

Yes, Love indeed is light from heaven; / A spark of that immortal fire with angels shared, by Allah given to lift from earth our low desire.
—Lord Byron (1788–1824), British Romantic poet

The spectacular ruins of this twelfth-century Norman monastery rest on a knoll in southern England that was considered sacred by pre-Christian pagan religions and that inspired medieval legends of Divine and romantic love. According to one legend, Joseph of Arimathea, a friend of the Holy Family, brought young Jesus to Somerset after Christ's Crucifixion and built a church on the site, where he also buried the Holy Grail. Another legend has it that King Arthur and Queen Guinevere are entombed there.

If your heart feels arid, visit Glastonbury ruins to inspire tender feelings of love. Open year-round, the site also features a museum, a large park, and a Saxon/Norman cemetery. The nearest airport is thirty minutes away in Bristol.

Soothe Your Spirit

Walk the ruins while contemplating the legends of romantic and Divine love associated with this ancient sacred site. As you breathe in the fragrance of roses, feel the cool wind on your face, and listen to the song of lovebirds in the trees; reconnect your senses to your heart.

A Deeper Look

Stones from what may have been the first Christian church in England (second century) form the base of the west end of the nave at Glastonbury Abbey (eleventh century). The abbey was once the second wealthiest monastery (after Westminster), before all of England's monastic churches succumbed to the Dissolution of the Monasteries enacted by King Henry VIII.

22. Iglesia y Convento de Santo Domingo (Church and Convent of Santo Domingo)

LIMA, PERU

Since love grows within you, so beauty grows.
—Saint Augustine (A.D. 396–430), bishop of Hippo

The Church of Santo Domingo in Lima (the "City of Kings") with its white façade and black wrought-iron fence is a stunning example of Spanish colonial architecture and dates to the late sixteenth century. This beautiful sanctuary enshrines a statue of the Virgin of the Rosary as well as two silver urns containing the relics of Saint Martin de Porres, the first black saint in the Americas, and Saint Rose, patron saint of Lima, venerated for her fervent love of the Holy Infant. After becoming a Dominican nun of the Third Order at age twenty, "Rosa" lived in a cottage in her parents' garden, where she said prayers and performed penance.

If you believe, as Saint Rose did, that working hard for God, for the poor, and for your loved ones is a path to spiritual development, come to the Church of Santo Domingo. From Jorge Chávez International Airport, you can easily get to the convent, located in Lima's city center, by taxi, automobile, or bus.

Soothe Your Spirit
Light a candle and vow that even as you work to support your family you will also do your inner spiritual work.

A Deeper Look
This old Dominican church, built roughly when Lima was established, has three naves, a large cupola, and Spanish-style patios (back gardens).

23. Kuan Yin Temple

HONOLULU, OAHU, HAWAII, UNITED STATES

In separateness lies the world's great misery, in compassion lies the world's true strength.
—Siddhartha Gautama, the Buddha (563–483 B.C.), father of Buddhism

*L*ocated in the heart of Honolulu's Chinatown, Kuan Yin Temple, painted a Chinese lacquer-box red with jade green roof tiles, is the oldest Buddhist temple in the Hawaiian Islands. An active center of worship, the interior is filled with the sweet smell of incense, fruit, and flowers—offerings to Guanshiyin, bodhisattva of *karunā* (compassion and mercy). Many images throughout the islands depict her holding a lotus, symbolizing purity of heart.

If you want to emulate the loving compassion of Kuan Yin, visit her temple in Honolulu, fifteen minutes from Waikiki. From the international airport on Oahu, rent a car or take a taxi to Chinatown. Dress modestly and show respect in this active place of worship. A temple monk may meet you to explain how to venerate this great being of a thousand hands (symbolizing her ability to help in myriad ways), whose name means "one who hears the cries of the world."

Soothe Your Spirit

Remove your shoes, light a stick of incense, and offer a prayer to open your heart to feelings of compassion and ever-greater love for humankind. Vow to lift the spirit of others.

A Deeper Look

At the altar, devotees offer fruit and flowers to demonstrate their hearts are open. Fruit symbolizes generosity and the goal of attaining enlightenment. Flowers, which are beautiful but impermanent, remind worshipers to value what is present in the moment. Those seeking wealth and luck burn symbolic paper money.

24. The Basilica Santa Maria sopra Minerva (Basilica of Saint Mary over Minerva)

ROME, ITALY

It is therefore true, indeed, that the soul unites herself with God by the affection of love.
—Saint Catherine of Siena (1347–1380)

This thirteenth-century church safeguards the tomb of the virgin Saint Catherine of Siena, whose love for Christ was so great that she believed she was mystically wedded to him. The basilica, named for Catherine but dedicated to the Virgin Mary, stands over the ruins of a Roman pagan temple of Isis (goddess of love) that was erroneously attributed to Minerva (goddess of wisdom). The church's baroque façade is plain, but the Gothic interior astonishes visitors with gleaming white marble floors, arched vaulting, brilliant frescoes, stained-glass windows, gold and lapis lazuli adornment, and priceless artwork—including *Christ the Redeemer*, a marble sculpture by Michelangelo.

If you long to deepen your Divine love or maternal love, visit this basilica venerating Saint Catherine and the Holy Mother. The church is one block from and directly behind the Pantheon. Stay in a nearby hotel and walk to the chapel, or travel by taxi, car, or bus from anywhere in Rome.

Soothe Your Spirit

Read *The Dialogue of the Seraphic Virgin Catherine of Siena* (which she dictated to her secretaries while in an ecstatic trance) and then visit her tomb to contemplate God's all-powerful love or to pray for your mother, children, or lover.

A Deeper Look

The Basilica Santa Maria sopra Minerva, the first (and only) Gothic church built in Rome, served as the Dominican Order's regional headquarters.

25. The Mildred B. Cooper Memorial Chapel

BELLA VISTA, ARKANSAS, USA

God writes the gospel not in the Bible alone, but [also] on trees and flowers and clouds and stars.
—Martin Luther (1483–1546), German priest and professor of theology

This nondenominational Christian church honoring Mildred B. Cooper, a deeply spiritual woman who loved nature, is tucked away in a wooded glen, where it invites quiet communion with the Divine under an intricately woven canopy of arches. Blending unobtrusively with the environment, and with floor-to-ceiling windows that allow natural light and shadow to dance in the interior, the chapel was designed by award-winning Arkansas architect Euine Fay Jones, a student of Frank Lloyd Wright.

If you love nature and are seeking a quiet setting for prayer and meditation or an intimate place to marry, this peaceful chapel with its stunning organic architecture can accommodate both. Visitors are welcome to enjoy the chapel daily between 9:00 A.M. and 5:00 P.M. (Reservations are required for weddings.)

Soothe Your Spirit

Take your time to appreciate the glory of God's earthly creation in this serene spiritual sanctuary in the woods. Offer a prayer for the love that flows from the Creator to all creatures.

A Deeper Look

The architect designed this chapel (as well as his other famed church in the woods, Thorncrown Chapel in Eureka Springs, Arkansas) to be a "light and airy structure that could engage the user with the spiritual qualities of nature" and to be used more for quiet contemplation than for communal worship.

26. Banteay Srei

ANGKOR WAT, SIEM REAP, CAMBODIA

Because thou are All-beauty and All-bliss, / My soul blind and enamoured yearns for Thee; . . .
—Sri Aurobindo (1872–1950), Indian yogi and poet

This tenth-century, red-sandstone temple in the massive Angkor Wat temple complex is consecrated to the Hindu deity Shiva, god of destruction. However, it is lovingly called Banteay Srei (Citadel of Women) in reference to the temple's abundance of delicately carved sacred feminine imagery, including Sita (goddess of purity and loyalty, an incarnation of Maha Lakshmi, goddess of prosperity), rosettes, lotuses, and *devatas* and *apsaras*, or dancing nymphs used by the gods to seduce ascetics, demons, and heroes to do their bidding.

If your spiritual practice could use the blessings of loyalty or sacred seduction, visit this temple of war and love, northeast of the main temple complex of Angkor Thom. A guided tour that includes transportation is the easiest way to visit Banteay Srei (also, Srey). Otherwise, from Phnom Penh take a bus, train, *tuk-tuk* (a three-wheel auto taxi), or boat (across Tonlé Sap Lake) to Siem Reap.

Soothe Your Soul

Steep your spirit in the subtle sacred energy described by some as Goddess energy in this ancient intricately carved temple. Issue a silent plea for the love, friendship, passion, or compassion you seek.

A Deeper Look

Surrounded on three sides by a moat, Banteay Srei has been praised as the precious "jewel of Khmer art" for the exquisite and amazingly well-preserved decorative carvings covering almost every inch of its red (the color of love/passion) sandstone walls.

27. Cathedral Rock

SEDONA, ARIZONA, USA

A pile of rocks ceases to be a rock when somebody contemplates it with the idea of a cathedral in mind.
—Antoine de Saint-Exupéry (1900–1944), French author

This butte of towering red-rock formations juts into the azure desert sky and stands upon one of the strongest energy vortexes on Earth, making it a favorite destination for New Age devotees. But the site has always been sacred to the Yavapai (Native Americans) who have occupied Sedona (*Wipik*) for centuries. According to legend, a couple who were deeply in love but arguing bitterly drew the attention of the Great Spirit, who chastised them for failing to appreciate the beauty of their union and the natural world around them. As a reminder to respect each other's views, he turned them into back-to-back pillars of stone—known as The Lovers, a smaller formation between the two large spires of Cathedral Rock.

Whether your path of spirituality resonates with New Age beliefs or you would like to venerate the holiness of nature with a meditation on love, visit Cathedral Rock, 110 miles from Phoenix.

Soothe Your Spirit
Hike the steep trail to one of the saddles (viewing points) with your lover or a beloved friend. Meditate on opening your *chakras* (energy centers in your ethereal body) to receive Divine love and to transmit love back into the universe.

A Deeper Look
The energy of the vortex is thought to flow upward, which is believed to help connect with the Divine.

CHAPTER 2

HEALTH, HEALING, WHOLENESS

The secret of health for both mind and body is not to mourn for the past, not to worry about the future . . . but to live in the present moment wisely and earnestly.

—*Siddhartha Gautama, the Buddha*
(563–483 B.C.), father of Buddhism

28. Mount Diablo

CLAYTON, CALIFORNIA, UNITED STATES

Climb the mountains and get their good tidings. Nature's peace will flow into you as sunshine flows into trees . . . cares will drop off like autumn leaves.
—John Muir (1838–1914), Scottish-born American naturalist

The Miwok and Ohlone tribes centered their creation myths on this isolated mountain towering 3,864 feet between the San Francisco Bay and California's Central Valley. For Wicca and New Age practitioners, this mountain heals and rejuvenates those who spend time exploring its wild woodlands, arid grasslands, and rocky ridgelines. If you seek spiritual, emotional, or physical healing or nourishment, take a day to experience this natural sanctuary. You can reach the mountain and 20,000-acre park by car from anywhere in the Bay Area. Park hours are 8:00 A.M. to sunset. Alcohol and fireworks are prohibited.

Soothe Your Spirit

Take your prayer rug and find a scenic spot where you can sit undisturbed. Invite a companion to join you (if you are concerned about personal safety). Listen to nature's sounds. Breathe in the scents and imagine that each of your inward breaths carries energy imbued with the mountain's strength. Affirm in each cycle of breath that you are being revitalized, healed, and made whole.

A Deeper Look

In 1805, according to legend, Spanish soldiers searching for Native Americans who had escaped from a mission during the night got caught in thick brush on the mountain, proclaiming *"monte del Diablo"* ("forest or thicket of the Devil"), which sounded like Mount Diablo.

29. Convento de Santa Teresa of Ávila (Convent of Saint Teresa of Ávila)

ÁVILA, SPAIN

Pain is never permanent.
—Saint Teresa of Ávila (1515–1582), Spanish-born mystic and Carmelite nun

When Teresa, daughter of a Spanish nobleman, prayed to Saint Joseph for a cure for the crippling illness that plagued her during childhood, she was healed. Perhaps this explains, in part, the young girl's fascination with saints (reading about them, pretending to be an aesthetic) as well as her decision to join a Carmelite convent as a teenager. She later reformed the convent into a stricter Discalced (shoeless) Carmelite convent.

If you desire Teresa's intercession to overcome illness, come to her convent. It's an easy day trip by train or bus from Madrid (68 miles). Erected in 1636 over the house in which Teresa was born, the convent is still an active religious facility. Certain areas are restricted, but you can enter the elaborately decorated chapel with a baroque altar and statue of the saint.

Soothe Your Spirit

Pray for Divine healing using the simple type of prayer Saint Teresa preferred: "Lord, hold me, love me, heal me." Tune into the subtle vibration that is said to permeate the convent and to which are attributed many miraculous healings.

A Deeper Look

A fragrance known to Catholics as the "odor of sanctity" filled Saint Teresa's monastic cell in Ávila on the night of her death (although she was traveling and not in the room when she died) and wafted from her coffin when it was exhumed 330 years after her death.

30. Pamukkale (Hierapolis)

DENIZLI PROVINCE, TURKEY

The drop dies in the river / of its joy / pain goes so far it cures itself . . .
—Ghalib (1797–1869), Turkish poet, tr. W. S. Merwin

*I*n an arid landscape the color of camels, Pamukkale (Cotton Palace) is a refreshing ancient thermal spa with mineral-rich waters that for millennia have tumbled down Caldag Mountain, leaving behind white travertine terraces. Here, too, are the ruins of Hierapolis (Holy City), a Greco-Roman community and religious retreat founded in the second century B.C. and later converted to Christianity by Philip the Apostle. The ruins include a cathedral, a baptistery, churches, and the tomb of the apostle Philip, who died there in A.D. 80.

Nestled in a surreal landscape of mineral forests, terraced basins, and petrified waterfalls, Pamukkale's sacred warm water can baptize the spirit, soothe the soul, and restore a weary body. Sitting and wading (shoes prohibited) is free, but you must pay to swim. You can reach Hierapolis-Pamukkale from Denizli, the nearest city, by car or local bus, but be sure to go early as the tour buses bring large crowds.

Soothe Your Spirit

Bathe in the springs as the faithful have been doing for thousands of years. Release all your worry and concerns. Pray for the restoration of perfect health in body, mind, and spirit, and offer a prayer of heartfelt thanks.

A Deeper Look

Since before the birth of Christ, the sick and infirm have come from far and wide to bathe in the warm waters of Hierapolis/Pamukkale, which are believed to have mystical healing powers.

31. Grace Cathedral

SAN FRANCISCO, CALIFORNIA, UNITED STATES

A peaceful heart leads to a healthy body . . .
—Bible, Proverbs 14:30

This Episcopalian treasure atop San Francisco's Nob Hill heals the heart while calling it to worship with its heavenly artwork (including replicas of Ghiberti's famed *Gates of Paradise*), stained-glass iconography (the most stunning: the Twenty-Third Psalm window), and choral concerts. But perhaps the major attraction for the millions who flock to the cathedral from around the world is the amazing indoor labyrinth modeled after the twelfth-century Chartres Cathedral in France and a newer outdoor labyrinth open twenty-four hours a day.

If you wish to experience the restorative and transformative powers of the labyrinth, go to this "house of prayer for all people," located at 1100 California Street. Parking is a major challenge, so unless you're familiar with the city, the easiest way to reach the site is by taxi or cable car (the nearest stop is two blocks away).

Soothe Your Spirit

Walk the labyrinth, focusing on your breath and meditating on what ails or troubles you. As you make your way to the center, release the disease (or dis-ease) within you (purgation). At the center, pause to receive the healing you seek (illumination). Feel the rejuvenation of your mind/body/spirit as you return to the beginning (union).

A Deeper Look

Grace Cathedral was built in 1964 on the site of the modest Grace Church, constructed during the Gold Rush. Among the cathedral's many artistic treasures is the Keith Haring AIDS Interfaith Chapel altarpiece.

32. Grotto of Massabielle

LOURDES, FRANCE

Let us draw near with a true heart in full assurance of faith . . . our bodies washed with pure water.
—Bible, Hebrews 10:22

When fourteen-year-old Bernadette Soubirous had a vision in which the Virgin Mary instructed her to dig in the earth until a puddle of water was revealed and to drink from it, she did as she was told. Today, the Grotto of Massabielle (or "old rock"), in southwestern France, with its bathing pools of sacred water fed by the spring exposed by that puddle, is the focal point of a large complex that attracts more than six million people yearly, many ill and praying for a miracle.

If you desire healing or to venerate Mary, visit the grotto. The closest airport, at Tarbes, is 13 miles from Lourdes; Paris is roughly 500 miles north. Take a tour or go alone, but be prepared for crowds since this shrine is the most sacred of all the Marion pilgrimage sites in the world.

Soothe Your Spirit

Pray the rosary in the Chapel of Mysteries inside the Basilica of the Rosary. Ask the Blessed Virgin to take your prayer of healing to the Lord on her heart before sliding into one of the nineteen pools of sacred water.

A Deeper Look

Stunning views of Lourdes—encompassing the Grotto of Massabielle, Basilica of the Rosary, and Basilica of the Immaculate Conception (built directly over the site of Bernadette's apparitions)—are afforded from the summit of Pic du Jer, rising 1,000 meters above Lourdes.

33. Charminar Mosque

HYDERABAD, ANDHRA PRADESH, INDIA

And know the help of God comes through patience and comfortable circumstances with distress and that difficulty is accompanied by ease.
—Shaikh Abdul Qadir Gilani (A.D. 1077–1166), Muslim cleric

When Indian ruler Sultan Muhammad Quli Qutub Shah prayed to stop the misery and suffering of his people from the plague, he vowed that, if his prayers were answered, he would build a *masjid* on the site of his prayers. His jewel in India, Charminar (Mosque of the Four Minarets), stands as an elegant sixteenth-century testament to the veracity of the sultan's promise. The mosque's Cazia (Indo-Islamic medieval) architectural style features four towering minarets (160 feet high) topped with bulbous domes that are embellished with petal motifs that may symbolize the first four caliphs of Islam.

If you seek spiritual rejuvenation, worship at this lovely mosque in the Old City of Hyderabad, in South India. Rajiv Gandhi airport is about 13 miles from the city. Local buses, taxis, and rickshaws will get you there from virtually anywhere in Hyderabad.

Soothe Your Spirit

Pray in the mosque's open area during Friday prayers (with larger numbers of people, men and women pray in separate areas) or in one of the four upper galleries inside the carved minarets (each gallery accommodates forty-five prayer spaces).

A Deeper Look

The Charminar Mosque, built in 1591, has been called the "Arc de Triomphe" of the East. See it at its most spectacular at night when the mosque is illuminated.

34. The Asclepeion of Kos

KOS, GREECE

The art of healing comes from nature, not from the physician. Therefore the physician must start from nature, with an open mind.
—Philippus Aureolus Paracelsus (1493–1541), German-Swiss physician, botanist, and alchemist

When the ancient Greeks needed healing, they would visit a temple of Asclepius (god of healing) much as people today go to a medical clinic. The lovely island of Kos, located in the Dodecanese chain of islands in the Aegean Sea off the Asia Minor coast, is home to the well-preserved ruins of the Asclepeion of Kos, covering three terraces. The island is also the birthplace of Hippocrates, the Greek "Father of Medicine."

Whether you seek healing for yourself or someone else, visit the sacred ruins of Kos. Walk or ride a bicycle the nearly flat 3 miles from the nearest town (Kos), enjoying the scenery and serenity the moderate exercise provides, or take a bus.

Soothe Your Spirit

Bring your journal. Pray for healing before going to sleep at night, and then write your dreams in your journal when you awake. As you walk through the ruins, contemplate the curative message the Divine delivered to you in your dreams.

A Deeper Look

Ancient Greeks and Romans believed that Asclepius, the healing god, would appear in the patient's dream to cure him or her. People would sleep in an Asclepius temple and the next morning report their dreams to a priest, who would prescribe a cure.

35. Saint Madron's Well

MADRON, CORNWALL, ENGLAND

. . . May the sacredness of your work bring healing, light, and renewal. . . .
—Celtic blessing

ornwall, as in other parts of Europe that once comprised the ancient land of the Celts, is home to several sacred spring-fed wells, such as this one in the village of Madron. Pre-Christian pagans believed the well's water healed infirmities and made the infertile fecund. The faithful would face the sun and plunge themselves (or their child) into the water three times, walk clockwise around the well nine times, rip a strip of cloth (*cloutie*) from their garments and hang it on a tree, and then dress and lie down on a nearby grassy hill (Saint Maderne's Bed). After Madron was Christianized, a small crude chapel was built near the well.

Whether you wish to perform a healing ritual at the well or to pray for wholeness of body/mind/spirit at the well-chapel, visit this ancient sacred site on a woodland path.

Soothe Your Spirit

Cut a small strip of cloth from clothing worn over the part of your body that needs healing, hold the strip to your solar plexus as you walk silently around the well nine times, and then tie the *cloutie* to a tree or bush. Or take the fern-lined footpath to the well-chapel and pray for the intercession of Saint Madron that the healing you need will be granted.

A Deeper Look

Pagan Celts believed their sacred wells had powers of both healing and divination (predicting the future) and were a spiritual portal to the Mother Goddess.

36. The First Church of Christ, Scientist (The Mother Church)

BOSTON, MASSACHUSETTS, UNITED STATES

Health is not a condition of matter, but of Mind.
—Mary Baker Eddy (1821–1910), founder of the Christian Science movement

When Mary Baker Eddy read a story about a miraculous healing performed by Jesus, she experienced an epiphany and became cured of her own disability, which inspired her to found the Christian Science movement, with its emphasis on faith healing and Jesus's healing works. The Mother Church, as this first church of the movement is called, is an architectural gem, built in the Romanesque Revival style with a later Renaissance-style extension featuring a gorgeous Byzantine-style dome. The plaza features a peaceful reflecting pool and fountain.

If you would like to learn more about the physical and moral healing practices and beliefs of the Christian Scientists, visit the Mother Church and its eleven-story library. Located in Boston's Back Bay neighborhood, it is easily reached by car or public transportation, including buses and the subway.

Soothe Your Spirit

Attend a Bible lesson-sermon by lay readers (there are no ordained ministers) and listen to hymns. Allow enough time to tour this lovely and large old church, soaking up its healing energy and letting it work its magic on you.

A Deeper Look

The First Church of Christ, Scientist that subsequently spawned 1,700 branch churches and societies has an amazing Aeolian-Skinner pipe organ that is several stories high, one of the largest in the United States.

37. Pipestone National Monument

MINNESOTA, UNITED STATES

When you pray with this pipe, you pray for and with everything.
—Black Elk (1863–1950), Oglala Lakota Sioux medicine man

*T*he Plains Indians of Minnesota describe the sacred Pipestone Quarry, named a U.S. Historical National Monument in 1937, as a "square jewel" because from a distance it looks like a giant square-cut ruby. Today, only Native Americans are allowed to quarry the catlinite, the red stone used to carve pipes for medicinal and peace ceremonies as well as for communing with the spirit world.

If you embrace the Native American belief that smoke from the sacred *calumet* (the pipe made from pipestone or catlinite) carries prayers for well-being to the Great Spirit, visit this national monument that has been sacred to indigenous people for thousands of years. The best time is late spring, early summer, or fall. Located in southwestern Minnesota at an elevation of 1,600 feet, this high plains site endures high winds and below-freezing temperatures in the winter and blistering temperatures (80–100°F) in the summer.

Soothe Your Spirit

Stand before the Three Sisters (large boulders) guarding the entrance of the quarry and offer prayers for healing and wholeness. Follow the paved Circle Trail to see Native Americans quarrying the red stone using only hand tools, Winnewissa Falls tumbling over massive boulders, and tall prairie grass swaying in the wind.

A Deeper Look

According to legend, the Great Spirit slaughtered buffalo on the site, turning the ground red, and from that sacred red earth the first human was formed.

38. El Santuario de Chimayó Shrine

CHIMAYÓ, NEW MEXICO, UNITED STATES

And behold a woman who was troubled with an issue of blood twelve years, came behind him, and touched the hem of his garment. For she said within herself: If I shall touch only his garment, I shall be healed. But Jesus turning and seeing her, said: Be of good heart, daughter, thy faith hath made thee whole. And the woman was made whole from that hour.
—Bible, Matthew 9:20–22

*J*n 1810, on Good Friday, Bernardo de Abeyta, a friar with the brotherhood of Penitentes, found a crucifix shimmering in the sunlight on a foothill near Sangre de Cristo Mountains. He dug it up and carried it to the altar of a church in Santa Cruz (7 miles away), but the cross disappeared only to reappear in the place where the friar first discovered it. Three times the friar took the cross to the chapel, and three times it mysteriously returned to the hillside. Finally, in 1814, the people of Chimayó built a chapel at the site, and miraculous healings began to occur when the faithful rubbed dirt from the hillside on the afflicted area of their bodies.

If you believe nature is holy and has the power to heal, visit El Santuario de Chimayó, the "Lourdes of America," about 30 miles north of Santa Fe.

Soothe Your Spirit
Kneel down and touch the dirt while offering a prayer of gratitude for good health or for Divine healing.

A Deeper Look
About 30,000 visitors visit the shrine each year on Good Friday.

39. Baths of Fordogianus

SARDINIA, ITALY

Health, the greatest of all we count as blessings.
—Ariphron of Sicyon, fourth-century B.C. Greek artist and poet

On the beautiful Italian island of Sardinia on the left bank of the Tirso, these Roman baths once served as a sort of ancient spa where people bathed in curative thermal waters and gathered for rituals of worship. As testament to the baths' spiritual sanctity, prayers to Asclepius, Greek god of healing, and to nymphs (water divinities) are carved into the stone walls, made of pink trachytes (igneous volcanic rock). The site has pools and springs of both cool and hot water, rich in minerals that were used to treat rheumatism and other ailments. Although today the baths are ruins of an ancient spa complex, they reflect the ancient Roman appreciation for water's healing properties.

Whether you seek curative treatment or rejuvenation near sacred water, give yourself plenty of time to visit the baths. A modern spa with restorative modalities and therapies is located nearby.

Soothe Your Spirit

Explore the historic ruins, and then ease your weariness in restful reflection on perfect health and wholeness. Consider indulging in a healing scented bath, followed by a massage at the state-of-the-art facility nearby.

A Deeper Look

The sulfur spring water in the thermal baths is about 129°F (54°C) and its palliative effect was no doubt enjoyed by the area's early inhabitants as well as by the Phoenicians, Romans, and subsequent residents and visitors.

40. Vailankanni Church

VAILANKANNI, TAMIL NADU, INDIA

It is not hard [to care for the terminally ill], because in each one I see the face of Christ . . .
—Mother Teresa (1910–1997), Albanian-born nun and founder of Missionaries of Charity, Calcutta

*T*owering above the Bay of Bengal, this Gothic-style Christian church with its graceful twin spires, alabaster-colored exterior, and red-tiled roof serves as a beacon to lost souls searching for spiritual fulfillment and healing. Built in the late sixteenth century, the church has been called "Lourdes of the East," because like the sacred spring in France, the Vailankanni (also known as Velankanni or Velanganni) Church is associated with water and the miraculous healing power of Mary. The church also maintains Our Lady of Good Health Hospital and Dispensary.

If you desire healing in body, mind, or spirit, visit the Vailankanni Church. Vailankanni is less than 8 miles south of Nagapattinam. The nearest international airport is at Tiruchirappali; the closest railway station is at Nagapattinam. Buses are available from Chennai and various major cities. Alternatively, you might rent a car and driver or take a taxi.

Soothe Your Spirit
Purchase a garland to offer the Holy Mother, light a candle, kneel, and ask Our Lady of Good Health to carry that prayer on her heart to the Lord. It is customary to promise to give something back when your prayer is answered. See objects others have donated in the church museum after being healed or cured.

A Deeper Look
In 1962, Pope John XXIII conferred the status of basilica upon the Vailankanni Church. More than 1.5 million pilgrims visit each year in August, for Mary's feast day.

41. Queen of Peace Shrine (Shrine of Medjugorje)

MEDJUGORJE, BOSNIA AND HERZEGOVINA

And a certain man was there, which had an infirmity thirty and eight years. When Jesus saw him . . . he saith, Rise, take up thy bed, and walk.
—Bible, John 5:5–8

On June 24, 1981, six Croatian children witnessed an apparition of a woman holding a child on a hillside. Although they were afraid, fear did not stop them from returning the next day. Upon seeing the apparition again, they prayed the rosary. On the third day, the apparition identified herself as the Blessed Virgin. On the fifth day, the children returned with villagers, but only the children could see and hear the lady. On the sixth day, the first of many miraculous healings occurred. Subsequently, a shrine dedicated to the Queen of Peace was erected in the square of the local parish church of Saint James.

Whether you desire a healing miracle or would like to venerate Mary, plan a pilgrimage to Medjugorje. No photos are allowed during worship services and periods of adoration; no lighting of candles is allowed on Apparition Hill and Cross Mountain; and no religious articles can be brought into those sacred sites.

Soothe Your Spirit

Climb Apparition Hill and meditate on holistic wellness. In Saint James Church, light a candle and pray near the wooden cross or attend the evening service when special healing prayers are said.

A Deeper Look

Millions of pilgrims visit the Marion shrine each year; the anniversary of the apparitions is a popular time of pilgrimage.

42. Sainte-Anne-de-Beaupré Sanctuaire (Shrine)

QUÉBEC CITY, QUÉBEC, CANADA

But I will restore health unto thee, and I will heal thee of thy wounds,
saith the Lord. . . .
—Bible, Jeremiah 30:17

When a fire destroyed the seventeenth-century church dedicated to Saint Anne—the grandmother of Jesus, the mother of the Blessed Virgin Mary, and patroness of the sick—in Québec City in 1922, a magnificent new house of worship was constructed in the shape of a Latin cross. Today, this holy sanctuary features 240 exquisite stained-glass windows in the basilica, gorgeous sculpted columns, and a dozen chapels where parishioners and pilgrims flock for worship and prayer. Locals join pilgrims from around the world for the nine-day novena preceding Saint Anne's feast day, July 26, when the sick and infirm come to pray for miraculous cures. There have been many, as any visitor can see by the collection of crutches, bandages, canes, and wheelchairs left behind near the main entrance.

Whether you seek the intercession of Saint Anne for an affliction or would like to venerate the mother of Mary and the grandmother of Jesus, visit this magnificent basilica in the French-speaking city of Québec.

Soothe Your Spirit

Light a candle for yourself or another, kneel, and recite the prayer of the sick.

A Deeper Look

The Redemptorist Order has administered and protected this shrine for 130 years. It attracts more than 500,000 pilgrims from all over the world, many seeking healing of body, mind, or spirit.

43. The Baths of Caracalla

ROME, ITALY

Health is the soul that animates all the enjoyments of life, which fade and are tasteless without it.
—Seneca (5 B.C.–A.D. 65), Roman dramatist, philosopher, and politician

This spectacular ruin in Rome was once a massive public bathing and entertainment complex constructed in the early third century A.D. The Baths of Caracalla reflect the fundamentals of good health promoted by Roman physicians: bathing, exercise, relaxation, and a good diet. The complex included a cafeteria, gymnasiums, a swimming pool, entertainment facilities, massage areas, two saunas, and three types of pools (tepid, hot, cold) seating 1,600 bathers. This ancient health spa was used until A.D. 537, when Witigis besieged Rome and destroyed the aqueducts supplying water to the site.

If you are intrigued with the connection between spiritual and physical well-being, you will be inspired by the Baths of Caracalla. Take Metro Line B to Circo Massimo Station; the ruins are at Viale delle Terme di Caracalla 52, south of the Colosseum.

Soothe Your Spirit

Walk around the baths and reflect on how improving your physical and mental health might enhance or work in harmony with your spiritual pursuits.

A Deeper Look

Over the centuries, priceless artwork was plundered from the site, including mosaics of athletes that covered the gymnasium walls and are now in the Vatican Museum, and a statue of a muscular Hercules that, along with other statues taken from the baths, is in the archaeological museum of Naples.

44. Basilica of the Born Jesus

VELHA GOA (OLD GOA), INDIA

And one of them, when he saw that he was healed, turned back, and with a loud voice, glorified God . . .
—Bible, Luke 17:15

*D*isplayed at the top of the baroque façade of this sixteenth-century church are the letters *IHS*, the first three Greek letters of the name Jesus and monogram of the Jesuit Order. Within the basilica lie the venerable remains of Saint Francis Xavier, Roman Catholic missionary and cofounder of the Society of Jesus, whose chosen mission was caring for the sick. The ailing and infirm pray for healing near the saint's silver casket, raised on a jasper and marble base with bronze side panels featuring events of Xavier's life. Every ten years or so (most recently, in 2004), the casket is lowered to permit viewing of the saint's incorruptible body through the casket's glass side panels.

If you seek Saint Francis Xavier's assistance in praying for healing or would enjoy seeing where he evangelized in India, come to this minor basilica dedicated to the Holy Infant. From the airport in Panaji, travel 6 miles east to Old Goa by bus, taxi, auto rickshaw, or guided tour.

Soothe Your Spirit
Pray for wholeness before the pulpit depicting the Four Doctors and Four Evangelists with Jesus. Attend the novena (a nine-day prayer of grace) that traditionally culminates in the saint's feast day on December 3.

A Deeper Look
So many Christian churches were built in Goa during Portugal's reign that it became known as the "Rome of the East."

45. Grotta del Genovese (Cave of the Genovese)

LEVANZO ISLAND, SICILY, ITALY

I want God to play in my bloodstream the way sunlight amuses itself on the water.
—Elizabeth Gilbert (1969–), American writer

*O*f the three Egadi Islands resting in the blue-green Mediterranean Sea off the coast of Sicily, Levanzo is the smallest. However, it is postcard-perfect with quaint houses hugging a tiny harbor overlooking the undulating sea and a backdrop of rocky hills dotted with sheep farms. Not far above sea level, and a twenty-minute walk down a steeply inclined walkway along the sea cliff, is the Cave of the Genovese—featuring Paleolithic engravings dating back 10,000 to 13,000 years and Neolithic paintings dating back 5,000 to 6,000 years, some thought to be spiritually symbolic.

If you feel the need to restore your health and nurture your spirit with the balm of peace and quiet, make your way to Levanzo Island and explore the prehistoric sanctuary. Get to this remote island by hydrofoil or ferry from the inland towns of Trapani or Marsala or the larger island of Favignana. You can see the grotto by guided tour only, once or twice daily, in July and August, so make your reservations in advance. The booking office is in Levanzo, just above the port.

Soothe Your Spirit

Put away your watch and alarms. Let the slower island rhythm adjust your body's internal clock. Affirm that your body has the wisdom to heal itself of everything, including the overworked, frazzled nervous condition. Offer a prayer of thanks for this beautiful, healthful island sanctuary.

A Deeper Look

Levanzo (population 200) is an idyllic place to fish, swim, and meditate on wellness and wholeness.

46. Saint Gabriel Church

KULUBI, ETHIOPIA

Blessed are the merciful, for these shall obtain mercy.
—Bible, Matthew 5:7

When the parishioners of the Orthodox Saint Gabriel Church in Kulubi desire to thank the archangel Gabriel for removing diseases and afflictions from their children, they embark on an end-of-the-year pilgrimage, bringing votive offerings along with spiritual vows and sacred promises. If a baby was born through Gabriel's intervention, parents also bring the infant for baptism. The muscular-looking church on a hill overlooking the dusty plain welcomes Orthodox Christians, Muslims (who call the archangel Gabriel "Gibral," as it is found in the Qur'an), and Animists who revere the sacred site where a tree once stood in place of the church.

If you desire to pray for healing for a child or for someone else, visit Saint Gabriel Church in Kulubi. Come in December when the weather is dry. From Addis Ababa, fly to Dire Dawa or take the overnight train or a daily bus. Minibuses also run from the nearby towns of Harar or Dire Dawa to Kulubi; the latter is roughly 42 miles. Dress appropriately. Bring the gift of a candle or umbrella, the most popular offerings along with livestock.

Soothe Your Spirit
Put on a *gabi* (white cotton shawl that Orthodox Christians in the area wear). Say prayers of thanksgiving for a healing, leaving behind your offering.

A Deeper Look
Kulubi is the largest place of pilgrimage in Ethiopia.

47. Basilica della Santissima Annunziata (Basilica of the Most Holy Annunciation)

FLORENCE, ITALY

If you ever feel distressed during your day—call upon Our Lady—just say this simple prayer: "Mary, Mother of Jesus, please be a mother to me now."
—Mother Teresa (1910–1997), Albanian-born nun and founder of Missionaries of Charity, Calcutta

The beautiful baroque-style Basilica della Santissima Annunziata is among the most revered churches dedicated to Mary. The lovely interior of shimmering marble, lavish gilded ceiling, patterned floor, and frescoes draw lovers of sacred art and architecture, the curious, and the faithful. However, it is the holy serenity of this sanctuary that soothes tortured minds, aching hearts, and weary bodies as the faithful petition the Blessed Virgin to assist them in praying for healing.

If you feel that praying in this church might heal you, hasten to Basilica della Santissima Annunziata. Located in the northeastern side of the Piazza della Santissima Annunziata, it is reachable by public transportation. Catch buses at Istituto degli Innocenti going to Piazza San Marco, take the train from Firenze S. Maria Novella Station, or hire a taxi.

Soothe Your Spirit
Light a candle and pray to the Blessed Mother, who suffered watching as her only Son was crucified, that she might carry your prayer for healing on her heart to Christ.

A Deeper Look
Founders of the Servite Order established the Basilica della Santissima Annunziata in 1250. Saint Juliana Falconieri (1270–1341), the patron saint of chronic illness, having suffered her entire life with a stomach ailment, was a Servite.

48. El Santuario de Las Lajas (Sanctuary of Las Lajas)

IPIALES, NARIÑO, COLOMBIA

The soul is healed by being with children.
—Fyodor Mikhailovich Dostoevsky (1821–1881), Russian novelist

*T*he neo-Gothic Las Lajas Cathedral on Colombia's border with Ecuador rises majestically from a deep, green gorge of the Guáitara River and its walkway spans the river. This glorious sanctuary commemorates the appearance of the Blessed Virgin on a cliff face in 1750. According to legend, a bolt of lightning illuminated a painting of Our Lady, revealing it to a deaf-mute girl, Rosa, and her mother, Maria Mueses de Quinones, local Amerindians who had taken shelter from the storm between two large *lajas* (sedimentary rocks). The painting of the Holy Mother and Holy Infant, located inside a cave high in the mountains, was reportedly unknown until Rosa spotted it. If you seek spiritual balm for an arid heart, weary spirit, or physical ailment, visit this sanctuary. Take a taxi to the cathedral from Ipiales, and on the return to the village share a taxi or catch a small bus (*colectivo*). Bring warm clothes as the area can be cold.

Soothe Your Spirit
Light a candle, kneel, and ask for spiritual or physical healing from Our Lady of Las Lajas.

A Deeper Look
On a wall along the road between the village and the church are hundreds of plaques thanking the Virgin for miraculous healings. The cathedral is a holy site of pilgrimage, especially on September 21.

49. Baca Grande

CRESTONE, COLORADO, UNITED STATES

Everybody needs beauty as well as bread, places to play in and pray in, where nature may heal and give strength to body and soul.
—John Muir (1838–1914), Scottish-born American naturalist

The small town of Crestone is situated on a convergence of ley lines (Earth's electromagnetic grids) in the western foothills of the Sangre de Cristo (Blood of Christ) Mountains. Here the meditative and healing qualities of the southern Rocky Mountains have long been a sacred pilgrimage site for Native American tribes such as the Ute and Comanche. Since the 1970s, the Crestone area has become a thriving spiritual center for many diverse traditions, an effort initiated by Maurice Strong, founder of the large, eco-friendly Baca Grande development, and his wife, Hanne Marstrand Strong.

If you think a retreat in a place of natural beauty and spiritual power might fix what ails you, find your way to Crestone and let the mountains work their magic.

Soothe Your Spirit

Choose a monastery, shrine, spa, or simply a quiet spot under a tree to meditate or pray. Do some breath work to discharge any negative energy and to fill your body with healing energy.

A Deeper Look

All spiritual paths are honored in Crestone, including Native American, Christian, Buddhist, Hindu, and New Age. Sacred sites include Crestone Mountain Zen Center, Karma Thegsum Tashi Gomang Stupa and Retreat Center, Haidakhandi Universal Ashram, Sanctuary House (with a sacred labyrinth), and Spiritual Life Institute and Nada Heritage Retreat Center (Roman Catholic).

50. Shiprock

NAVAJO NATION, NEW MEXICO, UNITED STATES

Be still and the earth will speak to you.
—Navajo proverb

The 40 million-year-old volcanic Shiprock Peak, rising out of the high-desert floor to an elevation of 1,800 feet, may look like a nineteenth-century ship to outsiders, but to the Navajo it looks like a winged rock. In fact, according to legend, *Tsé Bit'a'i* (as it is called by the Navajo) was once the dwelling place of a mythological great bird that carried the tribe's ancestors from their home in the north to their new home in the southwest. Another of the many myths associated with *Tsé Bit'a'i* is that it is a medicine pouch carried by a powerful mountain spirit.

If you would like to experience the Navajo healing ceremony known as *Ye'iibiche* (Night Way), visit Shiprock. It lies at the intersection of Highways 64 and 491, with the nearest towns being Cortez, Colorado, and Farmington, New Mexico.

Soothe Your Spirit

Find a guide willing to help you understand the portions of the ceremony you are allowed to see. Feel the healing energy of the chanting. Create a self-healing chant (for example, "My body is in the process of returning to perfection: every cell, every organ, every system").

A Deeper Look

Shiprock, in the Four Corners region, is the site of the Navajo Nation's annual October festival, which includes a nine-day healing ceremony. Photographs and videos of the sacred ceremony are prohibited, as are hiking and climbing on the sacred peak.

51. Basilica of Divine Mercy

LAGIEWNIKI DISTRICT, KRAKOW, POLAND

Jesus, I trust thee.
—Caption on the *Lord's Mercy* icon in Lagiewniki's sanctuary

After Sister Faustyna Kowalska, a Polish nun, passed away from tuberculosis, her relics were laid to rest beneath a painting of the image that had comforted and guided her throughout her spiritual life: her vision, in 1931, of the Merciful Christ. In the vision, the Lord instructed her to commission a painting of his likeness. In a later vision, Christ revealed His Dogma of Divine Mercy. The Merciful Christ painting was completed and the sister's relics were entombed beneath it in 1940, following her death in 1938. Since then, the faithful have flocked to the shrine to pray or to give thanks for healing.

If you suffer from an ailment and seek spiritual support for a healing, consider visiting the Basilica of Divine Mercy.

Soothe Your Spirit
Visit the church for the daily special prayer during the 3:00 P.M. "Hour of Divine Mercy" (a reference to the time Jesus is believed to have died on the cross) and stay for the Chaplet of Divine Mercy. Or light a candle and pray before the icon for the healing you seek. The church is about 2 miles from Krakow's Old Town.

A Deeper Look
Consecrated in 2002 by Pope John Paul II, a native of Poland, the modern, monolithic Basilica of Divine Mercy receives 2 million visitors each year. The shrine with the Divine Mercy painting and the nun's relics is in the chapel of the old convent.

52. Crater Lake National Park

OREGON, UNITED STATES

When one of the tribe felt called upon to become a teacher and healer, he spent several weeks on the shore of the lake in fasting, in communion with the dead, and in prayer.
—A. G. Walling (writing in 1884 about Crater Lake), nineteenth-century American historian

When southern Oregon's volcanic Mount Mazama erupted 7,700 years ago, the mountain collapsed, creating a caldera that heavy precipitation would fill to form Crater Lake, at 1,943 feet the deepest lake completely in the United States. Located in a wilderness preserve protected by the National Park Service, Crater Lake has been a *giiwas* (most sacred place) to Native Americans for more than 13,000 years. Klamath, Modoc, Yahooskin, Cow Creek, and other tribes traveled to the lake for vision quests. Many believed that swimming in the water or sleeping next to the lake with its volcanic Wizard Island would endow them with shamanic powers.

If you need to heal yourself in a peaceful and mystical natural sanctuary, visit Crater Lake—119 miles from Bend (north entrance) and 77 miles from Medford (west entrance). Though open year-round, the North Entrance Road and Rim Drive are closed mid-October through mid-June, when many trails and facilities are also closed due to heavy snowfall.

Soothe Your Spirit

Motor around the 33-mile Rim Drive, take a guided boat tour, or bike or walk along the lake. Feel the tension leave your body, mind, and spirit.

A Deeper Look

This most-sacred lake remained a secret of the Klamath Indians until it was discovered by gold prospectors in 1853.

53. Lake Baikal (Ozero Baykal)

IRKUTSK, SIBERIA, RUSSIA

One cannot reflect in streaming water. Only those who know internal peace can give it to others.
—Lao Tzu (600–531 B.C.), Chinese philosopher and father of Taoism

Lake Baikal, in southeastern Siberia, is 25 million years old, 1.2 miles deep, 400 miles long, and 500 miles wide, making it the world's oldest, deepest, and second-largest natural lake. This World Heritage Site is sacred to local Buddhists as well as to the region's indigenous tribe of Buryats, who leave monthly offerings at shrines around the lake and on the lake's islands.

If you are on a quest to restore or invigorate your sense of well-being, Lake Baikal offers many options. Book a packaged or customized tour (some even include shaman purification rituals and ancestor spirit rites), or explore the region by boat, horseback, or trekking. From Saint Petersburg, take a direct flight to Irkutsk, known as the "Paris of Siberia," which is the nearest town.

Soothe Your Spirit

Leave prayers for holistic well-being or of gratitude for good health at the sacred inlets, islands, and monuments of this enormous freshwater lake, also known as the North Sea in historical Chinese texts.

A Deeper Look

The most sacred area of Lake Baikal is Olkhon, an island 8 miles from the northern shore. A cave on the island is thought to be the earthly home of Burkhan, the supreme deity of the Buryats.

54. Belize Botanic Gardens

SAN IGNACIO, CAYO, BELIZE, CENTRAL AMERICA

God sleeps in the minerals, awakens in the plants, walks in animals, and thinks in man.
—Arthur Young (1741–1820), English writer

Located on 45 acres in the Cayo District of western Belize, the Belize Botanic Gardens is a showplace of indigenous vegetation. A popular ecotourism destination, the garden also features an Orchid House and a "Plants of the Mayan Trail"—which is actually two trails: one an easy walk through a garden, the other a more strenuous trek through a natural forest. Guided tours and a handbook provide detailed information about medicinal plants used by the ancient Maya.

If tropical flowers lift your spirit or you would like to learn more about the sacred healing properties of Mayan plants, visit the Orchid House and Botanic Gardens. Go in the driest months, February through April. There are direct flights from Miami, Houston, and New Orleans to Belize; then you'll need to rent a car or take a bus to Cayo.

Soothe Your Spirit

As you stroll through the gardens, meditate on the healthful harmony of mind, body, and spirit. At nighttime, offer a prayer of gratitude for the botanic medicines provided by the Creator as you stargaze from the garden's observation tower.

A Deeper Look

Also located in the Cayo District is Xunantunich, an ancient (A.D. 300–900) Mayan ceremonial center with a large plaza ringed by pyramids. The largest (130 feet high) is El Castillo, offering a panoramic view of the town and jungle beyond.

CHAPTER 3

STRENGTH, FORTITUDE, FORBEARANCE

Tenderness and kindness are not symptoms of weakness and despair but manifestations of strength and resolution.

—*Kahlil Gibran (1883–1931),*
Lebanese-born American poet

55. Machu Picchu

URUBAMBA VALLEY, PERU

Feeling important makes one heavy, clumsy, and vain. To be a warrior one needs to be light-hearted.
—Carlos Castaneda (1925–1998), Peruvian-born anthropologist

Perched on an emerald-green hilltop rising almost 8,000 feet above sea level and cradled between two craggy peaks of the Peruvian Andes, the famed "Lost City of the Incas" looms above the Urubamba Valley. Upon seeing the mist-enshrouded, fifteenth-century ruin with its remarkably preserved granite structures and terraced fields, travelers describe a sense of awe and intense spiritual power. Unknown to the outside world until 1911 (thus escaping Spanish conquistadors), Machu Picchu (Old Peak) was for centuries a secret Inca ceremonial center, retreat, and perhaps a fortress, and is now a New Age mecca and World Heritage Site.

You can journey to Machu Picchu to draw strength from the sacred mountain, the mystical Lost City, and its unspoiled 80,309-acre nature reserve. Go during the dry season, May through September. Wear sunscreen and comfortable walking shoes, take a hat, and explore this 5-square-mile wonder that is roughly 70 miles from Cuzco.

Soothe Your Spirit

As you explore the ruins, feel the spiritual potency of this fiercely beautiful mountaintop sanctuary. At *Intihuatana* (the Temple of the Sun), in what archaeologists call the "Sacred District" of Machu Picchu, offer a prayer for strength.

A Deeper Look

Machu Picchu, where some believe the energy of the world converges, has an urban section with temples, fountains, palaces, and homes and an agricultural section of terraced gardens (*andenes*).

56. Basilica di Santa Maria degli Angeli (Saint Mary of the Angels)

ASSISI, UMBRIA, ITALY

Start by doing what's necessary; then what's possible; and suddenly you are doing the impossible.

—Saint Francis of Assisi (1181–1226), founder of the Franciscans

*L*ike a heavenly beacon of strength, the gold statue of the Madonna of the Angels ascends from the façade of the blue-domed Basilica of Saint Mary of the Angels, constructed over the ninth-century Porziuncola (small church) where Saint Francis awakened to his ecclesiastical calling. For some the basilica's splendor and size (the world's seventh-largest Christian church) might seem grandiose, given the saint's vow of poverty, but for those who venerate Saint Francis, it is a fitting homage to this humble servant of God who worked tirelessly for the downtrodden and for animals.

If you want to awaken to your life's purpose or to strengthen your devotion to God, worship at the Basilica di Santa Maria degli Angeli near Assisi, 90 miles from Rome.

Soothe Your Spirit

Reflect on the purity of spirit and inner strength it took for Saint Francis, born into a wealthy noble family, to give away his riches to the poor and to devote his life to Christ and to helping others.

A Deeper Look

A few years after Saint Francis's death in 1226, a simple church was built around the Porziuncola. In 1569, the majestic Gothic basilica was built on top of the smaller (lower) church and its cupola was positioned directly above the Porziuncola.

57. Chaco Cultural National Historical Park

CHACO CANYON, NEW MEXICO, UNITED STATES

Life is not a continuum of pleasant choices but of inevitable problems that call for strength, determination, and hard work.
—Native American proverb

In Chaco Canyon in northwestern New Mexico stand the ruins of an Anasazi (Pueblo) cultural center that flourished from A.D. 850 to 1250. Although no one knows why the Anasazi left, all Southwest Indian tribes trace their ancestral roots to Chaco Canyon and consider it sacred. That the Chacoan people were able to build this highly advanced community and to thrive in this harsh environment for at least 400 years is a testament to their fortitude.

To fortify your spirit, take a day trip from Farmington, New Mexico (the nearest city, an hour away) to Chaco Canyon. Allow at least two hours to drive to and from this remote location and several hours to explore the vast ruins. Bring a picnic and water, and make sure to follow the advice given on the U.S. National Park Service website: *www.nps.gov/chcu/planyourvisit.htm*.

Soothe Your Spirit

Drive or bike the 9-mile paved loop, taking time to explore the guided trails of the five major Chacoan sites. Listen to the whispers of the ancients carried on the wind, offering encouragement or perhaps a solution to your problem.

A Deeper Look

This sacred gathering place for the Anasazi included fifteen complexes (Great Houses)—some several stories high, with hundreds of apartments (rooms) and dozens of *kivas* (circular ceremonial structures)—designed for celestial alignment and built from quarried sandstone and timber hauled from up to 70 miles away.

58. Winchester Cathedral

WINCHESTER, HAMPSHIRE, ENGLAND

Finally, be strong in the Lord and in the strength of his might.
—Bible, Ephesians 6:10

When Saint Swithun (Swithin), Anglo-Saxon bishop of Winchester and zealous builder and renovator of churches, died in A.D. 862, he was buried in the open—as he had adamantly instructed—between the Old Minster church and Saint Martin's Tower. A decade later, when an attempt was made to move his remains inside the church, legend has it that the saint caused it to rain for forty days, thus prohibiting his reburial. In 1093, the saint's relics were successfully transferred into Winchester Cathedral. Constructed of limestone that dazzles in the sunlight, this Romanesque sanctuary features soaring spires, flying buttresses, fourteen splendid church bells, and the longest nave (556 feet) of any cathedral in England.

Visit glorious Winchester Cathedral to pray for the spiritual conviction of Saint Swithun on July 15 (his feast day), throughout August when the weather is best (but the crowds are large), or at Christmas to hear the empowering chorale music.

Soothe Your Spirit
Reflect on the "raindrops" in your life and pray for the courage, patience, and perseverance to overcome them.

A Deeper Look
A popular pilgrimage site, especially during the Middle Ages, Winchester Cathedral venerates the Holy Trinity as well as Saints Peter, Paul, and Swithun. It safeguards the relics of numerous Saxon kings, members of the clergy, and writer Jane Austin in addition to those of Saint Swithun.

59. Masada

ISRAEL

When you have no choice, mobilize the spirit of courage.
—Jewish proverb

In A.D. 66, Jewish zealots (*Sicarii*) captured Masada, the virtually impenetrable fortress palace of Herod the Great, built on the summit of a mesa 30 miles southeast of Jerusalem. On that windy butte overlooking the Dead Sea and the Judean Desert, they established the last stronghold of Jewish rule in Palestine. After the fall of Jerusalem and destruction of the Second Temple four years later, the 960 *Sicarii* refused to surrender to the 15,000 Roman soldiers who besieged Masada. Drawing strength from their faith, they held off the invaders for two years before finally choosing death over life under Roman domination and enslavement.

Whether you want to strengthen your faith or to explore the ruins, Masada awaits. Book a day trip (from any of the local hotels). It's at least a two-hour drive from either Jerusalem or Arad.

Soothe Your Spirit

See the sprawling Judean desert from the crag of Masada at sunrise, as most pilgrims do. Take the Roman ramp, the serpentine Snake Path, or cable car to the summit and watch the sun rise spectacularly over the desert. Whisper a prayer for the courage and strength to remain true to your faith.

A Deeper Look

The remains of a synagogue built by the *Sicarii* still stand at Masada as do the palace Herod built, a couple of *mikvahs* (ritual baths), a church built by fifth-century monks, and other ruins.

60. Mount Desert Island

MAINE, UNITED STATES

Courage and honor endure forever. Their echoes remain when the mountains have crumbled to dust.
—Wiccan Code of Chivalry

*M*aine's spectacular Mount Desert Island with its crashing waves, sparkling waterways, forested mountains, craggy coastline, granite cliffs, and invigorating sea air became a refuge in the nineteenth century for wealthy families seeking solace and respite. For the indigenous Wabanaki (People of the Dawnland), the island they know as *Pemetic* (the sloping land) was sacred. For practitioners of Wicca and other Earth-based spiritual traditions, the island's wild beauty has ideal places to cast sacred circles for gathering spiritual strength.

To spend time in a restorative natural setting, you can't beat Mount Desert Island, home to Acadia National Park. The best time to visit is mid- to late summer. Drive to the island town of Bar Harbor from Bangor or Boston.

Soothe Your Spirit
Take a reflective stroll along a coastal path or one of the historical carriage roads used by walkers. Find a quiet spot and cast a magical stone circle. Commune with the energy of this island sanctuary and give voice to your desire or intention. Offer prayers of declaration, courage, and gratitude.

A Deeper Look
Mount Desert has only four towns and yet the island accommodates more than 2.5 million tourists annually. The island's Cadillac Mountain is the tallest on the eastern seacoast and where the sunrise is first seen in the United States.

61. Bighorn Medicine Wheel

YELLOWSTONE PARK, WYOMING, UNITED STATES

You have noticed that everything an Indian does is in a circle, and that is because the Power of the World always works in circles . . .
—Black Elk (1863–1950), Oglala Lakota (Sioux) holy man

An ancient Native American medicine wheel, 80 feet wide, lies in a desolate area of the Bighorn Mountains in Yellowstone National Park. Created by the Plains Indians but used by many Native American tribes, the wheel has a pile of stones at its center (*cairn*), from which spokes extend outward to a rim. Along the rim are six other *cairns*— possibly benches—that enable a person to face the center and see precisely the point on the horizon where the sun rises or sets during the solstice.

Whether you would like to learn about the medicine wheel's astronomy or tap into its sacred power, journey to Medicine Mountain in midsummer—the only time the site is accessible. Use the east entrance of Yellowstone National Park.

Soothe Your Spirit

Get an early start so you'll reach the medicine wheel before dawn. As the sun rises, declare what you desire and then pray for the forbearance and fortitude to make it so.

A Deeper Look

The Bighorn Medicine Wheel is part of an expansive sacred complex that has been used by various Native American tribes for more than 7,000 years. Prayer ribbons tied onto a fence are a visual reminder of their belief in the power of this sacred site.

62. Basiliek van het Heilig-Bloed (Basilica of the Holy Blood)

BRUGES, BELGIUM

But God is the strength of my heart, and my portion forever . . .
—Bible, Psalm 73:26

Since 1149, this pretty little basilica has been the home to a fragment of cloth said to contain blood wiped from Jesus's crucified body by Joseph of Arimathea (who also donated his own tomb, or sepulcher, for Jesus's burial). The sacred relic resides in a glass vial adorned with a gold crown on each end, which is housed inside the silver side altar of the upper chapel. Many people speak of having a spine-tingling experience in the presence of this icon.

If your spirit needs recharging, come to Basilica of the Holy Blood. Located in the southwest corner of Castle Square, the chapel is accessible by walking, cycling, buses, and trams.

Soothe Your Spirit

Visit any Friday 10:00–11:00 A.M. and 2:00–4:00 P.M., when the bishop of Bruges brings the relic out for public viewing, or on the Day of Ascension (forty days after Easter), when the bishop brings the vial out for a processional in the city. Let the relic work its magic on you and strengthen your spirit.

A Deeper Look

Presumably the relic was given to the count of Flanders by the patriarch of Jerusalem during the Second Crusade and was subsequently brought to the basilica in Bruges.

63. Sanjusangendo Hall

KYOTO, JAPAN

The secret of existence is to have no fear.
—Siddhartha Gautama, the Buddha (563–483 B.C.), father of Buddhism

This twelfth-century *heian* (temple) with vermilion columns, emerald roof, and serene gardens epitomizes Japanese court life in this bustling city from A.D. 794 to 1869. The spacious terrace offers stunning vistas of Sanjusangendo Hall with its 6-foot-tall statue of Kannon, goddess of mercy, who has eleven faces and a thousand arms. Flanking the large statue are 1,001 smaller Kannons, each having forty arms, and each arm has the power to save twenty-five worlds.

If you desire to be a force of good in the world, visit Sanjusangendo Temple. Located in the Higashiyama District of Kyoto, the temple is open 8:00 A.M. to 5:00 P.M. in summer, 9:00 A.M. to 4:00 P.M. in winter (November to March). From the Kyoto train station, Sanjusangendo is a fifteen- to twenty-minute walk; you can also take a city bus. No photography is allowed within the temple.

Soothe Your Spirit

In the hall of the Kannons, drop some money in a donation box, then strike the gong three times and say a prayer for the courage and conviction to do God's work. Light three sticks of incense: for the Buddha (the Divine one), the *dharma* (the law and discipline that guides one's life), and the *sangha* (the community).

A Deeper Look

The hall housing the Kannons is made in the Wayo Japanese style, long and large enough to house the statues and allow thirty-three spaces (a number sacred to Buddha) between the columns.

64. Schlosskirche (Castle Church)

LUTHERSTADT, WITTENBERG, GERMANY

Ein feste Burg ist unser Gott. (*A mighty Fortress is our God.*)
—Engraving encircling the steeple at Castle Church, from a hymn by
Martin Luther (1483–1546), German priest and professor of theology

*M*artin Luther, a German Roman Catholic priest, launched the Protestant Reformation in 1517 when he went to Schlosskirche and nailed his ninety-five theses to the church doors. The theses protested the Church's sale of indulgences (a practice that Luther regarded as corrupt) and called for a spiritual debate. The wood-paneled doors of the Gothic-style church burned in 1760, but the bronze replacement doors (1858) are engraved with Luther's theses in the original Latin text. The tympanum above the door depicts the crucifix, Martin Luther holding the German Bible, and Philipp Melanchthon holding the Augsburg Confession (confession of faith), which the two men composed.

If you desire the spiritual fortitude to face adversity, come to Castle Church. From either Berlin's Tegel or Schönefeld international airports, you can rent a car or taxi to take you to Lutherstadt Wittenberg, 45 miles southwest of Berlin. To go by bus, you will have to take a bus from the airport into the city and then change to another bus to reach the location.

Soothe Your Spirit
Inside this church venerating the father of Protestant Christianity, pray for inner strength and give thanks for your Lord's all-powerful Divine love.

A Deeper Look
Castle Church (officially named All Saint's Church) enshrines the tombs of Martin Luther, Philipp Melanchthon, and Frederick the Wise.

65. Great Pyramid of Khufu

GIZA PLATEAU, CAIRO, EGYPT

. . . the God sleeping in the soul of each person is awakened by the power of
the pyramid.
—Papyrus of Ani (1240s B.C.), Egyptian scribe

*R*ising almost 500 feet with a base covering 13 acres, the Great Pyramid of Khufu is the oldest, and only, survivor of the Seven Ancient Wonders of the World. Built around 2600 B.C., this pyramid was the largest human-made structure on Earth for forty-three centuries. A feat of engineering, construction, and astrological genius unknown for centuries, it is the only Egyptian pyramid with upper chambers and a passageway that descends 200 feet into bedrock and then ascends to a portal that aligns with the North Star once every 26,000 years. Innumerable mystical legends are associated with the Great Pyramid: such as, it was a temple for ancient Egyptian rituals, a prophetic monument, a giant sundial, and it was constructed by either extraterrestrials or an advanced race that mysteriously vanished.

If you seek personal or spiritual empowerment, make a pilgrimage to the Great Pyramid of Giza, 10 miles west of Cairo.

Soothe Your Spirit
Stand in the shadow of this ancient marvel and feel its monumental stability and powerful energy ground you and invigorate you.

A Deeper Look
The Great Pyramid of Khufu (Cheops in Greek) is at the north end of the Giza Plateau, on which also stands the rest of the Giza Necropolis—including the Pyramid of Khafre (Chephren, Cheops's son and successor), the Pyramid of Menkaure (Mykerinos, Chephren's son and successor), and the Sphinx.

66. Taos Pueblo

TAOS, NEW MEXICO, UNITED STATES

Hold on to what is good even if it is a handful of earth. / Hold on to what you believe, even if it is a tree that stands by itself . . .
—Pueblo Indian prayer

*T*aos Pueblo is the largest red-adobe *pueblo* (village) in North America—and one of the few continually occupied since its construction, one thousand years ago. Despite four centuries of European-American invasion and influence, the *Tuah-Tah* (Place of Red Willows) tribe of Pueblo Indians has held fast to this stunning structure and to their ancestral (and closely guarded) traditions.

To gain a new appreciation for the courageous spirit of the *Tuah-Tah* or to bolster your own spirit, visit the Taos Pueblo, one of the Eight Northern Pueblos. Drive or fly to Taos, an artistic mecca in northwestern New Mexico, which is only a few miles from the Pueblo, or take a day trip from Albuquerque or Santa Fe. Coach tours are available.

The site is open 8:00 A.M. to 4:30 P.M. daily, except for Pueblo holidays. Honor the visitors' guidelines: *www.indianpueblo.org/19pueblos/etiquette.html.*

Soothe Your Spirit

Tour the ancient *pueblo* with respect while contemplating the resilience of the Taos people. Write a prayer to the Great Spirit asking for strength to hold fast to your spiritual truth. When you return home, bury the note beneath a flowering plum, King protea, or borage; all three plants symbolize courage.

A Deeper Look

Taos Pueblo is a National Historic Landmark and a World Heritage Site. In 1970, the U.S. government returned 48,000 acres of sacred mountains and forests that included Blue Lake, a most sacred site to the Taos people.

67. Gingee Fort

GINGEE, VILLUPURAM DISTRICT, TAMIL NADU, INDIA

When restraint and courtesy are added to strength, the latter becomes irresistible.
—Mohandas K. Gandhi (1869–1948), Indian political leader and father of India

The thirteenth-century Gingee Fort, once called the "Troy of the East" because of its impenetrability, is actually a citadel complex built by the Chola Dynasty to protect a palace and temples, a mosque, granary, treasury, marriage hall, entertainment hall, "ladies' court," gymnasium, funeral pyre area, and sacred pool. Today, the ruins of these once-grand buildings occupied by Vijayanagara kings and then by French and British colonists remain a memorial to the fortitude of those who lived and worshiped there.

If you are inspired by symbols of power, consider a visit to Gingee Fort, now a national monument. The nearest airport is in Chennai (the capital of Tamil Nadu). The train station is in Tindivanam; from there, take a taxi, scooter, motorcycle, car and driver, or bus.

Soothe Your Spirit
Take your time walking the almost 3-acre site that covers three hills, each with its own citadel (fortress). Ask God, who bestows power and grace, to fill you with the kind of strength that fortified the inhabitants of this special place, attracting kings, foreign governments, and the faithful alike.

A Deeper Look
Occupation of the fortress-like hills of Gingee (also known as Chinji or Jinji) dates back to the Jains in A.D. 600. According to local legend, Gingee Amman was one of seven virgin goddesses who guarded the village.

68. Dom St. Peter (Trier Cathedral)

TRIER, RHINELAND-PALATINATE, GERMANY

His divine power has given us everything we need for a godly life through our knowledge of him who called us by his own glory and goodness.
—Bible, 2 Peter 1:3

According to legend, in the fourth century A.D., Constantine, the first Christian Roman emperor, accepted from his mother the sacred tunic Jesus wore during or just prior to his Crucifixion. Constantine installed the relic in his new church in Trier. Today, this red-brick Romanesque and Paleo-Christian–style church, rebuilt in the eleventh century, is a pilgrimage site for the veneration of the Holy Robe of Christ, safeguarded in its own chapel behind the high altar.

If you feel a resonance with the early Christians whose spiritual forbearance was perpetually tested and who drew strength from sacred artifacts associated with Jesus, come to Trier Cathedral. The next pilgrimage for the viewing of the Holy Robe is April 13 to May 13, 2012. The nearest airport is in Luxembourg, 31 miles away; Trier is also accessible by sea and land. From the airport, train and bus service connects to Trier, or you can drive. Bonn, Aachen, Wiesbaden, and Cologne are within 100 miles of the city.

Soothe Your Spirit

Meditate on the power of unity, symbolized by the seamless tunic. Feel the weight lift off your shoulders as you imagine being filled with strength and fortitude.

A Deeper Look

Over the arched south door of this church dedicated to Saint Peter is a lovely Romanesque tympanum depicting Christ, Mary, and Peter.

69. Temppeliaukio Kirkko (Rock Church)

HELSINKI, FINLAND

With this faith we will be able to hew out of the mountain of despair a stone of hope.
—Dr. Martin Luther King, Jr. (1929–1968), American clergyman and
civil rights leader

The Rock Church, looking a bit like a Neolithic tomb recast into a modern architectural structure, was cut from bedrock in the middle of a residential area in 1968 by brothers and architects Timo and Tuomo Suomalainen. The exterior of this underground Lutheran church reveals only a portion of its dome-shaped copper roof, doing little to prepare first-time visitors for the bold interior: an astonishing circular sanctuary of rough-hewn rock walls bathed in natural light, a copper-wire ceiling, a copper balcony, and dark wood furnishings with fuchsia cushions.

If you are inspired by images and sensations of strength, both tangible and intangible, visit Rock Church in the Etu-Töölö (southern district) of Helsinki. From the city's main tram station, take the 3T line and exit at the Sammonkatu stop.

Soothe Your Spirit

Attend a musical concert in this church (the acoustics are phenomenal), perhaps during the Easter or Christmas season. Cradled securely within the massive rock structure, feel the grounding strength of God's love and let the powerful sound of voices raised in fervent song connect you more firmly to your purpose.

A Deeper Look

The Rock Church has a structural collar (connecting the rock wall with the dome roof) that holds 180 vertical windows, allowing in natural light.

70. Mezquita-Catedral (Cathedral-Mosque)

CÓRDOBA, SPAIN

When you see the storm coming, if you seek safety in that firm refuge which is Mary, there will be no danger of your wavering or going down.
—Saint Josemaría Escrivá (1902–1975), Spanish Roman Catholic priest and founder of Opus Dei

*T*he Cathedral-Mosque of Córdoba began around A.D. 600 as a Visigoth monastery, which the Umayyad Moors converted to a mosque in the late eighth century. About 100 years later, the Moors built the new Great Mosque on the site, which the Roman Catholic Church reclaimed and consecrated to Saint Mary of the Assumption in 1236. In 1523, the Córdoba diocese removed the center of the mosque and inserted a lavishly ornamented cathedral. Today, this World Heritage Site stands as a monument to spiritual strength, both Muslim and Christian.

If you seek strength to deal with a radical change in your life or if you just want to experience a sacred site that has endured centuries of change, visit the Mezquita-Catedral. The nearest airport is Málaga (85 miles away), and the Córdoba Railway links to cities in Spain. In the city, hail a taxi, ride the local bus, or take a guided tour.

Soothe Your Spirit

Envision sustaining your spiritual equilibrium as you lean into the change you face or desire. Offer a prayer of gratitude to Mary for her strength in delivering her only Son to the world, that all may go forth in strength.

A Deeper Look

Mezquita-Catedral stands on a sacred site of pagan Roman worship, where a Roman temple to Janus once existed.

71. Tiwanaku (Tiahuanacu Spanish)

LA PAZ, BOLIVIA

. . . Be still until the sunlight pours through and dispels the mists / as it surely will / Then act with courage.
—Ponca Chief White Eagle (1800s–1914)

Tiwanaku, the sacred ruins of a pre-Columbian religious and political center in the Bolivian highlands, is surrounded by mountains on three sides and a lake on the fourth, features the ancients believed had protective and spiritual qualities. Prehistoric Andean people occupied this powerful city-state from A.D. 300 to 1000, when they suddenly disappeared. Five hundred years later, the sun-worshiping Incas laid claim to the abandoned city, which they believed was the birthplace of the Inca people and a gateway to their many gods. Purportedly a nexus for spiritual energy, Tiwanaku continues to be sacred to Andean people and now draws New Age devotees, scholars, and tourists from around the globe.

If you desire strength to endure adversity, make a pilgrimage to this sacred place high in the Andes (13,000 feet above sea level) that has endured for 14,000 years. Reach Tiwanaku by bus from La Paz, Bolivia's capital city, or take a guided coach tour.

Soothe Your Spirit

Join the thousands who come in June for the summer solstice. Dress warmly and find a spot with a good vista and good energy. As you watch the sun rise, feel the exhilaration rise in your soul and thank the Creator for the life-giving rays that warm your body.

A Deeper Look

Viracocha, the god of action, is one of many deities the Inca associated with Tiwanaku, now a World Heritage Site.

72. Sultan Ahmed Mosque (Blue Mosque)

ISTANBUL, TURKEY

In hardship I saw him on my side. In ease and well-being I beheld only God.
—Baba Kuhi of Shiraz (from *Rabi'a the Mystic*, tr. Aneela Khalid Arshed), ninth-century A.D. Iranian Sufi poet-saint

Named for the blue tiles covering the interior walls of the sanctuary, the Blue Mosque was built between A.D. 1609 and 1616 and is a grand representation of Byzantine and Ottoman religious architecture. The commanding mosque is framed by six tall, graceful minarets and surrounded by expansive courtyards. A massive circular chandelier illumines the cavernous domed interior, with its many smaller domes cascading from the main dome, and Arabic calligraphy and floral and geometric motifs embellish the ceilings.

Whether you seek the power of knowledge or spiritual recharging, travel to the Blue Mosque. Remove your shoes before entering. Women must cover their hair with scarves, and if not attired conservatively enough, don robes (available onsite at no charge). Non-worshipers must use the north entrance and are not allowed in during prayer times. Get to the mosque via taxi, tram, or bus T4 from Taxsim to Sultanahmet, Istanbul's tourist area.

Soothe Your Spirit
Fill the gaps in your spiritual knowledge by writing a question or two to ask one of the imams who lead the prayers and preach the sermon on Fridays. Be respectful; this is a holy place of worship.

A Deeper Look
The original seventeenth-century Venetian stained-glass windows have been replaced with replicas but still offer a lovely luminosity.

73. The Church of All Nations

JERUSALEM, ISRAEL

And they came to a place which was named Gethsemane: and he saith to his disciples,
Sit ye here, while I shall pray . . .
—Bible, Mark 14: 32–36

When Jesus was in the Garden of Gethsemane with his disciples before his arrest, he told them to sit while he walked off a short distance to pray. Today, the Church of All Nations, also known as the Basilica of the Agony, sits upon the site where Jesus prayed, and the sacred piece of bedrock upon which he prayed is enshrined in the church.

If you desire to cultivate the kind of spiritual strength that Christ exemplified, see the basilica that numerous nations helped build. Located at the base of the Mount of Olives, the Garden of Gethsemane is on many Jerusalem walking tours and is easy to reach by rental car or taxi.

Soothe Your Spirit

Reflect on the agony Jesus felt as he prayed. Notice the purplish-blue alabaster used in the basilica's windows to evoke a somber mood, indicative of Christ's agony even as he accepted God's will. Think of three ways you could work on developing that kind of spiritual resolve.

A Deeper Look

The Church of All Nations was built on a site once occupied by a fourth-century B.C. basilica that toppled in an earthquake and a twelfth-century Crusader chapel. The modern church was consecrated in 1924.

74. Oskar Schindler's Tomb at Mount Zion Catholic Cemetery

JERUSALEM, ISRAEL

The Unforgettable Lifesaver of 1200 Persecuted Jews.
—German inscription on Oskar Schindler's tomb

Oskar Schindler (1908–1974), an ethnic-German industrialist who saved 1,200 Jews from extermination by the Nazis, died in poverty in Hildesheim, West Germany. His body was buried in Jerusalem's Mount Zion Catholic Cemetery, where Jews pay their respects by leaving the customary stone or pebble on Schindler's grave as tokens of gratitude; others leave flowers.

Perhaps you want to cultivate the kind of courage and spiritual fortitude demonstrated by Oskar Schindler for those times when you see injustice, but do nothing. If so, consider visiting his tomb in the lowest portion of the Mount Zion Catholic Cemetery near a path on the right. The cemetery is adjacent to the Dormition Abbey, just outside the Old City and Zion Gate, on the Ma'ale HaSholom Road to the Mount Zion parking lot. You'll find it on maps of walking tours of Jerusalem, or take a taxi.

Soothe Your Spirit

Take a pebble or a flower to place on the grave of this Christian who became a Jewish hero. Think about how you might become more spiritually courageous and inspired to help others.

A Deeper Look

Oskar Schindler's dying wish was to be buried in Jerusalem. On his tomb there are two inscriptions: one in German and the other in Hebrew. The latter states, "Righteous among the Nations," an honor bestowed by Israel on Gentiles who risked their lives to save Jews during the Holocaust.

75. Lincoln Cathedral (Cathedral Church of the Blessed Virgin Mary of Lincoln)

LINCOLN, LINCOLNSHIRE COUNTY, ENGLAND

He giveth power to the faint; and to them that have no might he increaseth strength.
—Bible, Isaiah 40:29

When Remigius de Fécamp, the first bishop of Lincoln, ordered a cathedral to be built atop a hill facing Lincoln Castle in A.D. 1072, construction began on the Cathedral Church of the Blessed Virgin Mary of Lincoln. In 1092, just two days before the cathedral was to be consecrated, Bishop Remigius died. A fire destroyed the roof in 1141; forty years later, an earthquake all but destroyed the building. The spectacular Gothic cathedral that replaced it—and stands majestically today—is the result of the vision and fortitude of Saint Hugh, the medieval bishop of Lincoln who oversaw its construction but died before its completion.

If you find the collapse of old traditions to be disconcerting or seek inspiration in refashioning or rebuilding your life, visit Lincoln Cathedral to witness how vision and persistence can create something grand and enduring out of ruin.

Soothe Your Spirit

While touring the enormous cathedral, pause before one of the arched stained-glass windows in the towering nave to reflect on how faith can sustain you through difficult times and empower you to build anew.

A Deeper Look

Lincoln Cathedral—the seat of the Anglican bishop of Lincoln, Church of England—served as a set in the film version of Dan Brown's bestselling novel *The Da Vinci Code*, which some consider a blasphemous use of this holy site.

76. Bhimbetka Rock Shelters

ITARSI, RAISEN DISTRICT, MADHYA PRADESH, INDIA

Faith without thankfulness lacks strength and fortitude.
—Siddhartha Gautama, the Buddha (563–483 B.C.), father of Buddhism

Inside five clusters of caves believed to have been inhabited by prehistoric people in India's Vindhyan Mountains for more than 100,000 years is an incredible repository of ancient art, some sacred. The Bhimbetka Rock Shelters—discovered in 1957 and named for Bhima, the hero/deity of extraordinary strength from the *Mahabharata* epic—reveal religious and ritual symbols as well as scenes celebrating the abundance in ordinary life.

Whether you are inspired by cave art that has survived for millennia or wish to channel the superhuman strength of Bhima, journey to this World Heritage Site, 27 miles south of Bhopal, capital of Madhya Pradesh. From Bhopal, rent a taxi or a car and driver. The best time to go is during the dry season, December through May. Bring water and a snack, because (as of this writing) there are no services nearby; however, guards and guides are present to protect the site and educate visitors.

Soothe Your Spirit

Bring a journal or sketch pad to record affirmations or images of courage, strength, or fortitude that come to you as you examine the ancient cave paintings illuminating the enduring role of spirituality in humankind. Take strength from the abundance in your life.

A Deeper Look

Designated as a World Heritage Site in 2003, the caves were documented as a sacred Buddhist site in 1888, almost 100 years before the cave paintings were discovered by Indian archaeologist V. S. Wakankar in 1957.

77. Saint Cuthbert's Parish Church

EDINBURGH, SCOTLAND

Hope springs exulting on triumphant wing.
—Robert Burns (1759–1796), Scottish poet

Saint Cuthbert's Church sits in the shadow of Edinburgh Castle on the sacred site of the hut of Saint Cuthbert (the seventh-century Anglo-Saxon saint who eased the transition from Celtic to Roman rites) and of several other ancient sanctuaries. While the church's Renaissance design and artwork glorify Anglican traditions—including an interpreted version of Leonardo da Vinci's *Last Supper* created from alabaster in three parts to accommodate the curved wall in the apse—the parish embraces both Anglican and Celtic Christian spirituality. In addition to Saint Cuthbert, "Wonder Worker of Britain," the church venerates the Celtic saints Brendan the Bold, Brigid, "Mary of the Gael," and Columba, "Hope of the Scots."

Find inspiration to carry on and to celebrate God's grace at Saint Cuthbert's Parish Church where the Celtic spirit triumphantly endures. At 5 Lothian Road, the site is easy to reach by car from elsewhere in Edinburgh.

Soothe Your Spirit

Note the quiet beauty of this ornate church surrounded by a centuries-old graveyard where many notables of Scottish descent are buried. Consider how the Celts derived strength from their Earth-based spiritual beliefs and think of ways to generate strength of spirit in your life.

A Deeper Look

On the wall of a tower chapel built in 1775 are inscribed the names of Saint Cuthbert members who perished in the Great War of 1914–18. In 1930, the chapel was the wedding site of mystery novelist Agatha Christie and Max Mallowan.

78. Rollright Stones

LITTLE ROLLRIGHT, OXFORDSHIRE, ENGLAND

Strength of stone, refreshing water, / in peaceful place of green. Strength of water, fresher flowering, / Peaceful stone has ever been. / Strength of growth, refreshing stone, / Peace of water to be seen.
—Druid blessing

*N*othing epitomizes strength and staying power like stone, and the large upright stones in the little village of Oxfordshire form megaliths—large, upright stone monuments used for religious worship and ritual—dating from 4000 to 2000 B.C. (Neolithic to Bronze Age). The Rollright Stones include three megaliths: the Whispering Knights (the oldest and so named because the stones lean inward), the solitary King's Stone, and the King's Men (a circle of stones 104 feet in diameter).

If you long to develop the spiritual strength of a stone or to derive sacred energy from Neolithic ritual sites, journey to the Rollright Stones. Travel to the village of Little Rollright by automobile from Chipping-Norton, the nearest town. The site is open daily, sunrise to sunset. There is a small entrance fee. Note that Wyatt's Farm Shop (a mile away) and Cross Hands Inn (2 miles away) have restrooms and water, as neither are available at the site.

Soothe Your Spirit
Stroll around the Druidical megaliths, absorbing their ancient spiritual energy. Cast a sacred circle of small stones and pray that your faith will always sustain you.

A Deeper Look
The King's Stone monolith stands across the road in a different county (Warwickshire) from the King's Men circle.

79. Tel Megiddo (Mount Megiddo)

MEGIDDO NATIONAL PARK, ISRAEL

Be strong and of good courage, fear not, nor be afraid . . . for the Lord, thy God, he it is that doeth go with thee; he will not fail thee, nor forsake thee.
—Bible, Deuteronomy 31: 6

Not far from the city of Nazareth, an excavation is under way at one of Israel's most historic and ancient sites, Tel Megiddo, also known as *Tel-el-Mutesellim* (Hill of the Ruler) and the Solomonic "Chariot City." Located on this World Heritage Site are the ruins of twenty-six layers of ancient cities. One of many legends states that the Hebrew prophetess Deborah, "the Mother of Israel," camped at Megiddo before convincing General Barak to face the Canaanite armies of Sisera—one of many holy battles fought here.

If you wish to draw strength from a site of many spiritual victories, visit Tel Megiddo. Reservations are required, so book a guided tour. The nearest town is Afula; Taanach is 5 miles away and Haifa is 18 miles.

Soothe Your Spirit

Before entering the Solomonic gateway leading to the viewing area, offer a prayer of thanks for a life battle in which God was your strength. As you examine the religious complex and circular stone altar, contemplate the fortitude of the faithful who lived there.

A Deeper Look

The Book of Revelation prophesies that the world's last battle between good and evil will take place at Megiddo (known as the Plain of Jezreel and Armageddon).

80. Tikal

TIKAL NATIONAL PARK, EL PETÉN, GUATEMALA

The Track of the Sun / across the Sky / leaves its shining message, / Illuminating, / Strengthening, / Warming, / us who are here, / showing us we are not alone, . . .
—Atoni; Choctaw Native American blessing

Tikal, built in 600 B.C., was one of the most powerful kingdoms in Mesoamerica. The towering, 230-foot limestone temples left behind when the Maya people abandoned Tikal by the tenth century are monuments to the glory of their civilization at its peak. Archaeologists have found dozens of pyramids, some with stone implements that amplify the human voice, possibly enabling spiritual leaders to speak with godlike intonation from the top of the pyramids.

If you seek spiritual strength to empower your voice or message, visit Tikal. Book a guide tour at the site, near the museum. Fly from Guatemala City to Flores (on Lake Petén Itzá) and drive an hour to Tikal. From San Ignacio in Belize, Tikal is a two-hour drive.

Soothe Your Spirit
Climb to the top of a pyramid and offer a prayer for strength or a mantra affirming your great faith to the Divine. Let the words rise slowly from your heart to the top of your throat, out of your mouth, onto the wind, and toward the sun.

A Deeper Look
The abundant wildlife of Petén and the archaeological significance of the site prompted UNESCO to signify Tikal as both a Natural and a Cultural World Heritage Site.

81. Panagia Ekatontapyliani Church

PIRIKIA, PAROS, GREECE

If you are very valiant, it is a god, I think, who gave you this gift.
—Homer (800–700 B.C.), *The Iliad*, Greek epic poet

This fourth-century A.D. Orthodox Church complex, whose name means Our Lady of a Hundred Doors, is the oldest Byzantine Christian church in Greece. In 1962, a renowned Greek scholar confirmed Saint Helen and her son, the Roman emperor Constantine, as the founders of this marble monument venerating four saints (Anargiron, Philip, Theodosia, and Dimitrios) and a ninth-century nun, Osia. According to legend, pirates kidnapped several young nuns from a convent on Lesbos, and when they docked at Pirikia, which was deserted due to the frequent pirate raids, to allow the nuns to recover from seasickness, Osia escaped into the woods and hid in the abandoned church. She lived alone for thirty-five years, subsisting on wild plants and holy water.

If you wish to pay homage to Osia's bravery or to restore your faith, visit Our Lady of a Hundred Doors. From Athens, Mykonos, or Santorini, take a ferry to Paros, in the Cyclades Island group. Alternatively, you can take a small plane from Athens to Paros.

Soothe Your Spirit

Let the holy vibration of this elegant church strengthen your faith. In Osia's chapel, near where her relics are entombed, offer a prayer of gratitude for Divine protection.

A Deeper Look

There is evidence that a temple existed on the site as early as A.D. 326, where Saint Helen may have taken refuge during a storm while on a mission to find the Holy Cross.

82. Church of Mary Magdalene at Rennes-le-Château

LANGUEDOC, DEPARTMENT OF AUDE, FRANCE

Mary Magdalene reminds everyone of a fundamental truth: She is a disciple of Christ who . . . had the humility to ask for his help, . . . becoming a witness to the power of his merciful love . . .
—Pope Benedict XVI (1927–), elected to the Papacy in 2005

The restoration of the Church of Mary Magdalene at Rennes-le-Château was undertaken by Father Saunière in 1885, and the result seems designed to be a test of faith. On entering the church a statue of the devil holds the holy water *stoup* (or basin), raising the question of whether it is holy, and the plaques of the Stations of the Cross are out of sequence. Those are but two of the oddities that bedevil the 10,000 faithful each year who visit this remote sanctuary venerating Saint Mary Magdalene—a fierce disciple of Christ with mysteries of her own.

If you want to test the strength of your faith or bear witness to the unshakable faith of Mary Magdalene, visit this lovely church in the castle village of Rennes-le-Château, in southwestern France. Travel by train or rental car from Carcassonne.

Soothe Your Spirit

As you explore the renovated church, pay attention to whether the experience shakes or strengthens your beliefs. Notice, too, whether you feel called to show tolerance or to exercise constraint. Offer a prayer for forbearance or of gratitude.

A Deeper Look

The Latin inscription above the door states: "This place is terrible." Terribly holy, perhaps.

CHAPTER 4

FERTILITY, ABUNDANCE, GRATITUDE

Let us be grateful to the people who make us happy;
they are the charming gardeners who make
our souls blossom.

—*Marcel Proust (1871–1922), French novelist,*
critic, and essayist

83. Kūkaniloko Birthstones State Monument

WAHIAWĀ, OAHU, HAWAII, USA

Kapawa, the chief of Wai'alua, / Was born at Kūkaniloko; / Wahiawā the site; / At Lihu'e the placenta, / At Ka'ala the navel cord, / At Kapukapuakea (Heiau) the caul, (Heiau) of Kaiaka at Maeaea; / A chiefly child of Wai'alua, O'ahu.
—Hawaiian chant

*M*ost days, a soft, tropical Kona wind blows across mystical Kūkaniloko, a 5-acre historical preserve in central Oahu where 180 sacred lava stones lie on a half-acre grassy plot embraced by a grove of fragrant eucalyptus and coconut trees. The royal birthing stones mark the secret site where the wives of Hawaiian chiefs bore their children in the presence of thirty-six chiefs. The father then took the newborn royal (*ali'i*) to a nearby site where he ceremoniously cut the umbilical cord and performed purification rites in front of forty-eight chiefs, before the royal birth was announced by beating on ceremonial drums.

Whether you desire to bless the birth of a child or to give birth to a dream, come to Kūkaniloko, where the Kona wind seems to whisper the fertility secrets of the ancients. Rental car is the best way to get to Kūkaniloko, on the north side of Wahiawā, at Whitmore Avenue and Highway 99.

Soothe Your Spirit

As you look at (but don't touch) the sacred birthing stones, pray for fertility or abundance, or chant of the blessing of a child or sacred gift in your life.

A Deeper Look

Kūkaniloko translated from the Hawaiian means "to anchor the cry from within."

84. Church of Saint Anne

JERUSALEM, ISRAEL

Now there is at Jerusalem by the sheep market a pool, which is called in the Hebrew tongue Bethesda, having five porches.
—Bible, John 5:2–9

When Saint Anne and her husband, Joachim, observed their beloved daughter at play, most likely they needed to take only a few steps from the house in which Anne was born and later their child, the Blessed Virgin Mary. On the site, in 1130, the Crusaders constructed a Romanesque church featuring a domed basilica with a cross-vaulted ceiling supported by ornate columns and capitals. Nearby, you can still see the biblical Bethesda pool, where sheep were given purification baths before being sacrificed and where Jesus healed a man from an illness.

Whether you wish to conceive a child or to venerate the patron saint of childless and pregnant women, visit the Church of Saint Anne. The saint's feast day is July 26 (July 25 on the Eastern Orthodox calendar). Reach the church on foot or use local transportation as it is situated near the Lion's Gate near the Via Dolorosa.

Soothe Your Spirit

Breathe in the tranquility and pray or give thanks for the blessing of parenthood in this sanctuary honoring the grandmother of Jesus and mother of the Virgin Mary (in Roman Catholic and Islamic traditions) and the Forebear of God (in Eastern Orthodox tradition).

A Deeper Look

In 1856, the Ottoman sultan, appreciative of French support during the Crimean War, subsequently gifted the Church of Saint Anne to the Roman Catholic White Fathers.

85. Tomb of Sheikh Salim Chishti

FATEHPUR SIKRI, AGRA, INDIA

God is with those who persevere.
—Qur'an

*I*n the sixteenth century when Akbar the Great needed a male heir to succeed him, he sought the blessing of the Sufi mystic Salim Chishti. Subsequently, Akbar's wife gave birth to three sons. The first, named Salim (after the mystic), was raised by the holy man and later assumed his father's throne as the Mughal emperor Jahangir. The white marble mausoleum the grateful Akbar built for the saint stands in the center of the Jama Masjid complex at Fatehpur Sikri, now a World Heritage Site. The saint is entombed in an ebony chamber inlaid with mother-of-pearl. Pilgrims tie cotton string to the latticed exterior walls and kneel before the ebony crypt to pray for their heart's desires.

If you long to become fertile—with children, spirituality, or some other virtue—pray at the Tomb of Salim Chishti. Reach Agra by air, car, or rail from Delhi, then hire a cab or rent a car to travel 28 miles to Fatehpur Sikri.

Soothe Your Spirit

Stroll the complex, view the saint's tomb, offer a flower, and then say your prayer as you tie a symbolic thread through the lattice screen of the tomb. When your petition is granted, make a return visit to render thanks and remove your thread.

A Deeper Look

Akbar held the saint in such awe that he built an entire complex (Fatehpur Sikri) around the saint's camp and relocated his court there.

86. Stonehenge

AMESBURY, WILTSHIRE COUNTY, ENGLAND

Pile of Stone-hedge! So proud to hint yet keep / Thy secrets, thou lov'st to stand and hear / The plain resounding to the whirlwind's sweep / Inmate of lonesome Nature's endless year.

—William Wordsworth (1770–1850), English Romantic poet

Stonehenge's massive megalithic pillars and lintels, dating to 3200 B.C., were likely assembled for the purpose of worship. Today, this prehistoric monument in the quiet English countryside on the Salisbury Plain near Amesbury is a sacred destination for neo-Druids, pagan and neo-pagan worshipers, and New Age believers. Many come for summer solstice (June in the Northern Hemisphere), purportedly the most auspicious time for manifesting desires. At dawn on that day, the sunlight rises above the horizon, cuts across Stonehenge, and illuminates the pillars and field upon which thousands of believers gather. On winter solstice, the sun sets between the two biggest megaliths.

If you'd like to experience a magical summer or winter solstice or summon the magic of fertility or abundance, journey to Stonehenge.

Soothe Your Spirit
Bring an object symbolizing what you desire. Stand facing the sun in sight of the megaliths, holding the object in the open palms of your hands. Offer thanks to the Divine Source of All for the blessings in your life. Then pray for the magic you desire.

A Deeper Look
Some legends claim Stonehenge was built by King Arthur and Merlin, others point to the Druids, Danes, Saxons, Greeks, Romans, Atlanteans, even the Egyptians.

87. Lakshmi Narayan Temple (Birla Temple)

NEW DELHI, INDIA

In prayer it is better to have a heart without words than words without a heart.
—Mohandas K. Gandhi (1869–1948), Indian political leader and father of India

*J*n 1938 when the Birla family, wealthy Indian industrialists, decided to honor Vishnu (Narayan, the Preserver, when in the company of his goddess/consort Lakshmi, goddess of wealth), the family chose the site of an older temple on which to build. The Nagara-style Lakshmi Narayan Temple—with its generous use of polished marble and red sandstone, tall curved towers, lavish ornamentation, and exquisite shrines housing *murthis* (statues) of the deities—has been called an oasis of spiritual calm in an otherwise bustling city.

If you are experiencing uncertainty or scarcity in your life, pay your respects at the Lakshmi Narayan Temple. The temple is located near Connaught Place, an important thoroughfare in central Delhi, and is easily reached by taxi, three-wheel cycles, and buses. You will be required to remove your shoes and cover your bare arms, legs, and cleavage before entering the temple, and no cameras are allowed inside. Free lockers (with keys) are available for storing your camera, shoes, and other personal items.

Soothe Your Spirit
At the altar, offer a flower, and with folded hands, petition the Divine from the deepest recesses of your heart.

A Deeper Look
The temple was inaugurated by Mahatma Gandhi, "the Father of India," with the stipulation that all people would be welcome to worship there.

88. Ulun Danu Bratan Temple

LAKE BRATAN, BALI, INDONESIA

Water is life's mater and matrix, mother and medium. There is no life without water.
—Alfred Szent-Györgyi (1893–1986), Hungarian chemist and Nobel laureate

*U*lun Danu Bratan (also Beratan) Temple in Bali's Bedugul highlands is a stunning water temple situated on a shimmering lake surrounded by malachite green hills and thickly forested mountains frequently shrouded in mist. The temple takes its name from Dewi Danu (goddess of the lake), the source of fertility and prosperity, and from Lake Bratan, which nourishes life by irrigating rice fields throughout Bali. Inside the sanctuary of this important Buddhist-Hindu temple with its multilevel pagoda-shape (Meru) is a shrine dedicated to Brahma (the Creator) and a smaller temple honoring Dewi Shogawati, goddess of food and drink.

If you prefer sacred sanctuary in a fecund natural setting, visit Ulun Danu Bratan Temple. Getting there means traveling from south to north on a road that lifts gently through rice fields, terraces, and cocoa plantations, affording lovely coastal views. At certain times of the year, local people come to the temple to pray and receive blessings.

Soothe Your Spirit

This is not a public temple and since tourists and non-members are not allowed inside the temple, head for the lake's edge past the manicured gardens, stopping to meditate before the stunning Buddhist *stupa* (bell-shaped tower) along the way. Alternately, arrange for a small boat to take you out on the lake to view the temple at dawn, and pray or perhaps perform a fertility ritual.

A Deeper Look

Built in 1633 by the Raja (Hindu king) Mengwi, the temple is now a World Heritage Site.

89. Cozumel

QUINTANA ROO, MEXICO

*I'm aware of the mystery around us . . . coincidences, premonitions, emotions, dreams,
the power of nature, magic.*
—Isabel Allende (1942–), Peruvian-born American writer

When an ancient Maya woman wanted to become pregnant, she would appeal to Ix Chel, the moon goddess. From time immemorial, the effects of a full moon on sex and fertility have been observable: heightened romantic passion and increases in labor and childbirth. Since the entire island of Cozumel is the holy domain of the Mayan moon goddess, you might want to perform your own fertility ritual (perhaps with your lover) under a full moon on a romantic Cozumel beach.

Cozumel (Place of Swallows) is small: only 30 miles wide and not quite 10 miles across. Yet the island, which lies 37 miles south of Cancun, is one of Mexico's most popular tourist destinations because of its pristine beaches and incredible snorkeling on the Mesoamerican Reef.

Travel to Cozumel is easy now that the island has a small international airport with flights to and from mainland Mexico and many U.S. cities. Cruise ships also dock at one of three piers.

Soothe Your Spirit

As you sit under the stars sipping Mayan drinking chocolate spiced with chili and gazing at the moon, invoke the moon goddess's powers to bless you with motherhood as she has blessed Maya women for thousands of years.

A Deeper Look

The Maya believed the cacao tree was a gift from the gods and attributed eating and drinking chocolate to fertility.

90. Sri Senpaga Vinayagar Temple

SINGAPORE

Bountiful guardians of the world . . . when we long to win, may we be victors.
—Rig Veda, Book V, Hymn 62:9

If you arrive early enough at this lovely temple dedicated to Ganesh, the elephant-headed god of success, also known as Remover of Obstacles in the Hindu pantheon, you might see the priests ritually preparing the altar and statues for the morning worship (*puja*). Using jars of water poured amidst clouds of incense, the priests intone verses in Sanskrit and ring a bell while washing, drying, and then adorning the idols with brightly colored flowers.

If you seek Divine assistance in attracting success or removing obstacles to create a new beginning, come to Sri Senpaga Vinayagar Temple to pay your respects to Ganesh (also, Ganesha or Ganapati). The temple is in the Tanjong Katong area, twenty minutes from the airport and easily reached by taxi or rental car. No shoes or socks are allowed inside the temple.

Soothe Your Spirit

Offer a flower and ring the bell (if one is provided for devotees) as an invocation to the Divine. In a silent mantra, call his name, "*Aum Shri Ganeshaya Namah*" ("Praise to Lord Ganesha") and ask his assistance in clearing obstacles from within or without and in manifesting spiritual or material abundance.

A Deeper Look

The temple, the second oldest in Singapore, was originally created in the 1850s by the Ceylonese Tamils in the ancient south Indian ornate and intricately carved Chola style of architecture but has been reconstructed several times.

91. Temple of Tellus

DOUGGA, TUNISIA

Our duty, as men and women, is to proceed as if limits to our ability did not exist. We are collaborators in creation.
—Pierre Teilhard de Chardin (1881–1955), French philosopher and Jesuit priest

The Tunisian temple honoring Tellus (also Terra Mater), ancient Roman goddess of marriage (and fertility when coupled with Ceres), survives as part of a well-preserved third-century A.D. Roman town in northern Tunisia. The arid climate of Dougga, believed to have originally been a Berber village, preserves stunning pagan temples, baths, arches, theaters, cisterns, a forum, a market, and a mausoleum.

If you are drawn to the Earth Mother Goddess or to other cults predating the Judeo-Christian era and/or would like to pray in an ancient place of great spiritual and historical significance, visit Dougga. Take a day tour from Tunis or Le Kef; hire a taxi from the nearest town, Teboursouk; take the bus from Le Kef, disembarking at the Nouvelle Dougga stop and walking 2.5 miles to the temple.

Soothe Your Spirit

Explore the ruins, stopping to meditate before the capitol dedicated to Juno, Roman goddess who protected pregnant women and fetuses, delivering them into the light. Pray for fertility of mind, body, or spirit—for yourself, a loved one, or our leaders, for our earthly home needs solutions to its many problems in order to prevent our civilization from falling as did the Romans.

A Deeper Look

Dougga's capitol, dedicated to three Roman deities—Jupiter, Juno, and Minerva—was built in A.D. 166, and its walls (about 33 feet high) still support the breathtaking portico, where you can stand and look out over the vast desert landscape to blue-purple mountains rising far in the distance.

92. Giant Hill

CERNE ABBAS, DORSET, ENGLAND

It's easier to go down a hill than up it but the view is much better at the top.
—Enoch Arnold Bennett (1867–1931), British novelist

Cerne Abbas in northwest Dorset has a chalkstone giant carved into a hillock, waving his club and exposing an astonishing erection. Although the landmark's date of origin remains a mystery (possibly the Middle Ages or even the Iron Age), the giant has long been associated with fertility. According to legend, women who wanted to conceive would camp out alone and young couples would make love on the giant—most productively, within his enormous phallus. Today, women living in Cerne Abbas have more babies per capita than England's national average.

The best way to see the giant is from the air, across the valley, or from the east side parking area off the A352 highway. Walking on the giant is prohibited; as a National Trust ancient monument, he is fenced off from the public. Reach Cerne Abbas, between the towns of Sherbourne and Dorchester, by bus or car.

Soothe Your Spirit
Walk the Giant Hill Footpath, taking in views of the virile giant and the fertile English countryside. Make the act of loving a sacred sacrament (get a room first, perhaps in a lovely local B&B) and toast your fertility—in whatever manifestation you cherish or seek—with a cup of tea and a scone.

A Deeper Look
Some speculate that the giant represented the Greek god Hercules, who also held a club.

93. Temple of Artemis

I have seen the walls and Hanging Gardens of ancient Babylon, the statue of Olympian Zeus, the Colossus of Rhodes, the mighty work of the high Pyramids, and the tomb of Mausolus. But when I saw the temple at Ephesus rising to the clouds, all these other wonders were put in the shade.
—Philon of Byzantium (ca. 280–220 B.C.), Greek engineer and writer

On a marshy strip of river land near Ephesus stands a single column and a few fragments of a magnificent ancient temple honoring the Ephesian Artemis, goddess of fertility (also known as Diana, she is not the same as the Greek Artemis, who was goddess of the hunt). The marble temple was once the mother of all monuments, eclipsing even the Parthenon in Athens, testifying to the importance of this goddess of fertility. In fact, the temple was one of the Seven Wonders of the Ancient World.

Whether you wish to attract abundance or a grateful spirit, visit this temple at Ephesus, 2 miles from Selcuk. Go early to avoid the midday heat and tourists. The nearest ship harbor is Kusadasi, and the nearest airport is in nearby Izmir.

Soothe Your Spirit

Chant an affirmation of your desired fertility (whether it is to conceive a child, spawn income streams, or adopt new spiritual insight). Drink a sacrament of pomegranate juice to Artemis of Ephesus.

A Deeper Look

Pomegranate-shaped breasts (or eggs) cover the entire torso of the Ephesian Artemis. According to the Qur'an, pomegranates grow in the gardens of paradise and symbolize God's gifts to humankind.

94. Hal Saflieni Hypogeum

PAOLA, MALTA

First in my prayer, before all other deities / I call upon Gaia, Primeval Prophetess . . . / the Greek great earth mother.
—Aeschylus (ca. 525–456 B.C.), Greek playwright

*T*his prehistoric hypogeum is an underground labyrinth carved from limestone (symbolizing the Goddess's regenerative womb) with egg-shaped burial chambers. Its builders decorated the walls of the first level with a red-ochre wash and painted elaborate spirals on the ceiling of the second-level Oracle Room. But the heart of this sanctuary (and necropolis) is a trilithon (a structure consisting of two large vertical stones supporting a third stone set horizontally across the top) within a larger trilithon within a still larger trilithon—symbolizing progeneration.

Whether you feel drawn to the Mother Goddess or to sacred cave structures, visit Hal Saflieni Hypogeum, a World Heritage Site. From Malta International Airport, travel by bus, rental car, taxi, or motorbike. Order tickets (from the Archaeological Museum in Valletta, Malta) in advance; only eighty visitors are allowed in each day.

Soothe Your Spirit

After touring the hypogeum—pausing to issue a silent petition to Gaia in the Oracle Room—take off your shoes and embark on a barefoot walking meditation or meditate as you sit with your bare feet on the ground, absorbing the earth's regenerative energies. (Pressure points on the feet correspond to internal organs: reproductive, brain, heart.)

A Deeper Look

Hal Saflieni Hypogeum, discovered in 1902, dates from 3600 to 2500 B.C. *The Sleeping Lady of Malta*, a famous 5-inch sculpture found inside the cavern and now housed in the museum in Valletta, depicts a reclining woman, perhaps incubating a child or a dream of conception.

95. Temple of Heaven (more literally Altar of Heaven)

BEIJING, CHINA

Heaven means to be one with God.
—Confucius (551–479 B.C.), Chinese philosopher and teacher

When fifteenth-century Chinese emperors wanted to thank the gods for abundance, they journeyed to the Temple of Heaven to offer sacrifices upon the three-tiered Circular Mound Altar and prayers in the tri-level Hall of Prayer for Good Harvest. Just beyond the Imperial Vault of Heaven is Echo Wall, with acoustical properties that allow a whisper spoken at one end to be heard at the other end. The Triple Echo Stones in the courtyard have similar properties; the number of echoes (one, two, or three) depends on where the speaker is standing.

If you feel called to offer prayers of gratitude in a stunning representation of Chinese temple architecture, visit this ancient Taoist temple, built around 1420. Beijing Capital International Airport is about 10.5 miles from the city. From Beijing, take the subway, a taxi, or a city bus. The complex is open year-round from 6:00 A.M. to 10:00 P.M., but book a tour in advance because this World Heritage Site is one of the most visited sacred places in Beijing. Allow two hours to see everything.

Soothe Your Soul
Before or after touring the temple, take a leisurely stroll through the courtyard and gardens. Return the generous smiles of passersby with a smile of gratitude, and then bow your head in respect for this holy place venerating Divine abundance.

A Deeper Look
The Imperial Vault and Hall of Prayer are connected by the Vermilion Steps Bridge (Sacred Way).

96. Acropolis of Baalbek (also Temple of Heliopolis)

BAALBEK, LEBANON

Love is all we have, the only way that we can help each other.
—Euripides (ca. 480–406 B.C.), Greek playwright

After Alexander the Great conquered and Hellenized Baalbek, changing its name to Heliopolis, the Romans assimilated their deities Jupiter, Mercury, and Venus with the indigenous deities Baal (Lord), Aliyan (Baal's son), and Anat (Baal's daughter and Aliyan's consort). Then, on a hilltop in Heliopolis, the Romans spent 200 years building the Acropolis of Baalbek—one of the largest and finest temple complexes of the Greco-Roman period. For centuries, people worshiped at the monument and at the round Temple of Venus, goddess of love and tutelary deity of the acropolis.

If you wish to safeguard your love or to contemplate religious tolerance, journey to Baalbek. The best way to tour this World Heritage Site is with a local guide. Heliopolis is a major town in eastern Lebanon, accessible by road from Beirut (nearest airport) and Damascus, Syria.

Soothe Your Soul

Bring a small stone symbolizing romantic love (red, heart-shaped) or Divine love (white, thunderbolt-shaped). Carry your love talisman as you stroll around the site, soaking in the sacred power of this former city of love and grace.

A Deeper Look

In 1200 B.C., long before the Romans arrived, the Canaanites built a sanctuary here, where they honored Astarte, goddess of love and fertility. Archaeologists believe that the Assyrians, Phoenicians, and Israelites may have also worshiped at this site.

97. Saint Non's Chapel (also Capel Non)

ST. DAVIDS, PEMBROKESHIRE, WALES

Whoso loves, believes the impossible.
—Elizabeth Barrett Browning (1806–1861), English Victorian poet

Along a craggy coastline in Pembrokeshire lie the ruins of a church where Saint Non is said to have given birth in A.D. 500 to Saint David, patron saint of Wales. A large altar stone featuring an inscribed Latin cross dates from between the seventh and ninth centuries, suggesting the rectangular house of worship might be from the early medieval period and that the stone might not be original to the site. Whatever the date of origin, the church and nearby holy well (known for its healing properties) were pre-eminent sacred pilgrimage sites for healing, communion, and fertility for eons.

If your spirituality lacks fertility or if you'd like to explore the mystical spiritual heritage of Wales, visit the ruins of Saint Non's (and the quaint 1934 chapel nearby). From the Bristol or London airports, take the train to Haverfordwest, then catch the bus to St. Davids in West Wales (about 15 miles). The site is open year-round.

Soothe Your Soul
Pray that the seeds of your spiritual labors will bear abundant fruit.

A Deeper Look
A stone vault built over the well holds a statue of Saint Non. According to legend, she gave birth to David during a violent thunderstorm, leaving marks on the rock she clutched, so great were her labor pains.

98. Shri Mahalakshmi Temple

KOLHAPUR, MAHARASHTRA, INDIA

Even abundance and comfort are gifts of God.
—Rabindranath Tagore (1861–1941), Indian writer and Nobel laureate

The Hindu *puranas* (holy texts) designate this ancient temple in the holy city of Kolhapur as one of 108 *Shakti Peethas* where Shakti (goddess of empowerment) manifests and as one of only six sacred houses of Shakti where worshipers can either be freed from or granted their longings. The temple complex takes its name from Lakshmi, the four-armed, gemstone-adorned goddess of good fortune, the universal form of whom is Shakti. Lakshmi is endowed with six divine qualities, among them prosperity (spiritual and material). Her Sanskrit name in the Vandas (holy text)—*Lakshyayidhi Lakshmihi*—means "one whose aim is to uplift man."

If you need a lift or release from cravings, visit Lakshmi's temple in Kolhapur. Come for Diwali, the five-day Hindu festival of lights when the goddess is worshiped in her eight forms as Asta Lakshmi. Kolhapur is about 140 miles south of Pune. Travel from Mumbai, Bangalore, or New Delhi to Kolhapur via train, public buses, or auto.

Soothe Your Spirit

Present Lakshmi with yellow fruit or flowers. Pray for what you seek. Then offer thanks for Divine generosity (another of the deity's graces).

A Deeper Look

The lavish icon of Mahalakshmi enshrined in the temple is carved from black gemstone and embellished with gold. On Fridays and full-moon days, the idol is taken out of the temple in a processional around the courtyard.

99. Wat Phra Kaew
(Temple of the Emerald Buddha)

BANGKOK, THAILAND

We have more possibilities available in each moment than we realize.
—Thich Nhat Hanh (1926–), exiled Vietnamese Buddhist monk, scholar, poet, and peace activist

The holiest *wat* in Thailand, the Temple of the Emerald Buddha is situated on the Grand Palace grounds in Bangkok's historic center (Phra Nakhon) and safeguards a seated Buddha carved out of a single green stone (jasper) and dating back six centuries. The 2-foot tall Buddha—a talisman of prosperity and protection for the Thai people—can only be touched by the Thai king when he changes the icon's gold garments at the heart of Thailand's three seasons (hot, rainy, cold).

If you wish to attract abundance into your life, visit Wat Phra Kaew. Take a taxi or *tuk-tuk* (a three-wheel auto taxi) or walk to the site. There is a fee for non-Thai visitors. Photography inside is forbidden. Dress appropriately (no revealing clothing) and remove your shoes. When praying, do not point your feet toward the Emerald Buddha.

Soothe Your Spirit

Allow at least two hours at the temple and the Grand Palace to soak up the palpable peace that seems to emanate from this holy place. Make an offering, light a stick of incense, and meditate on the Divine provider and protector.

A Deeper Look

According to legend, the Emerald Buddha was created by the Indian sculptor and Buddhist sage Nagasena in 43 B.C. to bring prosperity, protection, and pre-eminence to the kingdom (country) in which it resides. The icon came to Thailand in 1432 by way of Cambodia and before that Laos (fifth century), after spending 300 years in its birthplace, Pratna, India.

100. Petra

WADI ARABA, JORDAN

What you leave behind is not what is engraved in stone monuments, but what is woven into the lives of others.
—Pericles (495–429 B.C.), Greek politician

*P*etra's ornate carvings in pink sandstone glisten under shafts of brilliant sunlight, showcasing the ornamented façade of the 2,000-year-old Al-Khazneh (the City Treasury) in the dark canyons of southern Jordan. In a landscape where you might expect to see Bedouins tending their sheep or a camel caravan ambling past, the spectacular Treasury and other amazing structures carved by ancient Arabs, the nomadic Nabataeans, might seem like a mirage—or perhaps a miracle of human ingenuity and prosperity.

If you seek creative inspiration or spiritual enrichment, journey to this sacred treasure. Petra is 162 miles south of Amman (Queen Alia International Airport) and 82 miles north of Aqaba in a mountainous desert between the Red Sea and the Mediterranean Sea. Take a guided coach tour to Petra. Once there, stop at the visitor's center. Walk (or hire a horse-drawn carriage) to traverse the *siq* (canyon) into the ancient city, and then hire a horse, camel, or donkey to tour the ruins. Wear comfortable walking shoes, loose conservative clothing, and a hat, and bring bottled drinking water.

Soothe Your Spirit
Find inspiration in the brilliant work of the ancient Nabataeans, and bring along a journal to capture your impressions and inspirations.

A Deeper Look
Petra has been inhabited since prehistoric times and was a flourishing trading center when the Nabataeans masterfully executed their elaborate carvings.

101. Mar Elias Monastery

JERUSALEM, ISRAEL

A good man leaves an inheritance to his children's children, but the sinner's wealth is laid up for the righteous.
—Bible, Proverbs 13:22

On a ridge with panoramic views of the ancient road between Bethlehem and Jerusalem, the twelfth-century Greek Orthodox monastery of Mar Elias stands like a fortress, in stark contrast to the three-story Byzantine building with a bell tower that once stood on the site. In that original sixth-century church, the prophet Elijah (Elias) found shelter while fleeing the vindictive queen Jezebel. Elijah performed many miracles, including raising a child of a poor widow from the dead. Today, the monastery is a popular pilgrimage site, especially for infertile women and sick and infirm children, who believe that here their prayers are answered.

Whether you seek Elijah's assistance in bringing health to a child or bringing a child into your home, come to Mar Elias. The monastery is 3 miles from central Jerusalem and roughly a mile from the checkpoint into Bethlehem from Jerusalem. Get there by rental car, taxi, or guided tour.

Soothe Your Spirit
Cover you head, light a candle, and pray for the blessing of good homes and good health for all children.

A Deeper Look
A stone bench memorializing the pre-Raphaelite painter William Holman Hunt in front of the monastery reads: *Thou shalt love the lord thy God with all thy heart and with all thy soul, and thy neighbor as thyself* (Bible, Luke 10:27).

102. Domkirche (Graz Cathedral)

GRAZ, AUSTRIA

But the fruit of the Spirit is love, joy, peace, longsuffering, gentleness, goodness, faith.
—Bible, Galatians 5:22

*G*raz Cathedral sits on the site of a previous church dedicated to Saint Giles, a seventh-century A.D. Athenian noble whose reputation of sanctity has grown through the centuries with each new miracle attributed to his intercession. Located in the central Austrian city of Graz, known for its extravagant architectural styles dating to the fifteenth century, Domkirche features a magnificent baroque interior; the eighteenth-century high altar, constructed of beautiful marble, has a stunning altarpiece depicting the miracles of Saint Giles.

If you seek Divine intervention for a financial or fertility problem, visit Domkirche. Graz is located 124 miles southwest of Vienna in the Old Town District, the entirety of which is a World Heritage Site. The address is Burggasse 3, Graz, Austria. To get to Graz from Vienna, take the Autobahn 2 south. The nearest airport is Graz Thalerhof, 11 miles southwest of the city. Graz is connected to other major cities in Austria by rail service. The easiest way to reach Domkirche within the city is to take a taxi to Burggasse 3.

Soothe Your Spirit
Inside the chapel, light a candle and dedicate your prayer to Saint Giles, asking for the fulfillment of your heart's dream of fertility or financial stability.

A Deeper Look
On September 1, Domkirche celebrates the feast day of Saint Giles, patron saint of people afflicted with mental and physical disabilities, sterility, and breast cancer.

103. Mono Lake

MONO LAKE STATE NATURAL RESERVE, MONO LAKE COUNTY, CALIFORNIA, UNITED STATES

The trees reflected in the river
—they are unconscious of a spiritual world so near to them. So are we.
—Nathaniel Hawthorne (1804–1864), American fiction writer

*M*ono Lake, formed eons before humans walked on Earth, is a sacred site to diverse groups of people, from Native American tribes to conservationists, New Age believers, and practitioners of Wicca, Animism, and Paganism. This Northern California lake fed by runoff water has no outlet (such as a river, stream, or ocean) and high salinity. The combination has created a fertile ecosystem that supports brine shrimp, which, in turn, feed more than 2 million migratory birds.

If evidence of Creation's ancient fertility might invigorate fertility in your spiritual, creative, charitable, or vocational endeavors, visit Mono Lake. The lake sits right on Highway 395 between the towns of Mono Lake City and Lee Vining (which has a small airport) on the eastern side of Northern California near the Nevada border.

Soothe Your Spirit

Take a guided nature hike to learn about this ancient place of fertility so revered by many spiritual traditions. Cast a sacred circle and invoke the Goddess to inspire you with ideas on how to be more fertile in all areas of your life.

A Deeper Look

In December 2010, NASA scientists discovered a new life form in Mono Lake: the rod-shaped bacterium GFAJ–1, an extremophile that is not adversely affected by arsenic, which is poisonous to many living creatures.

104. Milk Grotto

BETHLEHEM, ISRAEL

To hope means to be ready at every moment for that which is not yet born, and yet not become desperate if there is no birth in our lifetime.
—Erich Fromm (1900–1980), German-American Jewish psychologist and philosopher

The Milk Grotto, a holy shrine venerated by Muslims and Christians and dedicated to Our Lady of the Milk, safeguards a rock that purportedly was formed from a few drops of milk that fell from the Blessed Virgin's breast as she nursed the Holy Infant. The grotto, also believed to have been a place of hiding for the Holy Family during the Slaughter of the Innocents decreed by Herod, sheds a limestone dust that the faithful have pinched and taken with them in the hope of experiencing fertility through ritual use.

If you desire fertility but have lost hope, visit the Milk Grotto to ask for help from Our Lady of the Milk. Take a day trip (by rental car) to Bethlehem from the West Bank of Jerusalem.

Soothe Your Spirit

Pray for the fertility you desire. If you feel inspired, you might also purchase a small packet of the "milk" limestone powder from the Franciscans, complete with directions for use.

A Deeper Look

Although the Grotto is 2,000 years old, pilgrims have prayed at the site for fertility since the fourth century and nuns pray around the clock in shifts behind a glass screen in the grotto. According to a 2007 CNN report, 1,700 babies were born to parents who had prayed at the shrine over the previous ten years.

105. Hill of Ward

ATHBOY, COUNTY MEATH, IRELAND

Life is always a rich and steady time when you are waiting for something to happen or to hatch.
—E. B. White (1889–1985), American writer, author of *Charlotte's Web*

The Hill of Ward was a site of Goddess worship for thousands of years as well as the center of the Celtic veneration of Tlachtga (Hill of Ward), an Irish Druidess who gave birth to triplets on the hill. During Samhain (All Hallows' Eve), celebrated by the Celts on the night of October 31, the Great Winter Fire would be lit on the hill, symbolizing the beginning of the shorter, darker, colder half of the year—a time of magic, mischief, and chaos, when the veil separating the worlds grows thinner and the energy of life draws inward into Earth's womb to rest.

If you enjoy Celtic spiritual traditions and desire fertility, visit Ireland's Hill of Ward. Medieval Athboy is near the Yellow Ford River at the junction of N51 and R154. The nearest airport is in Dublin, 30 miles away. Rent a car or take a Route 111 Bus Éireann from Dublin to Athboy.

Soothe Your Spirit
Join in the Samhain celebration on Hill of Ward. Meditate on the fertility or rebirth you seek. Write your name and desire on a stone to toss into the bonfire.

A Deeper Look
The Hill of Ward has an Iron Age ring fort, as does its neighbor, the town of Tara, 12 miles away.

106. Temple of Isis

PHILAE, NUBIA, EGYPT

A grateful mind is a great mind which eventually attracts to itself great things.
—Plato (ca. 428–347 B.C.), classical Greek philosopher, writer,
and mathematician

The ancient Egyptians built a stunning temple for Isis (wife of Osiris) on the holy island of Philae in the middle of the River Nile, where they worshiped her as goddess of motherhood, magic, fertility, children, and protector of the dead. Recently, the temple had to be moved due to yearly flooding, so the temple complex was deconstructed and painstakingly transferred to another island, where it was reconstructed and the island was renamed Philae.

If you seek fertility of spirit or body and believe that being in the Temple of Isis might benefit your aspirations, visit this site. From Aswan, take the road 4 miles south to a boat landing and then hire a boat to take you to the island. There is an entrance fee to tour the temple and to see the light-and-sound show.

Soothe Your Spirit

Take as much time as you need to absorb the magical energy of the temple. As you walk, think about how you might attract or manifest the blessing of fertility in your life. When you are ready to leave the site, offer a heartfelt spiritual thank-you to this ancient goddess for any inspiration that came to you during the visit.

A Deeper Look

The towering walls of the temple are covered top to bottom with intricate reliefs depicting scriptural stories sculpted into the stone walls and painted in now-fading, but once brilliant colors.

107. Temple of Demeter

SANGRI, NAXOS ISLAND, GREECE

Take full account of the excellencies which you possess, and in gratitude remember how you would hanker after them, if you had them not.
—Marcus Aurelius (A.D. 121–180), Roman soldier

Arising from the fertile fields of Naxos in the Cyclades chain of Greek Islands is the partially reconstructed Temple of Demeter, whom the ancients worshiped as goddess of fecundity and grain. Several important and secretive rituals were associated with Demeter, including one performed in autumn to promote a good harvest. However, the most famous rituals to Demeter were the Eleusinian Mysteries, in which the worshiper petitioned for "prosperity before death."

If you believe the fecund energy that is said to permeate the ruins of Demeter's temple might increase the productivity of your spiritual life or other endeavors, come to Greece. Once on the island, the best way to get to the temple is by rental car or car and driver. Start from Hora, drive to Filoti, and follow the signs.

Soothe Your Spirit

Enjoy an hour of downtime in the open air, walking around or sitting and gazing at the temple. If no one else is around, take time to meditate, and once your mind is calm, ask for inspiration to start flowing. Record your ideas in a notebook.

A Deeper Look

This temple, unlike many of its ancient counterparts, has a square-shaped floor. A portion of the floor, a wall, columns, and a doorway give an idea of the splendid white-stone temple built in the sixth century B.C.

108. Sheela Na Gig (Kilpeck Church)

HEREFORD, HEREFORDSHIRE COUNTY, ENGLAND

If facts are the seeds which later produce knowledge and wisdom, then the emotions and the impressions of the senses are the fertile soil in which seeds must grow.
—Rachel Carson (1907–1964), marine biologist and ecological writer

Sheela Na Gig, viewed alternatively as a plumpish and sensual goddess or a thin and menacing hag, always exhibits an exaggerated vulva—a surprise for many people who do not expect such exhibitionist art on a church. However, Sheela Na Gig is associated with childbirth and is a medieval embellishment on many churches throughout England and Ireland. The Kilpeck Church (formerly the parish church of Saints Mary and David in Kilpeck), which sits in the English countryside bordering Wales, has some of the country's most notable Romanesque adornment, dating from 1140, including a well-preserved carving of Sheela Na Gig among the corbels of the apse.

If you are interested in Celtic ideas of fertility, come to Kilpeck village to visit this Anglican church. It's located about 8 miles southwest of Hereford in Herefordshire County.

Soothe Your Spirit

Soak up the peace and quiet in this lovely little church in the most rural county in England, and then walk around outside. Open your creative mind to the fecundity that surrounds you: sketch images, jot notes, read about Celtic beliefs, and see what develops.

A Deeper Look

Many of the church's Romanesque carvings feature sacred images of nature, including a Tree of Life carved on the south door tympanum.

109. La Dama de Elche (Lady of Elche)

NATIONAL ARCHAEOLOGICAL MUSEUM, MADRID, SPAIN

. . . Come, Blessed Goddess, and hear the prayers of your children, / And make the increase of the fruits and grains your constant care, with the fertile seasons your handmaidens, / Draw near and bless your supplicants.
—"Orphic Hymn to Gaia," tr. Virginia Stewart

The Lady of Elche is a magnificent Iberian sculpture discovered in 1897 during an archaeological excavation on a private estate at L'Alcúdia near Valencia. Dating to between the fourth and fifth centuries B.C., the Dama de Elche bust represents a sacred pre-Roman fertility goddess so exquisitely carved that her beauty transcends time.

If you are intrigued by pre-Christian and pagan Goddess worship, especially by those to whom prayers for fecundity and fertility were offered, come see La Dama de Elche at the National Archaeological Museum. Madrid has an international airport. The museum shares a building with the National Library in Columbus Square (Plaza de Colón), reachable by rental car, taxi, or local transportation.

Soothe Your Spirit

Enjoy the museum artifacts but focus on La Dama de Elche. Imagine those who prayed to her for fertility and offer your own prayer if you are inspired to do so.

A Deeper Look

Although the museum is not a sacred site, the thirty-four exhibition rooms display numerous holy artifacts that are as sacred as the places they were found—including Visigoth votive crowns dating to the eighth century, a fourteenth-century choir stall, and an elaborate Islamic-Spanish astrolabe (bronze plate) from the eleventh century.

CHAPTER 5

SPIRITUAL SUCCOR, GUIDANCE, INSIGHT

Your word is a lamp to my feet
and a light to my path.

—*Bible, Psalm 119: 105*

110. National Shrine of Our Lady of Prompt Succor

NEW ORLEANS, LOUISIANA, UNITED STATES

My good Mother, if you will promptly remove these obstacles, I shall carry this image of you to New Orleans where I promise to do all in my power to have you honored.
—Mother Saint Michel Gensoul (1758–1822), French-born American nineteenth-century Ursuline nun

When French Ursuline nun Michel Gensoul prayed to the Blessed Virgin that she would honor Mary as "Our Lady of Prompt Succor" if given a quick response to her request to serve the mission in New Orleans, she soon received papal permission. Sister Gensoul commissioned a statue of Mary cradling the Holy Child to be carved and painted gold and personally delivered it to the Ursuline Sisters in New Orleans in 1810. Since then, Our Lady of Prompt Succor has provided miraculous interventions for many faithful who turn to her in time of crises—including the 6,000 American soldiers who fought against 15,000 British soldiers in the fierce Battle of New Orleans, January 7–8, 1815. The battle was won, as General Andrew Jackson had petitioned. Thereafter, Our Lady's feast day has been January 8.

If you seek a rapid response to your prayers, travel to the National Shrine of Our Lady of Prompt Succor.

Soothe Your Spirit
Slow your breathing to generate feelings of calm and then pray from your heart.

A Deeper Look
Originally installed in the Old Ursuline Convent in the French Quarter, the statue is now enshrined at the Ursuline Academy and Convent on State Street.

111. Gandhi Mandapam

KANYAKUMARI, TAMIL NADU, INDIA

Each one prays to God according to his own light.
—Mohandas K. Gandhi (1869–1948), Indian political leader and father of India

When a hole was cut into the pale pink and white ceiling of the Gandhi Mandapam shrine, some may have questioned why. All doubt disappeared on October 2, Gandhi's birthday, when every year the midday sunlight streams through the hole and falls precisely on the holy spot that had held his ashes (before they were distributed), thus symbolizing the emerging light of independence that Gandhi's selfless efforts helped manifest. As India metamorphosed from an outpost of the British Empire to a free nation, the Mahatma became the holy beacon of hope for worldwide nonviolence until, and ever since, his assassination in 1948.

If you desire to pay homage to the Mahatma (great soul) or to pray at the shrine that held his sacred ashes, visit the Gandhi Mandapam in Kanyakumari, at the tip of the Indian subcontinent. Reach the city by rail or air from other parts of India, and then use local buses and taxis to visit the shrine.

Soothe Your Spirit

Stand before the black four-sided column on which the ashes of Gandhi were kept to reflect on the Mahatma's life and ideals. Ask for spiritual succor and guidance for yourself, the ones you love, and your nation.

A Deeper Look

The Gandhi Mandapam shrine finds resonance in Orissan temples, with its columns, towers, elaborate sculptural treatments, pilaster decoration, capitals, and needlepoint spires.

112. Norwich Cathedral

NORWICH, NORFOLK, ENGLAND

All shall be well, and all shall be well, and all manner of thing shall be well.
—Dame Julian of Norwich (1342–1416), English mystic

*A*s if the astonishing beauty and enormous size of the 900-year-old Norwich Cathedral in eastern England weren't enough to draw pilgrims over the Atlantic and across the English Channel, its rich chorale music, treasury of sacred art, labyrinth, verdant gardens, and enthusiastic welcome to people of all faiths surely add to the allure. This Romanesque cathedral where open-armed spiritual succor is a governing principle draws tens of thousands of worshipers every year.

Whether you would like to learn more about the cathedral's Benedictine heritage and historical medieval buildings or give your spirit a boost, Norwich Cathedral will inform and inspire you. Located in the heart of Norwich, the cathedral is best reached by taxi or public transportation; parking in the Close is not permitted, except in special cases of disability if you've made previous arrangements.

Soothe Your Spirit
Light a candle and pray silently that your heart may find comfort, your mind may find peace, and your soul may find guidance.

A Deeper Look
Among the religious figures commemorated at Norwich Cathedral are Herbert de Losinga, the Norman monk who was the first bishop of Norwich and founded the church in A.D. 1096, and Julian of Norwich, who "exemplifies the very best in the English mystic tradition of the fourteenth century and lay ministry at its most refined." Dame Julian's birth name is unknown; she is named for the church at which she lived as an anchoress, or hermit.

113. Russian Church of Mary Magdalene

GETHSEMANE, JERUSALEM, ISRAEL

Jesus saith unto her, Mary. She turned herself, and saith unto him, Rabboni; which is to say, Master.
—Bible, John 20:16

*C*zar Alexander III of Russia's vision of a splendid church honoring his mother, Empress Maria Alexandrovna, named for Saint Mary Magdalene, on the Mount of Olives in Gethsemane (near where Jesus prayed), materialized as this incomparable Russian Orthodox church dedicated to the saint. Built in 1888, the Muscovite-style church is a notable landmark with a dazzling white sandstone façade, a circular blue and gold mosaic iconostasis of Mary Magdalene, gabled roof adorned in faux lace trim, seven gilded domes crowned with crosses, and glorious sacred art, including the sixteenth-century icon of the Virgin with Child lovingly called *Prompt Succor*.

If you wish to see incredible sacred artistry or to summon the spiritual steadfastness of Mary Magdalene or the Divine succor of the Holy Mother, visit the Russian Church of Mary Magdalene. Travel to the church by rental car or local public transportation. Visiting hours are 10:00 A.M. to 12:00 P.M., Tuesday through Thursday.

Soothe Your Spirit
As you explore this peaceful sanctuary, feel Mother Mary's nurturing presence and Mary Magdalene's indomitable spirit. Offer a prayer of gratitude for the comfort and support of your faith.

A Deeper Look
The church's crypt contains the relics of the martyred Orthodox saint, the Grand Duchess Elizabeth Feodorova of Russia, and her niece, Princess Alice of Greece, mother-in-law of Queen Elizabeth II and a rescuer of Jews during the Nazi occupation of Greece.

114. Al-Aqsa Mosque

A good word is like a good tree whose root is firmly fixed and whose top is in the sky.
—Qur'an, 14–Ibrahim

Al-Aqsa, the second-oldest and third–most sacred mosque in Islam, stands on a holy site of prayer once occupied by the Crusaders and later by the Knights Templar. Built in A.D. 1033 after an earthquake demolished the existing mosque, Al-Aqsa is also one of Islam's most important learning and worship centers and the largest mosque in Jerusalem, with the capacity to accommodate 5,000 worshipers.

If you seek spiritual guidance or increased knowledge of the Islamic faith, visit this mosque. Located on Temple Mount in Jerusalem's Old City, Al-Aqsa and the Dome of the Rock form the centerpieces of the Noble Sanctuary (Haram al-Sharif), 35 enclosed acres of sacred gardens, fountains, and structures.

Worshipers are expected to ritually purify themselves before entering the mosque. A woman's body and hair must be covered, and men and women pray in separate areas. The mosque's main ablution fountain, al-Kas (the Cup)—situated between the Dome of the Rock and the Al-Aqsa Mosque—has taps and stone benches.

Soothe Your Spirit

Stand attentively, quietly disconnecting from the world, and consider that you are standing in the presence of Allah or God. After the traditional ritual prayer, issue your personal prayer of petition or gratitude.

A Deeper Look

Al-Masjid El-Aqsa in Arabic means "farthest mosque" and alludes to Prophet Muhammad's legendary Night Journey from Mecca to Jerusalem, which the Dome of the Rock venerates.

115. Bahá'í House of Worship

WILMETTE, ILLINOIS, UNITED STATES

O God, guide me, protect me, make of me a shining lamp and a brilliant star . . .
—Àbdu'l-Bahá (1844–1921), Persian theologian and eldest son of Bahá'u'lláh
(founder of the Bahá'í faith)

*L*ike the other six Bahá'í Houses of Worship in the world, this temple's beauty is circular, has nine sides, and is surrounded by expansive gardens with walkways. Yet, like each of the others, it has its own distinctive—and breathtaking—design. Lacy claddings of ornamental white Portland cement cover the exterior and interior walls, columns, and the ceiling of the dome rising 135 feet above the auditorium. Per Bahá'í tenets, the temple welcomes people of all faiths and is used exclusively for worship and learning; no sermons are allowed.

To learn about Bahá'í principles or to worship in a place of tranquil beauty, visit the Bahá'í House of Worship in Wilmette, along Lake Michigan outside Chicago.

Soothe Your Spirit

Sit with your eyes closed and meditate on the Bahá'í belief that we all are of the same God who desires for us to become a unified, egalitarian global society.

A Deeper Look

Founded in Iran in 1844, Bahá'í is the youngest monotheistic religion, and today has more than 5 million adherents. The "Mother Temple of the West" in Wilmette, built from 1920 to 1953, is the oldest surviving temple. The first, built during the years 1902 to 1908 in Turkmenistan, was destroyed in 1948. The other temples are in Australia, Germany, India, Panama, Samoa, and Uganda. A ninth is underway in Chile.

116. Cathedral of Saint James

INNSBRUCK, AUSTRIA

Forsake me not, O Lord: O my God, be not far from me. Make haste to help me, O Lord my salvation.
—Bible, Psalm 39:12–13

The Cathedral of Saint James (Domkirche zu St. Jakob) astonishes visitors with its ornate four-tiered façade, clock towers, dramatic domes, ceiling murals, high marble altars, lavish gilt, carved altar, and lavish embellishments throughout. However, one of the most outstanding treasures of this angelic, eighteenth-century baroque masterpiece is an exquisite painting entitled *Mary Hilf* (Mary of Succor) by the German master Lucas Cranach the Elder on the main altar.

If you need aid or answers at this time in your life, visit the Cathedral of Saint James and view the icon. During the summer the cathedral opens from 7:00 A.M. to 7:00 P.M., except on Fridays when it is also closed from 12:00 to 3:00 P.M. No tours or visits are allowed during services, and no photography is allowed inside the cathedral.

Soothe Your Soul

Attend Mass and then sit quietly for a few moments gazing at the icon of Mary of Succor as you pray for the guidance or assistance you seek.

A Deeper Look

Built in 1717 to 1724, the cathedral's sumptuous interior was created by two Munich artisans, brothers Cosman Damian (a painter) and Egid Quirin (a sculptor).

117. Temple Emanu-El

NEW YORK CITY, NEW YORK, UNITED STATES

It is written, "Love the Lord your God and serve Him with all your heart."
—Bible, Deuteronomy 11:3

Temple Emanu-El is the world's largest Reform Jewish synagogue, accommodating 2,500 worshipers inside the Moorish and art deco interior embellished with handsome mosaics. The exterior limestone walls with Romanesque Revival detailing suggest a building from the medieval period rather than one built in 1928 to serve a growing progressive-minded community that had also assimilated Conservative Jews from Eastern Europe (in the 1930s)—a blending of new, old, West, and East. Today, the "spirit of the congregation" is one of "inclusion, flexibility, and sensitivity to the needs and desires" of worshipers.

If you seek a place that can lift your heart and help you find meaning or would enjoy attending a service in a beautiful, welcoming synagogue, visit Temple Emanu-El. It is located at One East 56th Street, in New York City's Upper East Side, across from Central Park, an easy walk from several subway trains and bus lines.

Soothe Your Soul

Attend a service and experience the power of prayer embraced by this congregation. Perform a traditional ritual or one of your own urging, as allowed and encouraged here.

A Deeper Look

The Temple Emanu-El complex includes the smaller Beth-El Chapel, a six-story religious school. The temple also has a world-class collection of Judaic art that provides spiritual succor through its aesthetic, social, and religious context.

118. Basilique du Sacré-Coeur de Montmartre (Basilica of the Sacred Heart)

PARIS, FRANCE

If any man thirsts, let him come to me and drink.
—Bible, John 7:37

The white travertine dome of the Basilica of the Sacred Heart shimmers in the light—and its panoramic views rival those of the Eiffel Tower. Few buildings in Paris can surpass the beauty of this Romanesque-Byzantine church rising regally from Montmartre, drawing admiring eyes throughout the city. The treasures inside are no less alluring; for example, the mosaic, *Christ in Majesty*, in the apse is one of the largest mosaics in the world. However, it is the emphasis on devotion and prayer that beckons worshipers from near and far. Since 1885, the monstrance containing the Holy Sacrament has been perpetually on display over the high altar. Parishioners and Catholic pilgrims come day and night to receive the succor of Christ's body (the consecrated host) and blood (consecrated wine).

If you yearn for deep communion with the Divine or for an answer to a prayer, visit the Basilica of the Sacred Heart in Paris. For an unforgettable experience, come during Holy Week (Easter) or Christmas. The nearest metro station is Abbesses, Line 12. No recording devices are allowed inside the church.

Soothe Your Soul
Contemplate the symbolic meaning of the communion ritual. Pray for the insight or support you desire, and then light a candle to perpetuate your prayer.

A Deeper Look
Montmartre was sacred to the Druids, the Gauls, the Romans, and early Christians (Saint Peter's). The cornerstone of Sacré-Coeur was laid in 1875; the basilica was completed in 1881, but wars delayed its consecration until 1919.

119. The Abbaye de Notre-Dame-de-Sénanque (Abbey of Sénanque)

GORDES, PROVENCE, FRANCE

Faith has to do with things that are not seen, and hope with things that are not at hand.

—Saint Thomas Aquinas (1225–1274), Italian Christian theologian and philosopher

After French noblemen donated land in the valley north of the medieval village of Gordes in Provence for a monastery, Cistercian monks took up residence and built a simple sanctuary. Consecrated in 1178, the abbey endured centuries of turmoil, occupancy, abandonment, and reclamation. Today, Cistercian monks again occupy the honey-colored stone monastery nestled amid rolling hills of aromatic lavender bordered by a forest of fragrant pine.

Whether you seek the comfort of a heaven-scented spiritual retreat or the sheltering walls of a humble monastery, visit the Abbey of Sénanque. Visitors may attend services, which are posted at the entrance. Go in June or early July, when the lavender is in full bloom and before farmers begin harvesting. From Gordes, take D177 road approximately 2 miles.

Soothe Your Soul

Book a retreat, and bring along some spiritual books. As you explore the abbey, tune in to the sounds of monks as they perform a Gregorian chant. Walk to the cloister in the enclosed courtyard, taking in nature's scents and scenes. Settle into a quiet place and read for a while, and then meditate for deeper understanding of what you've read and experienced.

A Deeper Look

This abbey is one of the medieval Romanesque Cistercian monasteries known as the "Three Sisters of Provence." The others are Thoronet Abbey and Silvacane Abbey. For a guided tour, the fee is 7 euros.

120. Lichfield Cathedral

LICHFIELD, STAFFORDSHIRE, ENGLAND

Sometimes the Lord rides out the storm with us and other times He calms the restless sea around us. Most of all, He calms the storm inside us in our deepest inner soul.
—Dr. Lloyd John Ogilvie (1930–), American Presbyterian minister and former chaplain of the United States Senate (1995–2003)

*L*ichfield Cathedral with its Flemish stained-glass windows, octagonal Chapter House, beautiful Lady Chapel, and three spires affectionately called "the Ladies of the Vale" dominates Lichfield's architecture, even though it is one of England's smallest cathedrals. This tiny hamlet in the English Midlands has been a center of worship and religious teaching since A.D. 669. So it's not surprising that one of its most impressive buildings, Lichfield Cathedral, safeguards numerous sacred treasures: among them, the *Litchfield Gospels*, an eighth-century illuminated manuscript; a fifteenth-century mural of the Crucifixion; and the shrine of Saint Chad, the seventh-century bishop of Mercia.

If your heart yearns for spiritual knowledge and you find medieval religious art fascinating, visit Lichfield Cathedral. Travel from Birmingham (17 miles north) or London (124 miles south) to Lichfield by bus, taxi, rental car, or coach tour.

Soothe Your Soul

Walk around the cathedral, enjoying its beauty and bounty. Take time to visit the tearoom and the bookshop. Offer a departing prayer of gratitude for God's omnipresence.

A Deeper Look

The visitor's study center, tearoom, and bookshop in the Close were established to share information with tourists, pilgrims, school groups, and others interested in the cathedral, ecclesiastical literature, and the history of Lichfield.

121. Dhamekh Stupa

SARNATH, UTTAR PRADESH, INDIA

Bring us, Powerful One, all blessings, all facility . . . the best of treasures: the efficient mind and spiritual luster . . .
—Rig-Veda, Book II, Hymn 21:6

After Buddha attained enlightenment, he received Divine inspiration to impart spiritual wisdom to his five disciples. At a deer park in Sarnath, roughly 8 miles from Varanasi, Buddha shared his Divine knowledge of the Middle Way. Today, Dhamekh Stupa sits upon the holy site of Buddha's first sermon, looking like a giant red-brick cylinder with a collar of lighter stones encircling its base.

If you seek inner guidance or want to begin sharing your spiritual insights with others, visit this sacred pilgrimage site. The best months to go are August through March. The nearest airport is in Babatpur (18 miles from Sarnath), with daily service to major Indian cities. Trains from Varanasi also stop at Sarnath.

Soothe Your Spirit

Circumambulate Buddha's ancient *stupa* (bell-shaped tower), spinning the prayer wheels as you pass the entrance and allowing your mind to receive insights and inspiration. For Tibetan Buddhist practice, walk counter-clockwise while chanting *"Om mani padme hum"* to open your mind to Divine inspiration.

A Deeper Look

Built by the Indian emperor Ashoka, Dhamekh Stupa measures 143 feet tall and 92 feet in diameter. Just before his death, Buddha named Sarnath as one of four holy places, which accounts for all the monastery ruins in the area. Although the site is often filled with tourists and pilgrims, it still radiates serenity.

122. Avebury Henge

AVEBURY, WILTSHIRE COUNTY, ENGLAND

Some keep the Sabbath going to Church, / I keep it staying at Home
— / With a bobolink for a Chorister, / And an Orchard, for a Dome.
—Emily Dickinson (1830–1886), American poet

*R*oughly 4,500 years ago, Neolithic people formed a community in what is now the lovely farming village of Avebury in southern England, constructing massive megalithic monuments and a stone circle 1,401 feet in diameter and covering 28 acres. Today, the site is important for its archaeological and anthropological information as well as for its enigmatic and spiritual properties. It is especially venerated by modern Earth-based spiritual traditions, such as Wicca and neo-Druidism, whose rituals often involve stone circles from which to draw spiritual strength and succor.

If you feel spiritually aligned in natural settings or are intrigued by stone circles and megaliths, visit Avebury Henge—90 miles west of London and 20 miles north of Stonehenge. From London, take a coach tour to Avebury, Stonehenge, and other mysterious sites. From Bath, go by car, bus, or train.

Soothe Your Spirit

Draw in energy as you walk the circle. Holding a crystal pendulum, begin asking questions for guidance—a clockwise-swinging pendulum means yes; counterclockwise means no.

A Deeper Look

Avebury's stone circles consist of an outer ring of ninety-eight slabs of sarsen (the sedimentary rock found in the region) and two inner rings comprised of thirty stones each. This World Heritage Site is protected by Britain's National Trust.

123. Beth Sholom Synagogue

ELKINS PARK, PENNSYLVANIA, UNITED STATES

*And one cried unto another, and said "Holy, holy, holy, is the Lord of hosts: the whole
earth is full of his glory."*
—Bible, Isaiah 6:3

When asked about the hexagonal element in the Beth Sholom temple design, the renowned architect Frank Lloyd Wright responded that when you enter a house of prayer, you place yourself in God's hands. Further, he explained the six-sided structural shape that you see as you look down while leaving the synagogue resonates with the shape of hands folded in prayer. This architectural masterpiece has even greater resonance in the shape of Mount Sinai (a flat top, tentlike, strong as stone but beautiful in the light and spiritually significant), where the great Jewish liberator and patriarch Moses received the light and wisdom of the Divine.

If you seek to widen your spiritual network and to understand or more fully embrace Jewish belief and tradition, visit Beth Sholom Synagogue, a National Historic Landmark. Elkins Park is a thirty- to forty-five-minute drive from Philadelphia International Airport, and there is train service between Philadelphia and Elkins Park.

Soothe Your Spirit

Visit the temple for a service. Fold your hands in your lap and pray deeply for the wisdom and spiritual succor your heart seeks. Expand your spiritual network by meeting the congregants and the rabbi.

A Deeper Look

Downstairs, and also designed by Frank Lloyd Wright, is a smaller synagogue known as the Sisterhood Sanctuary that accommodates 250 people and has a beautiful black walnut ark that holds seven Torah scrolls.

124. Temple of Apollo

DELPHI, GREECE

I am in you and you in me, mutual in divine love.
—William Blake, English poet and mystic

*B*efore Apollo, the sun god of light, could establish the Oracle at Delphi, he first had to defeat the python that guarded the spring. Apparently, that was handily accomplished, because the Temple to Apollo and the Oracle at Delphi became the most sacred sites in the ancient world. People of all classes and ranks undertook the pilgrimage to Delphi (which some believe to be the center of the world) to ask the Oracle for advice and guidance.

If you feel as though you've lost your inner compass, come to Delphi to reset it. The nearest international airport is in Athens; the Temple of Apollo and Oracle of Delphi are in central Greece. The easiest way to see the sight is with a tour. Alternatively, you could rent a car or hire a car and guide to show you around this sacred site.

Soothe Your Spirit

As you stroll, let your mind and body slow to the pace of the ancients, whose only timepiece was the sun. When you feel calm, ask for Divine counsel and wait for a reply from your intuition.

A Deeper Look

A priestess known as the Pythia was the only person allowed to enter the *adytum*, a sacred chamber where the Oracle was given.

125. Ek Balam

VALLADOLID, YUCATÁN, MEXICO

. . . From above, House of Heaven, where star people and ancestors gather, may their blessings come to us now . . .
—Mayan Prayer of the Seven Galactic Directions

The open mouth of a jaguar forms the entrance to the gigantic Acropolis pyramid at the ancient Mayan city of Ek Balam (Black Jaguar) deep in the Yucatán jungle. The ruins of this once-flourishing city also include ceremonial temples, a massive tower, and the ruler's tomb.

If you believe each human has an animal spirit for guidance and protection or if you are inspired by the highly spiritual Maya, journey to Ek Balam, open 8:00 A.M. to 5:00 P.M. daily. From Valladolid, drive north to Ek Balam, hire a car and guide, or book a tour.

Ek Balam receives fewer visitors than similar Yucatán ruins, partly because of its remote location and lack of facilities. The excavation is also less complete than other sites—hence, less crowded and less developed—making it more peaceful and more authentic to the time of the Maya. The site has one restroom, but no refreshments. However, in the nearby village of Ek Balam is a refreshing surprise: Dolce Mente, a charming hotel and Italian restaurant serving homemade pasta and its own organic vegetables and honey.

Soothe Your Spirit
As you explore the ruins, breathe deeply and let the spirit of the jaguar fill you. Offer a red flower in gratitude.

A Deeper Look
To the Maya, the jaguar symbolized Divine protection, spiritual strength, and earthly connection to the Great Spirit.

126. Durham Cathedral

DURHAM, ENGLAND

I pray thee, loving Jesus . . . Thou wouldst mercifully grant me to attain one day to Thee, the fountain of all wisdom and to appear forever before Thy face.
—Venerable Bede (A.D. 672–735), English scholar, teacher, and writer

Durham Cathedral, rising majestically from a hill in northeastern England overlooking the River Wear and ancient Durham, is a stunning example of Norman architecture. Although the cathedral, built in the middle of the tenth century, no longer holds the eighth-century illuminated *Lindisfarne Gospels* that combine Christian and Celtic themes, it does safeguard other treasures, including the tomb of medieval scholar Bede, author of *The Ecclesiastical History of England*, and the relics of Saint Cuthbert, the bishop of Lindisfarne, described by Bede as "afire with heavenly love, unassumingly patient, devoted to unceasing prayer and kindly to all who come to him for comfort."

If you feel a spiritual link to Saint Bede or Saint Cuthbert and would like to pray for guidance, visit Durham Cathedral. From London, reach Durham by plane, train, ferry, bus, or car (A1M motorway). No interior photography is permitted.

Soothe Your Spirit

Attend a traditional service or the special service for peace and justice. Pray for Saint Cuthbert's comfort, insight, and guidance.

A Deeper Look

Cuthbert was so revered for his spiritual succor to others that when he died in A.D. 687, the wandering monks of Lindisfarne carried his body with them until they reached Durham in 995, where they enshrined him in the White Church, which is the site of Durham Cathedral.

127. Agii Apostoli (Church of the Holy Apostles) Solaki

ATHENS, ATTICA, GREECE

Give me where to stand, and I will move the earth.
—Archimedes (ca. 287–212 B.C.), Greek scientist and intuitive

*T*his Byzantine church stands below the ancient Acropolis of Athens and along the Agora (open-air place of assembly), where saints, philosophers, and orators imparted their ideology and insights to all within earshot. The rose-colored brick exterior features lovely crenulated arches over narrow wooden doors and a heavy metal bell hanging from a large protruding stone (as no bell tower exists) as well as white stone benches in the courtyard. Inside, ornate Corinthian columns support the arches of a dome adorned with frescoes of cherubs, angels, John the Baptist, and the Christ Pantocrator (Almighty, or Sustainer of the World).

Whether you seek spiritual sustenance or enlightenment, include this lovely church in your visit to Athens. Agii Apostoli Solaki, in the heart of the city, is best seen on foot. Entrance is free.

Soothe Your Spirit

Take refuge from the sun's heat and your racing thoughts in the church's cool, calm interior. Standing under the dome's frescoes, pray for the assurance or guidance you seek. Before continuing your exploration of Athens, sit on one of the outside benches and reflect on the sacred message sent to your heart by the apostles, or perhaps Christ Pantocrator.

A Deeper Look

The church was built in the tenth century A.D. over a second-century *nymphaion* (sacred spring) honoring nymphs, the nurturing water deities of Greek mythology.

128. Sanchi Stupa (also Sanchi Hill)

SANCHI, MADHYA PRADESH, INDIA

Peace comes from within. Do not seek it without.
—Siddhartha Gautama, the Buddha (563–483 B.C.), father of Buddhism

The Great Stupa of Sanchi, built by Emperor Ashoka in the third century B.C., is a large hemispheric dome of mud-colored brick crowned with a *chatra* (resembling a parasol or umbrella) inside a *harmika* (a small platform with a railing). This is the oldest, largest, grandest, and most sacred of several *stupas* (bell-shaped towers) on Sanchi Hill, which also includes temples, megalithic pillars, and other sacred structures constructed over a period of 1,300 years. Unique to these *stupas* is that not one bears the image of Lord Buddha; instead, he is represented by carvings of symbolic images such as wheels (teaching) and the lotus (enlightenment).

Whether you seek spiritual insight or assurance, visit Sanchi Stupa, a World Heritage Site. The nearest airport (29 miles) is in Bhopal; the nearest rail station (6.5 miles) is in Vidisha. From Bhopal, Vidisha, or Indore, you can travel to Sanchi by taxi, rental car, bus, or auto rickshaw.

Soothe Your Spirit
Circumambulate the Great Stupa, mindful that you are moving ever closer to your spiritual solar plexus: the source of Divine "gut" messages. At the center, stand or sit in lotus position in *zazen* (quiet meditation) to receive the whisper of wisdom or succor you seek.

A Deeper Look
In the Vihara (Buddhist monastery) on Sanchi Hill, a glass chest enshrines the holy relics of Buddha, which originally were interred in the Great Stupa.

129. Apamea

SYRIA

I have found power in the mysteries of thought.
—Euripides (ca. 480–406 B.C.), Greek playwright

The once glorious Greco-Roman city of Apamea now lies in rubble—except for remnants of the main boulevard and the Cardo Maximus (Grand Colonnade) that ran alongside it—a grand procession of 400 granite fluted columns connected by lavishly carved granite lintels. Located at a critical Middle Eastern intersection overlooking the verdant Ghab Valley, Apamea was a major center of trade, politics, and religious thought—including Monophysitism (the doctrine that Christ had only one nature, divine)—from 300 B.C. to A.D. 1157. At its peak, it was home to half a million people and enjoyed a constant flow of visitors (including Cleopatra).

If walking along an ancient road where myriad religious thoughts were examined and sometimes threatened might help you to understand or to strengthen your faith, come to Apamea. Book a tour (several are available in-country; English guidebooks are available), or hire a guide and car in Hama, 35 miles to the south. Women are advised to travel with a male companion or by group tour. Bring bottled water. Dress appropriately for the culture (Muslim), for the climate (hot, dry), and for walking (lots of it).

Soothe Your Spirit

As you walk this sprawling intersection of sacred beliefs, examine your own, staying open to whatever Divine truths are whispered on the wind.

A Deeper Look

Human occupation at this site dates to the Stone Age and extends to the Middle Ages. During the Christian period, Saint Paul (Saul before his conversion on the road to Damascus) passed through Apamea (then Phrygia).

130. Ajanta Caves

AJANTA, MAHARASHTRA, INDIA

Be a lamp unto yourself. Work out your liberation with diligence.
—Siddhartha Gautama, the Buddha (563–483 B.C.), father of Buddhism

On the cliff of a deep forest ravine overlooking the Waghora River in the Sahyadri Hills of southern India is a sacred treasure: twenty-nine rock-cut caves used as Buddhist monasteries and temples from the second century B.C. to the seventh century A.D. The tenacity it took to chisel these monuments out of volcanic rock is testament to spiritual devotion. The beauty of the friezes of the Buddha and bodhisattvas adorning the walls and ceilings of the caves speaks to the liberating light of such devotion.

If you want to clear your mind of worldly woes and open your heart for inner guidance, visit the Ajanta Caves. Fly into Mumbai (international airport) or Aurangabad (domestic airport). From Aurangabad, take a coach tour, bus, rental car, hired driver/car, or taxi to the caves, which are about an hour away. The caves are open 9:00 A.M. to 5:30 P.M. Tuesday through Sunday and are closed Mondays.

Soothe Your Spirit
Explore the caves mindfully, absorbing the beauty and serenity of this holy place. Focus on your breath, exhaling the stale air of doubt, inhaling the fresh air of knowing.

A Deeper Look
Around A.D. 650, the monks abandoned their Ajanta sanctuary in favor of the Ellora Caves, 62 miles away. The Ajanta Caves faded into obscurity until they were rediscovered in 1819 by a British hunting party that chased a tiger into one of the caves.

131. Umayyad Mosque
(Grand Mosque of Damascus)

DAMASCUS, SYRIA

And your Lord said, "Invoke me. I will respond . . . "
—Qur'an, 40:60

*B*efore this triumph of Islamic mosques was built in A.D. 705, the land on which it stands held a succession of sacred structures. First, there was an Aramaic temple to Hadad, which gave way to a Roman temple exalting Jupiter. In the fourth century B.C., Byzantines converted the temple into a church, which, after the fall of Damascus in A.D. 661, they shared with Muslim worshipers: Christians on the west, Muslims on the east. By 670, the Christians had moved into Saint John the Baptist Cathedral nearby. The small church was stripped of its Roman and Byzantine features, and construction of the grand mosque ensued.

Umayyad Mosque stands today as the ultimate in Islamic mosque design; it is artistically superior, with a large domed nave and an open courtyard with three porticos. Among the 777 monuments enshrined in this grand mosque are one of the three original copies of the Qur'an and the relics of Saint John the Baptist.

Whether you wish to seek guidance from Allah or to see one of Islam's most important places of worship, visit Umayyad Mosque. Fly into Damascus International Airport and take a taxi to the mosque in the Old City section of Damascus. Observe all Islamic customs.

Soothe Your Spirit
Pray, asking Allah for the spiritual succor you seek.

A Deeper Look
One of the mosque's minarets is believed to be the passage through which Jesus (Issa) will return to Earth.

132. Mitrópoli Cathedral

PLÁKA, ATHENS, GREECE

Whatsoever that be within us that feels, thinks, desires, and animates, is something celestial, divine, and, consequently, imperishable.
—Aristotle (384–322 B.C.), Greek philosopher

When Athens became the capital of Greece, King Otto decided a cathedral was needed. To construct the massive metropolitan (*mitrópoli*) cathedral of Athens, seventy-two churches were demolished. In 1862, the Mitrópoli Cathedral was dedicated to the Annunciation of the Virgin. The Byzantine-style blue-and-rose interior showcases splendid religious art and enshrines the tombs of two saints: Gregory V, patriarch of Constantinople (hanged in 1821 on orders of Ottoman Sultan Mahmud II), and Agía Filothéi, believed to have paid for the release of Greek women kept as sex slaves in Turkish harems.

If you appreciate the Orthodox Christian tradition and believe that the veneration of saints helps you further your spiritual goals through their assistance and intercession, check out Mitrópoli (as it is commonly known). It is located at Plateía Mitropóleos, Pláka, in Athens and is easy to get to by taxi or the metro (get off at the metro stops for Syntagma or Monastiráki).

Visit in the morning; the Mitrópoli is closed in the afternoon.

Soothe Your Spirit
Pass through the lovely triple-arched entrance, leaving your worries and cares outside. At the tombs of the saints, pray about how best to achieve your spiritual goals. If you feel inspired to do so, light a candle and sit for meditation, basking in the presence of the Divine in the temple of your heart.

A Deeper Look
Mitrópoli is the largest church in Athens.

133. Panagia Gorgoepikoos
(Church of Our Lady Who Hears Swiftly)

PLÁKA, ATHENS, GREECE

Before, by yourself, you couldn't. Now, you've turned to Our Lady, and with her, how easy!

—Saint Josemaría Escrivá (1902–1975), Spanish Roman Catholic priest and founder of Opus Dei

The tiny church of Panagia Gorgoepikoos is revered by Athenians for its icon of Theotokos (the Mother of God), to whom many miracles have been attributed, including swift responses to petitions. The lower walls of this elegant cross-in-square church are constructed of unadorned marble. In contrast, the upper portions display ninety bas reliefs, replete with pagan symbols—remnants of an ancient temple razed to build the church—that were Christianized with the insertion of crosses.

Whether you want to make a supplication before the holy icon or to see and learn more about this historic church, pay a visit to Panagia Gorgoepikoos. It is located at Plateía Mitropóleos, adjacent to the Mitrópoli. Take a taxi or the metro rail (get off at the metro stops for Syntagma or Monastiráki).

Soothe Your Spirit
Offer your prayer before the icon, petitioning Mother Mary to assist you in your quest for Divine understanding and nurturance.

A Deeper Look
The Church of Panagia Gorgoepikoos served as the National Library from 1841 (after the foundation of Greece as a state) until 1863, when its use as a church was restored and it was rededicated to Saint Eleftherios, venerated for his pastoral virtues. The ancient temple from which the church's friezes were repurposed was founded by Athenian-born empress Irene, credited with restoring the Greek Orthodox veneration of icons.

134. White Horse Temple

LUOYANG, HENAN PROVINCE, CHINA

He who depends on himself will attain the greatest happiness.
—Chinese proverb

*L*egends abound regarding the establishment of China's picturesque White Horse Temple; one of the most prominent involves two Indian monks who traveled on white horses along the Silk Road from Afghanistan to China carrying ancient Buddhist scriptures, sacred icons, and holy relics. When they arrived in the capital city of Luoyang in A.D. 68, the Chinese constructed the White Horse Temple outside the city walls. There, on the lush grounds of the 32-acre compound, which today is a popular pilgrimage site, the monks stayed and translated the *sutras* (a type of Hindu literary composition).

If you seek spiritual insights or knowledge about Buddhism or Chinese history, visit White Horse Temple. English signage explains the halls and their treasures. The temple sits 8 miles east of Luoyang, where the nearest airport is located. It is China's fourth busiest airport, with flights from Beijing, Zhengzhou, and other major cities. From Luoyang train station, it's a forty-minute ride on bus 56 to the temple.

Soothe Your Spirit
Light a stick of incense in the courtyard, remove your shoes, and enter the main temple to worship. Reflect upon the happiness and knowing that comes from within. Trust your intuition to guide you to the knowledge you seek.

A Deeper Look
The compound includes many worship halls, including Hall of the Jade Buddha, Hall of Mahavira, Hall of Heavenly Kings, and Hall of Changing Ge, which is the repository of the ancient manuscripts.

135. Dura Europos

SALHIYÉ, SYRIA

I circle around God; around the primordial tower . . . circling for thousands of years . . . and I still don't know: am I a falcon, a storm, or a great song?
—Ranier Maria Rilke (1875–1926), Austrian-German poet

*I*n the sweltering desert of Syria where sandstorms have circled and whirled for time immemorial, an ancient city lay buried along the Euphrates River, hiding the world's oldest synagogue and house-church. In 1920, during the Arab Revolt following World War I, a soldier digging a trench unearthed brilliant tempera wall paintings of biblical figures (now in the National Museum of Damascus), which later archaeological excavations (1920s–1930s) identified as ruins of an ancient temple. Other sacred treasures found on the site include a synagogue roof and papyrus scriptures in Greek, Aramaic, Hebrew, and Latin. Numerous historical artifacts and structures have also been recovered.

If you are spiritually edified by early Judeo-Christian religious and cultural history, visit Dura Europos, bordering Iraq on Syria's eastern flank, near the village of Salhiyé. Book a coach tour or day trip from the town of Dayr az-Zawr, north of Dura Europos.

Soothe Your Spirit

As you explore the ruins, envision a deep spiritual connection with ancient Judaic or early Christian culture. Offer a prayer of hope or gratitude for God's guidance and grace.

A Deeper Look

Visit the National Museum of Damascus, perhaps before visiting Dura Europos, to learn about the spiritual, cultural, and historical significance of this ancient city.

136. Basilica de la Macarena (Our Lady of Hope)

SEVILLE, SPAIN

To be prepared is half the victory.
—Miguel de Cervantes (1547–1616), Spanish author

*P*rotected behind black wrought-iron fencing, the white-and-mustard colonial-style Basilica de la Macarena (built in 1949) welcomes worshipers inside to venerate the seventeenth-century icon of the weeping Virgin Mary, lavishly dressed in gold and white, adorned in jewels, and bearing a crystal teardrop on her cheek. At her feet pray Spain's faithful, particularly her matadors and the Roma, who favor the Virgin's blessings upon their fate in the bullring or on their business agreements.

If you would like to pray for guidance in a spiritual undertaking or a business venture, visit the Basilica de la Macarena. It's only a twenty-minute walk from downtown Seville, or various buses will take you to the church as well as to Murillo Gardens and the Triana District in a loop. The Seville International Airport is 6 miles south of the city.

Soothe Your Spirit

Enjoy the holy ambiance of this church, its sacred art, and the chapel of Christ. Light a candle and pray before the Macarena, asking specifically for the counsel you seek.

A Deeper Look

The beautiful wooden statue of the Virgin Mary, believed to have been sculpted by Luisa Roldán and with hair purportedly fashioned from real human hair, is the crowning highlight of an enormous parade of floats from the church (other churches participate as well) and through the streets, starting on Friday during Holy Week (*Semana Santa* in Spain).

CHAPTER 6

RELATIONSHIPS, MARRIAGE, FAMILY

Oh, the comfort—the inexpressible comfort of
feeling safe with a person—having neither to weigh
thoughts nor measure words, but pouring them all
right out, just as they are, chaff and grain together;
certain that a faithful hand will take and sift them,
keep what is worth keeping, and then with the
breath of kindness blow the rest away.

—Dinah Craik (1826–1887), A Life for a Life

137. Amorgos

CYCLADES ISLANDS, GREECE

The dream is realized where you do not expect it.
—Greek proverb

*A*round the Greek island of Amorgos, the royal blue hue of the Aegean Sea shifts to the brilliant turquoise of a Byzantine tile, in stark contrast to the gray-green and ruddy brown vegetation on the island's tallest mountain, Kroikelos. Inhabited since prehistoric times, this breathtaking sanctuary stretching more than 20 miles long and almost 4 miles wide has a wild, unrestrained beauty that is quintessentially Greek— inspiring spiritual seekers, poets, lovers, nature buffs, and globe trekkers alike.

If a nature retreat might help you cultivate a more intimate relationship with the Divine or rejuvenate a personal relationship with a lover, friend, or family member, visit Amorgos in the spectacular Cyclades, the most easterly of the Greek Islands. From Piraeus, the port of Athens, take the ferry to Amorgos to either the village of Katapola (in the central and more populous part of the island) or Aigiali (in the north).

Soothe Your Spirit

Make your way to Chora by car, bus, bike, or on foot, depending where you stay on the island. Take a stroll through this bougainvillea-covered village, where you will find many small churches and other quiet places conducive to prayer. When a spot calls to you, bow your head and pray for your relationship needs.

A Deeper Look

The most dazzling feature on Amorgos is the white-washed monastery of Panagia Chozoviotissa, built on a sheer cliff 186 feet above the Aegean.

138. Tulum

YUCATÁN, MEXICO

Tell me who you live with and I will tell you who you are.
—Hispanic proverb

The once-jungle-covered, late-Mayan city of Tulum stands on a cliff overlooking a white powder beach stretching along the sparkling blue Caribbean Sea, like a sacred gift from the gods to whom the Maya prayed for bountiful crops, healthy families, and good marriages. The temples, sanctuaries, and offertories of the Tulum ruins, once a place of worship for Maya kings, provide a view into their civilization, when family and friendship were as important to the ancient Maya as they are to their descendants.

If you want to share a spiritually enriching experience with your spouse or to take a solitary retreat in order to gain perspective on a personal relationship, come to Tulum. From Cancún, take a bus, rental car, tour package, or hired car and driver. Allow two hours to get there and a few hours to see everything.

Soothe Your Spirit
Walk around the ruins, soaking up the peaceful beauty and spiritual energy of this sacred site. Climb the steep steps to the top of the main temple; sit in quiet meditation or prayer. Later, go for a refreshing swim.

A Deeper Look
Tulum has three areas: Tulum Pueblo (the town, with markets, hostels, hotels, restaurants, etc.), Tulum Playa (the beach area and ecology reserve), and Tulum Ruins (the archaeological site); none are within walking distance of each other. The ruin is the third most visited archaeological site in Mexico.

139. Basilica di San Marco (Saint Mark's Basilica)

VENICE, ITALY

We are each of us angels with only one wing, and we can only fly by embracing one another.
—Luciano de Crescenzo (1928–), Italian writer, filmmaker, and engineer

Once called *Chiesa d'Oro* (Church of Gold) because of its gilded Byzantine mosaics and status as a chapel to the ruling Venetians, this magnificent five-domed Gothic cathedral has long been a symbol of wealth and power. However, the multitudes who flock here to worship or to wed speak more to its holiness and sacred beauty.

Built to safeguard the relics of the Evangelist Saint Mark, Saint Mark's Basilica dominates Piazza San Marco (San Marco Square), where *The Tetrarchs* statue anchors the church's southwest corner. Among the basilica's many treasures, the statue represents the interdependence of the four rulers of the Roman Empire.

Whether you wish to sanctify your romantic relationship or your love for the Divine, go to Saint Mark's Basilica. Fly to Venice's Marco Polo Airport, and then take a water bus or ferry to the island.

Soothe Your Spirit
Attend Mass at 6:45 P.M. if you want to see the mosaics illuminated. Pray with (or for) someone you love.

A Deeper Look
Saint Mark's Basilica, consecrated in A.D. 1094, is the seat of the Venetian archbishop and the third church built on the site. The first was in A.D. 828, when San Marco's body was supposedly found in a pillar in Alexandria and brought to Venice. The golden pillar (*Pala d'Oro*) is enshrined behind the high altar.

140. Kamakhya Temple

GUWAHATI, ASSAM, INDIA

Tantra loves and loves unconditionally. It never says no to anything whatsoever . . .
—Osho, or Bhagwan Shree Rajneesh (1931–1990), Indian mystic and spiritual leader

According to myth, when the womb of Sati (the Hindu Mother Goddess) fell to Earth as the result of a chain of events stemming from her father's disapproval of her husband, a large cleft occurred in the bedrock. On that holy site, a temple was built to venerate the goddess, thereafter known as Kamakhya (One Worshiped by the God of Love). The eye-catching temple—with seven oval spires, three golden pitchers, and inner walls covered with carvings of Hindu deity—is among the most sacred to practitioners of Shakti Tantra.

If you wish to meditate on a family conflict or learn more about tantrism, visit Kamakhya Temple, which welcomes people of all beliefs. Located 5 miles from the railway station in the Kamrup District of Guwahati, the temple is open from 8:00 A.M. until sunset most days, with a break for lunch.

Soothe Your Spirit

Place your fingertips on the *yoni* (cleft in the bedrock, representing the origin of life in Tantra) and say your prayer. Outside, light a ghee lamp or incense and walk around the temple clockwise.

A Deeper Look

Built in the sixteenth century and rebuilt in the seventeenth century, Kamakhya Temple sits high on a hill looking every bit the medieval Hindu temple it is. Its *sanctum sanctorum*, located in a cave, is one of the most venerated Shakti shrines in India.

141. Cathedral Basilica of Saint Joseph

SAN JOSE, CALIFORNIA, UNITED STATES

May he [Saint Joseph] always guard, protect and enlighten families.
—Pope John Paul II (1920–2005)

In 1801, the Franciscans built a modest adobe church dedicated to Saint Joseph (the husband of the Virgin Mary) in what is now the city of San Jose. Earthquakes destroyed that church and then another. When fire destroyed a third church, a temporary church was built nearby. The cornerstone of the fifth (and current) church was laid on March 19, 1876 (Saint Joseph's feast day); since then it has undergone several renovations, most recently in preparation for receiving minor basilica status in 1997. With each incarnation, Saint Joseph's has grown bigger and more beautiful—and provided an even more nurturing spiritual home to the families and faithful of sprawling Santa Clara Valley.

Whether you seek a loving connection to your birth family or to a spiritual family, visit the Cathedral Basilica of Saint Joseph, with its emphasis on families, located in downtown San Jose.

Soothe Your Spirit

Attend the Misa Familiar or Family Mass on the first Sunday of every month to hear the church's Coro de Niños or children's choir. Or drop in anytime to say a heartfelt prayer for your family.

A Deeper Look

The tower bell from the first adobe church has been hung in each of the succeeding churches. In deference to its large Hispanic congregation, the church honors traditions such as the Feast of the Vírgen de Guadalupe and Día de los Muertos (Day of the Dead).

142. Temple Square (Mormon Temple)

SALT LAKE CITY, UTAH, UNITED STATES

The church exists to exalt the family. And the family is the fundamental unit of the church.
—Russell M. Nelson (1924–), American physician and LDS elder

It is no wonder Temple Square—world headquarters of The Church of Jesus Christ of Latter-day Saints (Mormons)—receives millions of visitors each year. The 10-acre complex is beautiful and welcoming, and it features a dozen historical and sacred sites. Among those open to the public are Assembly Hall (a lovely Gothic church with exquisite stained-glass windows); Mormon Tabernacle (a dome-shaped auditorium, where the famed Mormon Tabernacle Choir performs); Joseph Smith Memorial Building (the location of the Family Search Center); and Family History Library (huge repository of genealogy records). The most sacred site—Salt Lake Temple, the "House of the Lord"—is not open to the public, but it is a glory to behold.

Whether you yearn to connect with your ancestral family or to deepen your connection to your church family, try visiting Temple Square in downtown Salt Lake City. Take a shuttle, rental car, taxi, or bus from Salt Lake City International Airport. The visitors' center at Temple Square has information on guided tours, shuttles within the complex, guidebooks, concerts, and more.

Soothe Your Spirit

Explore the site that calls to you. Enjoy a concert or a quiet meal with your family. Gaze at the sacred temple (lit like the North Star at night), and pray for help in finding, healing, or strengthening your family.

A Deeper Look

The Humanitarian Center is open to the public and provides resources to help strengthen families.

143. Saint Patrick's Cathedral

NEW YORK CITY, NEW YORK, UNITED STATES

. . . If two of you agree on earth about anything they ask, it will be done for them by thy Father in heaven. For where two or three are gathered in my name, there am I among them.
—Bible, Matthew 18:29–20

Approaching Saint Patrick's Cathedral on busy Fifth Avenue in midtown Manhattan, you may be struck by how different it is from the surrounding cityscape. The cathedral appears to be more medieval European than the nineteenth-century New Yorker it is. Built in 1858, Saint Patrick's is a neo-Gothic masterpiece with a lavishly decorated marble façade and many squared spires, including two flanking the grand front entrance and rising 330 feet from street level. You will feel as if you are entering a different world as you step from the bustling city street through the entrance and inside the nave. Cavernous and quiet, this sanctuary surrounds its visitors with peace as the sunlight shimmers through exquisite stained-glass windows and reveals soaring arches and stunning artwork. So it is that 5.5 million faithful and hopeful from around the globe are drawn to Saint Patrick's Cathedral in midtown Manhattan.

Whether you seek deeper communion with the universal family or your own family, come to Saint Patrick's Cathedral. Find it in midtown Manhattan on Fifth Avenue between Fiftieth and Fifty-first streets, 6 blocks from Grand Central Station (rail), near subway and bus stops, or you can always hail a taxi.

Soothe Your Spirit
Light a candle and pray for a special intention for loved ones.

A Deeper Look
Among the cathedral's extraordinary works of sacred art are two altars by Tiffany & Co., Charles Connick's *Rose* window, and a *Pietà* by Araldo Perugi that is three times larger than Michelangelo's original.

144. Basilica of Our Lady of the Rosary (Basilica at Fátima)

FÁTIMA, PORTUGAL

Mother is the name for God in the lips and hearts of little children.
—William Makepeace Thackeray (1811–1863), Indian-born English author and novelist

In 1982, Pope John Paul II gave thanks to the Virgin Mary for saving his life from an assassination attempt the previous year by embedding the bullet taken from his chest into the crown of Our Lady of Fátima. Built in 1928, the cream-colored neoclassical basilica stands on the site where, in 1917, three children saw six consecutive apparitions of the Virgin Mary, the third prophesying the death of a pope in 1981. The tombs of two of the children (Jacinta and Francisco) are housed in the basilica, and stained-glass windows depict narrative scenes of the apparitions. At the center of this cathedral that has fifteen altars honoring the mysteries of the rosary is the Chapel of Apparitions, where a marble pillar marks the spot of the appearances.

If you wish to pray on behalf of your child or children everywhere, visit Our Lady of the Rosary, Fátima. Travel from Lisbon by rental car, or from Lisbon to Caxarias by train and then by taxi.

Soothe Your Spirit
Pray the rosary for peace, or offer the simple prayer Mary gave to the three children at Fátima: "My God, I believe, I adore."

A Deeper Look
Four million people visit Fátima each year, with crowds swelling on May 13, the day of the first apparition, and on October 13, the day of the last appearance.

145. Great Mosque of Kairouan

KAIROUAN, TUNISIA

Friendship is honey, but don't eat it all.
—Moroccan proverb

The Great Mosque of Kairouan, built around A.D. 670 and rebuilt around 863, is the fourth holiest site of Islam and the oldest in Africa. The fortress-like mosque is constructed of dressed stone bricks. The interior's marble columns, stone floor, pyramid-shaped chandeliers, tiled *mihrāb* (a niche that indicates the direction of Mecca), and carved teak pulpit were created with ninth-century materials from Mesopotamia. Porticos created with recycled Roman and Byzantine pillars frame the marble-slab courtyard. The north portico houses the oldest minaret in Maghreb, and the current minaret is a massive square-based tower with three stories of diminishing size.

Whether you wish to ask Allah for wisdom regarding an uneasy relationship or to see an ancient Islamic site where the *muezzin* continues to call the faithful to *adhān* (prayer), visit the Great Mosque of Kairouan, located in the city's historic district, Medina. The mosque is an easy day-trip by car or bus from Monastir or Sousse, but a guided local or packaged coach tour is best. Kaftans are available if you come improperly attired. Remove your shoes and perform the ritual ablution. Non-Muslims may look inside the prayer hall but may not enter.

Soothe Your Spirit
Pray for a healing or a blessing. Show your gratitude by leaving an offering of food for the poor.

A Deeper Look
Some Muslims believe that making seven pilgrimages to the Great Mosque at Kairouan is the equivalent of a *hajj* (annual pilgrimage) to Mecca.

146. Brigit's Garden (Gairdín Bhríde)

GALWAY, COUNTY GALWAY, IRELAND

I will smoor the hearth / As Brighid the Fostermother would smoor /
The Fostermother's holy name / Be on the hearth, be on the herd /
Be on the household all.
—*Carmena Gadelica*, vol. 3, ed. Alexander Carmichael (1832–1912),
Scottish folklorist

The ancient Celts revered Brigit, the "Exalted One," as a goddess of creativity, poetry, childbirth, and the hearth and as a patron/protector of children, home, and nature. Brigit's Garden—11 magical acres with gardens, ponds, woodland, a discovery trail and a willowed play area for children, a *crannog* (round gathering house), and Celtic ceremonial sites—invites celebration and contemplation of all Brigit's Divine attributes. The four themed gardens reflect Celtic cycle-of-life mythology, which aligns with the four seasons, and the four Celtic festivals: *Samhain* (winter/death, rebirth; the beginning of the Celtic yearly cycle), *Imbolc* (spring/birth), *Bealtaine* (summer/youth), and *Lughnasa* (autumn/maturity).

If you wish to celebrate the blessings of a warm home or inspire your children to honor Mother Earth, come spend the day at Brigit's Garden, located twenty minutes north of Galway. There are restrooms and a café onsite.

Soothe Your Spirit

Explore the gardens, mindful of your soulful connection with your child and Mother Earth. Stand on the sundial, raise your face and arms to heaven, and give joyful thanks for the family that sustains you.

A Deeper Look

Some believe the Celtic goddess Brigit and the Christian saint Brigid of Kildare (Mary of the Gael) are one and the same.

147. Cathédral Saint-Mammès de Langres

LANGRES, CHAMPAGNE-ARDENNE, FRANCE

Children are the hands by which we take hold of heaven.
—Henry Ward Beecher (1813–1887), clergyman and social reformer

The Cathédral Saint-Mammès de Langres, in the Champagne-Ardenne region of France, has twin towers that jut heavenward like outstretched arms beckoning angels to draw near to hear whispered prayers and to soothe the souls of families and children. Welcoming all who come to pray through its festive red doors, the cathedral is dedicated to Saint Mammès of Caesarea, a child whose parents were executed for being Christians. After his own teen martyrdom, Mammès's relics were taken to the cathedral in Langres in 1209 to be safeguarded along with those of martyred Cappadocian triplets, Saints Speusippus, Eleusippus, and Melapsippus.

If you are inspired by the faith of a child and wish to pray for children or for the souls of the child-saints whose relics are enshrined in the Cathédral Saint-Mammès de Langres, visit the cathedral, which is roughly an hour's drive northeast of Dijon or 183 miles from Paris and is easily accessible by car or bus.

Soothe Your Spirit

Hold love in your heart for children of all nations as you light a candle and pray to Holy Mother Mary that your faith be as strong as a child's love for his or her parents and for protection and love for all God's children.

A Deeper Look

Dedicated in 1196, the cathedral straddles two styles: Burgundy-Romanesque and Gothic. It is a national monument of France and the seat of the bishop of Langres.

148. La Sagrada Família (also Basílica y Templo Expiatorio de la Sagrada Família)

BARCELONA, CATALONIA, SPAIN

A cathedral open for every buddy [sic], a place of spirituality with the Christian message, a place of fraternity for all.
—Antoni Gaudí (1852–1926), Catalan architect and designer of
La Sagrada Família

*L*a Sagrada Família (Church of the Holy Family) is an exuberant architectural allegory to Christianity that fuses Gothic, baroque, and modernism styles and makes dramatic use of religious symbolism. It is also gargantuan—with more to come. Although under construction almost continuously since 1882, the structure will not reach completion until 2017 to 2026. Then, architect Antoni Gaudí's "masterpiece" will have three grand façades—Nativity (completed in 1930), Passion (nearing completion), and Glory (begun in 2002)—and eighteen spires (eight completed) in ascending heights: twelve Apostles, four Evangelists, the Virgin Mary, and Jesus Christ (the tallest spire at 560 feet).

Meanwhile, worshipers and visitors continue to throng to Basílica y Templo Expiatorio de la Sagrada Família. The church's crypt is among the "Works by Antoni Gaudí" designated a World Heritage Site in 1984.

Whether you wish to attend Mass, to pray for loved ones, or to see Gaudí's "Cathedral of the Third Millennium," plan a journey to La Sagrada Família. Travel from Barcelona International Airport or within the city by rental car, taxi, sightseeing coach, or public transportation.

Soothe Your Spirit

Tour the church with your family or a group of friends. Say a grateful prayer before whatever image calls you.

A Deeper Look

The consecration mass in 2010 was attended by 6,500 faithful inside and 50,000 outside, with 100 bishops and 300 priests serving the Eucharist.

149. Notre-Dame-de-la-Mer

SAINTES-MARIES-DE-LA-MER (CHURCH OF SAINT MARYS FROM THE SEA), CAMARGUE, FRANCE

It is virtue, virtue, which both creates and preserves friendship. On it depends harmony of interest, permanence, fidelity.
—Cicero (106–43 B.C.), Roman statesman and philosopher

According to legend, in A.D. 40, three saints—Mary Magdalene, Mary Jacobé, and Mary Salomé—were set adrift in a boat with no oars and washed ashore at Saintes-Maries-de-la-Mer. The twelfth-century fortified church of Notre-Dame-de-la-Mer—sacred to Celts, Romans, and Christians—venerates the three Marys as well as Sarah (patron saint of Gypsies), thought to be their Egyptian servant.

If you are inspired by the friendship of the three Marys, whose bond included their devotion to Jesus or by the hospitality of southern France, come to the church of Notre-Dame-de-la-Mer. Travel to Saintes-Maries-de-la-Mer by rental car, taxi, or bus from one of three regional airports: Avignon, Marseille-Provence, and Nimes-Garon. Alternatively, you can take a bus from Aigues Mortes (16 miles away) or Arles (23 miles away), or rent a car. There is also rail service from Paris to Nimes, which is 42 miles from Saintes Maries-de-la-Mer.

Soothe Your Spirit

Meditate on your spiritual connection to your closest friends. Ask the Marys to take your prayer of petition for loving relationships on their hearts to the most Sacred Heart.

A Deeper Look

The church hosts an annual *Pélerinage des Gitans* (Pilgrimage of the Gypsies) in May to honor their patron saint Sarah and to seek blessings on their contracts, engagements, and baptisms.

150. Temple De Hirsch Sinai

SEATTLE, WASHINGTON, UNITED STATES

And give unto Solomon my son a perfect heart, to keep thy commandments, thy testimonies, and thy statutes, and to do all these things, and to build the palace for which I have made provision . . .
—Bible, 1 Chronicles 29:19–20

*B*uilt in the 1960s, this Reform Jewish synagogue makes a modernistic architectural statement with its use of concrete and functionality, yet the focus of this progressive spiritual community is as old as time—families. Through examination of Jewish history and celebration of sacred and cultural traditions, the congregation of this lovely synagogue emphasizes dialogue with God through prayer, song, study, community, sacred space, and the authenticity of intention.

If you feel kinship with spiritual communities that respect both diversity and tradition or if you would like access to a Judaic lending library, visit Temple De Hirsch Sinai in Seattle. Although located on East Pike Street, the sanctuary entrance is on Sixteenth Avenue. Getting to the temple by city bus, taxi, or rental car is easy.

Soothe Your Soul
Attend the service as a guest or become part of this family of families. Engage at least one other person in conversation on a spiritual topic, whether about Hebrew history, a tradition, or a sacred holiday such as Hanukkah, Rosh Hashana, Yom Kippur, Sukkot, or Purim.

A Deeper Look
Temple De Hirsch Sinai has a number of community outreach programs wherein members of the synagogue help the less fortunate in Seattle.

151. Basilica de Nuestra Señora de Guadalupe (Basilica of Our Lady of Guadalupe)

MEXICO CITY, MEXICO

So your strength is failing you? . . . Mother! Call her with a loud voice. She is listening to you . . .
—St. Josemaría Escrivá (1902–1975), Spanish Roman Catholic priest and founder of Opus Dei

One of the holiest places in the Western Hemisphere—the Basilica of Our Lady of Guadalupe—might not exist if it weren't for an Aztec peasant. Juan Diego, a newly converted Christian, went to his bishop in Mexico City to request a church be built at Tepeyac, where he had seen an apparition of Virgin Mary. He was told that a heavenly sign was needed. The Virgin made roses bloom in the snow and told Juan to wrap them in his *tilma* (cloak) and take them to the bishop. When Juan delivered the gift, the *tilma* was miraculously imprinted with an image of the Virgin. That miracle of faith continues to give strength to the church community of the Basilica of Our Lady of Guadalupe.

If you wish to strengthen your spiritual bonds or to see the miraculous cloth, travel to the basilica. The church is located in the Villa de Guadalupe Hidalgo area of Mexico City. Travel by metro to La Villa Station, and then walk two blocks to the church.

Soothe Your Soul

Light a candle and pray in thanksgiving to Mary for the faith that sustains you and your church community.

A Deeper Look

Digital technology reveals that the image reflected in the Virgin's eyes on the *tilma* is of the bishop receiving the roses.

152. Basilica di Santa Maria del Fiore (Duomo)

FLORENCE, ITALY

The soul that can speak through the eyes, can also kiss with a gaze.
—Gustav Adolfo Bécquer (1836–1870), Spanish poet

*O*f the most spiritual and romantic places in the world, few can rival Florence, in the beautiful Italian countryside of Tuscany. The most recognizable structures in the Florence skyline are the octagonal dome of the Duomo (designed by Filippo Brunelleschi) and the Gothic Campanile di Giotto, the bell tower named after the painter and sculptor who designed it for the cathedral.

Whether you yearn for more depth in your spiritual life or more intimacy with your life partner, plan a lover's trip to Florence's Duomo. Go in September when the tourists have gone home and the Tuscan weather is wonderful. Get a walking map and explore this incredible city on foot. You can fly into Pisa, which has the nearest major airport, and then take the train to Florence's SMN railway station (under an hour), the bus, or rent a car. Florence also has a regional airport.

Soothe Your Spirit

Climb the narrow steps to the marble observation tower of the cupola to see spectacular views of the city, even on a gray day. Face your lover, and looking deeply into each other's eyes, offer a prayer of thanks for God's blessings.

A Deeper Look

The massive dome features a fresco, *The Last Judgment*, which took more than ten years to paint. Giorgio Vasari started the fresco, and Federico Zuccari finished it in 1579.

153. Valle dei Templi (Valley of the Temples)

AGRIGENTO, SICILY

O Friends, ye who inhabit the great city of sacred Akragas up to the acropolis, whose care is good deeds, who harbour strangers deserving of respect . . .
—Empedokles of Akragas (ca. 492–432 B.C.), Greek philosopher, physician, and politician

Cerulean skies, azure seas, and sun-drenched beaches have long attracted tourists to Sicily, but spiritual seekers have discovered something else here: the Valle dei Templi (Valley of the Temples), the sacred ruins of an acropolis (Akragas) dating to fifth century B.C. For most of its history, Akragas was ruled by tyrants. From 471 to 406 B.C., however, the city enjoyed a period of democracy that promoted the *eudaimonia* (well-being) of all people, thanks to Empedokles, a political leader who advocated working together for the benefit of each and all.

If you are seeking insight for resolving a power struggle with your boss, spouse, teenager, or conscience, visit the Valley of the Temples. Take advantage of the guided tours; the ruins cover a large area. Fly to Palermo International Airport (also known as Falcone-Borsellino Airport) or Catania Fontanarossa, and take a bus or rental car to Agrigento.

Soothe Your Spirit

As you explore the temples, contemplate the concepts of individual and universal well-being espoused by Empedokles and how you might facilitate those qualities in your spiritual community and in the world.

A Deeper Look

This World Heritage Site includes Doric temples to Juno, Concordia, Asclepius, Heracles, Olympia, the Dioscuri (twins Castor and Pollux), and Vulcan.

154. Whitefriar Street Carmelite Church

DUBLIN, IRELAND

What greater thing is there in life than for two human souls to feel that they are joined for life . . .
—George Eliot (1819–1880), pseudonym for Mary Ann Evans, English novelist

When Father John Spratt, an Irish Carmelite, returned to his parish in Dublin from preaching in a Jesuit church in Gesu, Italy, he brought the sacred relics of Saint Valentine, given to him by Pope Gregory XVI. These relics were enshrined in Whitefriar Street Carmelite Church. Today, couples visit the Shrine of Saint Valentine on February 14 (the saint's feast day), when the reliquary is taken from the side altar and placed in front of the high altar. There they pray for blessings on their marriages or enjoy the Eucharistic celebration, which includes the Blessing of the Rings (for engaged couples).

Whether you are engaged or married and desire to pray for the intercession of Saint Valentine, visit Whitefriar Street Carmelite Church in Dublin, at 56 Aungier Street. The international airport is in Shannon. From there, rent a car or take a shuttle bus or taxi into Dublin.

Soothe Your Spirit

Light a candle, kneel before the saint's reliquary, and pray with your beloved for what you want or need in your relationship.

A Deeper Look

Built in 1825, Whitefriar Street Carmelite Church was enlarged in 1856 and again in 1868. Today, the church has numerous chapels, including one dedicated to Saint Albert of Sicily, who healed with water.

155. Baths of Aphrodite / Fountain of Love

PAPHOS, CYPRUS, GREECE

Even if you gods, and all the goddesses too, should be looking on, yet would I be glad to sleep with the golden Aphrodite.
—Homer (800–700 B.C.), *The Iliad*, Greek epic poet

*J*ust north of Paphos is a site sacred to the ancient Greeks—the Baths of Aphrodite, where the Olympian goddess of love and sexual rapture bathed in a pool of a natural grotto under a fig tree. Today, the Aphrodite and Adonis walking trails along the Akamas Peninsula merge between the Baths of Aphrodite and Pyrgos tis Rigenas (Tower of the Queen), offering spectacular views.

If you desire to awaken or reawaken intimacy in your relationship, grab your partner and head for the Baths of Aphrodite. Winter, spring, and autumn are the best times to go, as Cyprus is hot in summer. No bathing is allowed in the pool, but there are great swimming beaches and coves just beyond the fountain. Fly into Paphos Airport and drive north along the coast about 29 miles, 2 miles past Latchi. Daily buses (except on Sundays) also link Paphos and Latchi.

Soothe Your Spirit

Walk the sacred lovers' trail hand-in-hand with your beloved. Sit on one of the benches overlooking the sea, wrapped in each other's arms, mindful to keep the passion of Aphrodite/Adonis alive in your relationship.

A Deeper Look

Adonis and Aphrodite's complicated love story is told in Ovid's *Metamorphoses*.

156. Temple of Hera (Heraion)

OLYMPIA, ATHENS, GREECE

We learn by practice. . . . One becomes in some area an athlete of God.
—Martha Graham (1894–1991), American ballerina and choreographer

The Temple of Hera in Olympia, one of the earliest Greek temples with Doric columns, honored both Hera and Zeus (wife and husband supreme deities) until the Great Temple to Zeus was completed, after which only women worshiped at Hera's temple. Today, the temple is the site where eleven women (representing the Vestal Virgins) ignite the Olympic Torch with the sun's rays, in a ceremony that signals the opening of the Olympic Games. The games are a testament of athletic excellence as well as of respect and cooperation among athletes and countries of the world.

If you seek the focus and dedication of an Olympic athlete in your spiritual life or in your personal relationships, visit the Temple of Hera. From Athens International Airport, travel by bus or train to Olympia.

Soothe Your Spirit

Energize your body and your spirit with a devotional walk amid the sacred ruins of ancient Olympia. At Hera's temple, pause to absorb the heartfelt energy that ancient athletes poured out in prayer and supplication to the deity.

A Deeper Look

The Temple of Hera (ca. 590 B.C.) was among several temples as well as altars, statues, treasuries, and other structures in the *Altis* (sanctuary, or sacred precinct) of Olympia. The *Altis* originally included the Olympic Stadium, where people watched the competitions from the hill of Kronos, but the arena was gradually moved east to its present location.

157. Parish Church of Saints Peter and Paul

OBERAMMERGAU, BAVARIA, GERMANY

Nothing great in the world has ever been accomplished without passion.
—Georg Wilhelm Friedrich Hegel (1770–1831), German philosopher

The villagers of Oberammergau, after suffering the ravages of the bubonic plague, promised God to put on a Passion Play every 10 years if they were spared further strife from the scourge. Their prayers were answered, and they have kept their promise since 1634. In gratitude, those who survived also helped the next generation build the breathtaking rococo church dedicated to Saints Peter and Paul and finished in 1749. Today, the church stands as a testament of God's grace and of the faith and cooperation of an entire village that keeps their ancestral promise.

If you seek inspiration for committing to a worthy cause or to your faith, visit the Church of Saints Peter and Paul. The nearest international airport is in Innsbruck (43 miles away), with another in Munich (64 miles away). Oberammergau also has a railway station with service to Murnau and on to Munich. From the town center, travel by rental car, bus, or taxi to the church, on Dorfstrasse.

Soothe Your Spirit

Visit this church alone or with family or friends. Pray for the vision, passion of purpose, and/or spiritual collaboration you seek.

A Deeper Look

The church features a gorgeous fresco by Matthaeus Guenther of Saint Dominic receiving the rosary from the Blessed Virgin. Notice, too, there are plaques in the churchyard that commemorate those who perished during the plague.

158. Yochanan ben Zakai Synagogue / Four Sephardic Synagogues

JERUSALEM, ISRAEL

There may be times when we are powerless to prevent injustice, but there must never be a time when we fail to protest.
—Elie Wiesel (1928–), Romanian-born Jewish-American Holocaust survivor, writer, and Nobel laureate

When the Romans besieged Jerusalem in A.D. 70, Talmudic sage Yochanan ben Zakai stole out of the holy city in a coffin for a clandestine meeting with Vespasian, the conquering Roman general. Ben Zakai was able to convince the general (who later became emperor) to spare the Judaism academy at Yavne'el (Jabneel). He subsequently moved his school to Jamnia, where it became the leading Judaic cultural and scholastic center. There, he led the transformation of Judaism from a temple/priest to a shul/rabbinical tradition and promoted the more liberal Hillel teachings.

Yochanan ben Zakai Synagogue is one of the Four Sephardic Synagogues in Old Jerusalem. Each temple was built at a different time according to the changing beliefs and practices of the Jewish Sephardic community.

If you would like to pay homage to a hero of the Jewish people or to learn more about Judaism, plan to visit Yochanan ben Zakai Synagogue. Go to Hurva Square and find the synagogue below street level, on Mishmeret HaKehuna Street.

Soothe Your Spirit

Vow to gain a deeper knowledge of your faith and to share it. Pray for greater understanding and tolerance of all faiths.

A Deeper Look

During the War of Independence in 1948, more than a thousand Jews took refuge in the Four Sephardic Synagogues.

159. Church of Saint Nikolaos (Nicholas)

DEMRE (ALSO KALE OR MYRA), ANTALYA PROVINCE, TURKEY

The stockings were hung by the chimney with care / In hopes that St. Nicholas would soon be there.
—Clement Clarke Moore (1779–1863), author of "A Visit from St. Nicholas," American professor of literature and theology

Nikolaos of Myra—the Christian saint now commonly known as Saint Nicholas and Santa Claus—was born in A.D. 300 in the town of Myra (Patara) in what is now Turkey. As bishop of Myra, Nikolaos was revered for his anonymous gift-giving and for numerous miracles attributed to his intercession. Upon his death in 350, he was buried on the site where the existing church, built in the fifth century to house his tomb, now stands. Although the Byzantine church has faded with age and the tomb is empty, the colored-marble mosaic floor is still splendid and the church receives thousands of visitors each year.

Whether you wish to honor the patron saint of children or to ask for his intercession on behalf of a child, come to Church of Saint Nikolaos in Demre. Rent a car with a guide or take a coach tour or guided day trip to Demre, 56 miles from Patara.

Soothe Your Spirit

Pray on behalf of a child or for the blessing of a child in your life.

A Deeper Look

In the eleventh century, the emperor of the Eastern Roman Empire lost control of the area to the Seljuk Turks. In the confusion, and over the objections of the Orthodox monks, sailors from Bari, Italy, confiscated the saint's remains, which were entombed in a church in Bari, where they remain today.

160. Shepherds' Fields

BEIT-SAHOUR (BAYT SAHUR), EAST JERUSALEM, ISRAEL

Glory to God in the highest, peace on earth and good will toward men.
—Bible, Luke 2:14

On the holy night of December 25, while three shepherds watched over their flock from the mouth of an underground cave less than a mile from Bethlehem, an angel appeared proclaiming the birth of the Savior. There are two caves at Shepherds' Fields—one sacred to the Greek Orthodox, the other to the Franciscans. Both groups claim rights to the holy birth announcement, with favor going to the Orthodox grotto. From the early fifth century to 1955, the Orthodox used Kanisat al-Ruwat (Place of the Shepherds' Shelter) as a church dedicated to Mary. The sanctuary the Franciscans built over the other cave in 1954—the Church of the Angels—is still in use.

Whether you are traveling to the Holy Land on a discovery journey with your family or on a spiritual discovery of your own, be sure to include Shepherds' Fields on your itinerary. Both churches are open throughout the year; entry is free. Catch the bus or walk from Bethlehem.

Soothe Your Spirit

Reflect on the story of the birth of Jesus (Luke 2:8–20) and on how you might extend good will to others. Give praise to the Holy Family or offer a thankful prayer for your own.

A Deeper Look

King David wrote some of his psalms beneath two of the 2,000-year-old olive trees here. The site also contains the remnants of a stone memorial Jacob erected on the spot where God spoke to him, naming it "Bethel."

161. Pura Luhur Uluwatu Temple

BALI, INDONESIA

Of one seldom seen.
—Polynesian proverb

*B*ali's warm hospitality, Technicolor sunsets, and gorgeous beaches are a few of the many splendors that have earned Indonesia the name "Land of Smiles." Another reason is its spectacular temples, and one of the most amazing and sacred is Pura Luhur Uluwatu. Facing southwest and perched on a cliff more than 200 feet above the Indian Ocean, Uluwatu (as it is known locally) is one of nine directional temples that protect the island from evil spirits. Built in the eleventh century, this Balinese sea temple is made of black coral.

If you yearn for a spiritual island getaway with your lover or your closest friend, travel to Bali and visit Uluwatu Temple. Fly into Bali Ngurah Rai Airport (Denpasar International Airport), 8 miles south of Denpasar in southern Bali. Half-day minivan tours are available, or reach the temple by auto, taxi, or motor scooter.

Soothe Your Spirit

Join with your partner or friends in a meditation or devotional walk, envisioning or praying for a long and joyful relationship. Hold hands and watch the sun set over the Indian Ocean, stretching as far as the eye can see.

A Deeper Look

Every night, locals gather at Uluwatu Temple for *kecak* (sarong) and fire communal dances, which begin at sunset and culminate in a ceremonial bonfire.

162. Holy Trinity

HEADINGTON QUARRY, OXFORD, OXFORDSHIRE, ENGLAND

An open door between heaven and earth, showing God's love for all.
—Aim of the Holy Trinity parish church

Holy Trinity Headington Quarry, a parish church of the Church of England, is nestled in a residential neighborhood with houses, some dating to 1396, constructed of stone extracted from nearby quarries. The stone was used to build Holy Trinity (1848–1849), which bills itself as a "village church in the city" and, indeed, resembles a lovely old English country manor. However, the building, for all its fine features, is not Holy Trinity's main attraction. Nor is it that famed novelist and Oxford academic C. S. Lewis was a parishioner for three decades, until his death in 1963. Those who worship and are drawn to Holy Trinity come for its open-minded, open-hearted, open-armed celebration of God's love for all and its deep connection with the community.

If your soul longs for spiritual belonging or you would like your children to experience spiritual diversity, visit Holy Trinity, east of Headington in Oxford. London International Airport is 50 miles away. Oxford Bus Company runs from Heathrow and Gatwick airports to Oxford.

Soothe Your Spirit

Attend a service to experience firsthand the warm embrace of this church community. Pray for the faith family you seek.

A Deeper Look

The pew where C. S. Lewis worshiped for so long bears a plaque with his name. In 1991, the *Narnia* stained-glass window, fashioned and named for his beloved children's classic, *The Chronicles of Narnia*, was installed.

163. Moku'ula

LAHAINA, MAUI, HAWAII, UNITED STATES

We have to learn to become better ancestors.
—Jonas Salk (1914–1995), American medical researcher and virologist

For more than a thousand years, Moku'ula was a *piko* (umbilicus) of the Hawaiian Kingdom. The acre island surrounded by a 76-acre spring-fed "fish pond" (moat) served as a royal residence and political/spiritual center for indigenous Hawaiians until 1845. Now, it lies buried under a baseball field in a county park. Native Hawaiians believe their ancestors are living gods whose *mana* (spiritual power) is passed on to their progeny upon their death. Kihawahine, golden lizard goddess and protector of home, is the deification of Lala'iheana, daughter of a Moku'ula chief. In 1990, Kihawahine's *mana* manifested in the Friends of Moku'ula, who rallied to protect their sacred ancestral home. The excavation and preservation of Moku'ula is now underway.

If you would like to learn about Native Hawaiian spirituality and see an active archaeological dig, visit the ruins on Front Street in Lahaina. Observe the ongoing excavation or join in (reservation required). Fly to Maui, rent a car, and follow the signs west to Lahaina.

Soothe Your Spirit

Put on a yellow lei and feel Kihawahine's protective spirit embrace you. Pray for the restoration of her spiritual home and the preservation of your own home.

A Deeper Look

In 1919, sugar-plantation owners leveled the island and filled the moat, burying a wealth of sacred and historical structures, artifacts, and documents along with the life-sustaining fish pond and taro gardens (to Hawaiians, taro represents the staff of life).

CHAPTER 7

PEACE, PROTECTION, SAFE PASSAGE

We do not understand the intricate pattern of the stars in their courses, but we know that He who created them does, and that just as surely as He guides them, He is charting a safe course for us.

—Reverend Billy Graham, Jr. (1918–),
Southern Baptist Evangelist

164. Our Lady of Częstochowa (Black Madonna)

MONASTERY OF JASNA GÓRA, CZĘSTOCHOWA, JASNA GÓRA, POLAND

Madonna, Black Madonna, in her arms you will find peace . . . and be protected . . .
—Polish song, "Black Madonna"

In 1650, Grand Chancellor George Ossoliński was so inspired by the Black Madonna of Częstochowa that he made as his votive offering an ebony and silver altar. Today, the altar and the much-revered painting—said to have been painted by Saint Luke the Evangelist on a tabletop made by Jesus—are enshrined in the small fifteenth-century Gothic chapel adjoining the majestic sixteenth-century baroque monastery of Jasna Góra. Many miracles are credited to the icon of the Black Madonna, including the safety of Jasna Góra during threatened invasions in the seventeenth century by the Swedes and later in the twentieth century by the Nazis. Today, millions of Christians from around the world come to Our Lady of Częstochowa, whose images of Madonna and Child have blackened from centuries of votive smoke.

Whether you seek safe passage during your sacred travels or protection from religious oppression, visit the Black Madonna of Jasna Góra. Located in south-central Poland, Częstochowa can be reached from all major cities by rail, bus, or rental car.

Soothe Your Spirit

Light a candle, pray for what you wish to safeguard, and leave a votive offering.

A Deeper Look

In 1430, a thief twice slashed the Black Madonna with his sword. As he raised his arm to deliver a third gash, he purportedly fell to the ground in pain and died. The icon still bears the scars of that defacement.

165. Futarasan Shrine

NIKKŌ, TOCHIGI PREFECTURE, JAPAN

A single, sincere prayer moves heaven.
—Shinto proverb

Futarasan, a Shinto shrine on the slopes of Mount Nantai (also Futarasan) north of Tokyo, rises like a shimmering ruby above the misty haze at the top of a deep gorge of the Daiya River. The shrine's vermilion-lacquered *Shinkyo* (Sacred Bridge) straddles the river in a graceful arch, affording safe passage to this peaceful eighth-century A.D. Buddhist sanctuary. The temple venerates the *kami* (Shinto deities) of Nikkō's three most sacred mountains: Mount Nantai (or Futarasan), Mount Nyoho, and Mount Taro.

If you yearn for a peaceful retreat from the turbulence in your life or for peace within on your path to enlightenment, visit Futarasan Shrine, which together with nearby Nikkō Toshō-go and Rinnō-ji form the Shrines and Temples of Nikkō, a World Heritage Site. The best time to visit is in April, cherry blossom season, or early October, when the leaves change color. The train trip from Tokyo is about ninety minutes; the walk from Nikkō Station to the Sacred Bridge takes about twenty minutes, or you can take the five-minute bus ride. Or you can walk 220 yards from Toshō-go, a forty-minute walk or ten-minute bus ride from Nikkō Station.

Soothe Your Spirit

Meditate or pray for release from whatever obstructs or threatens your spiritual or inner peace.

A Deeper Look

The *kami* of Futarasan were the tutelary (protective) gods of the Tokugawa shogunate, and the shogunate's founder and first shogun, Tokugawa Ieyasu (1543–1616), rests in eternal peace in Futarasan Shrine.

166. Basílica de Nuestra Señora de La Altagracia (Higuey Basilica)

SALVALEÓN DE HIGUEY, DOMINICAN REPUBLIC

Men do not fear a powerful hostile army as the powers of hell fear the name and protection of Mary.
—Saint Bonaventure (1221–1274), Italian medieval scholastic theologian, philosopher, and Doctor of the Church

In 1502, the Trejo brothers came from Spain to the island of Hispaniola, bringing with them a painting of *La Virgen de la Altagracia* (Our Virgin of High Grace). After the painting disappeared from their house and miraculously reappeared in an orange tree, they erected a chapel at the place of the tree. Today, an elaborate frame holds the painting, now enshrined above the altar of a basilica built in 1972 on the same site. The monolithic Roman Catholic cathedral draws millions of pilgrims and visitors each year, many waiting in long lines to climb the stairs to worship one by one before the icon.

Whether you wish to pray for a loved one's safekeeping or to develop the fierce faith of Mary, come to Higuey Basilica. Three hours from Las Americas International Airport and an hour from Bávaro, the basilica can be reached by public transportation or rental car from anywhere in the country.

Soothe Your Spirit

Place your hand on the icon and pray for the safekeeping you seek. Outside, light an orange candle in gratitude for Mary's holy grace.

A Deeper Look

In 1922, Pope Pius XI crowned Virgin Mary the patron saint of Higuey.

167. Borobudur (Borobudur Park)

JAVA, INDONESIA

Even death is not to be feared by one who has lived wisely.
—Siddhartha Gautama, the Buddha (563–483 B.C.), father of Buddhism

When viewed from above or a distance, Borobudur looks like a lavishly decorated, giant stone multilayer wedding cake whose round edges have been gently squared. This ancient (ca. A.D. 750) Buddhist temple is a nine-step pyramid carved out of a crag of volcanic basalt to form a three-dimensional *mandala* (diagram of the universe) topped by a Mahayan *stupa* (bell-shaped tower). Adorning the walls of the massive temple are 2 miles of carved reliefs (1,300 friezes) depicting the Buddha's journey from *Samsara* (birth/knowing) to *Nirvana* (rebirth/ enlightenment). In Mahaya tradition, Nirvana is not a Divine end, or heaven, where eternal safekeeping/well-being is bestowed. Rather, safekeeping/well-being is achieved through the infinite/circular journey of Oneness (sacred living).

Whether you would like to see an astonishing sacred structure or to take a step forward in your journey to inner peace, visit Borobudur on the Kedu Plain of eastern Java. Fly from Jakarta or Bali to Yogyakarta Airport; travel by rental car, coach tour, bus, or taxi to the park.

Soothe Your Spirit

Take a sunrise tour and watch the mist rise from the ruins along with the sun. As you circumambulate your way through the temple, release your fears and feel the peace of faith fill you.

A Deeper Look

No one knows when or why the temple was abandoned; most likely, it was due to the eruption of one of three surrounding volcanoes. In 1914, a British statesman discovered Borobudur covered in volcanic ash.

168. Our Lady Gate of Dawn (Shrine)

OUR LADY OF ŠILUVA (MONASTERY), VILNIUS, LITHUANIA

Call upon Mary . . . if she walks before you, you shall not grow weary; if she shows you favor, you will reach your goal.
—Saint Bernard of Clairvaux (A.D. 1091–1153), French Cistercian abbot, and Doctor of the Church

The sacred *Blessed Virgin Mary Mother of Mercy* icon was once embedded in a gate on a stone wall encircling Vilnius, the capital of Lithuania. Of the wall's nine gates, only one was adorned with art. The side facing outward held a painting of Jesus, protecting those within. The side facing inward held the Virgin Mary, blessing those who traveled beyond. When the wall was destroyed in 1795, only the gate bearing the paintings of Jesus and Mary remained standing.

The icon is now enshrined in Our Lady Gate of Dawn Chapel, adjoining Our Lady of Šiluva Monastery (1726), on the site of the original gate. For centuries, pilgrims have come to Our Lady for protection and blessings; several miracles have been attributed to the icon.

Whether you seek safe passage through difficulty or peace of mind regarding a spiritual redirection, come to Our Lady Gate of Dawn, in old-town Vilnius. The nearest international airport is in Vilnius (VNO). Another major airport is in Kaunas, an hour by car, taxi, or bus. You can travel by train between the major cities.

Soothe Your Spirit
As you gaze at the icon, pray for courage to follow your heart or to face adversity with grace.

A Deeper Look
Pope John Paul II said rosary at the chapel in 1993.

169. Church of Madonna del Ghisallo (Chapel of the Madonna of Ghisallo)

MAGREGLIO, COMO, ITALY

Love conquers all.

—Encryption on dedication stone of the Museo del Ciclismo, Pope Benedict XVI (1927–), elected to the Papacy in 2005

*T*his tiny chapel on the summit of Madonna del Ghisallo—a steep hill in the Lombardy region of Northern Italy—is legendary among cyclists around the world. The legend originated in the seventeenth century after Count Ghisallo ran toward an apparition of Mother Mary as he was being attacked by highway robbers, saving his life. In gratitude, he built the church on the hill named for his Marion apparition, who became the local patroness of travelers. Later, cyclists adopted the icon as their patroness, and in 1949, Pope Pius XII decreed Madonna del Ghisallo the patron saint of cyclists. At the church's center is an "eternal flame" bestowing blessings on the thousands of cyclists—and other travelers—who happen by.

Whether you seek the courage to pursue your passion or blessings of your trek through God's country, take a road trip to Madonna del Ghisallo. From Como or Bellagio, travel by rental car, local guide, or bicycle (fit, trained cyclists only).

Soothe Your Spirit

Pray for safe passage as you follow your bliss or continue your cycling adventure in Italy.

A Deeper Look

In 2000, when the building of the Museo del Ciclismo (next door) was approved, cyclists conducted a torch relay from the church to the Vatican. In 2006, Pope Benedict XVI laid the final stone.

170. Rosslyn Chapel (Collegiate Chapel of Saint Matthew)

ROSLIN, MIDLOTHIAN, SCOTLAND

The whole value of solitude depends upon oneself; it may be a sanctuary or a prison, . . . a heaven or a hell as we ourselves make it.
—John Lubbock (1834–1913), English biologist and politician

On a hill above Roslin Glen stands a somber fifteenth-century church, the Collegiate Chapel of Saint Matthew. Rosslyn Chapel, as it is commonly known, was intended as a sanctuary where the church's founder, William Saint Clair, could say Divine Office and restore his soul. That makes the chapel's unusual interior all the more so, for the walls are covered with a strange assortment of ornate carvings, including images of knights, Lucifer, corn (unknown to Europe at that time), and the Green Man, a pagan deity. Famous for its alleged connections with the Knights Templar and the Freemasons, the chapel remains shrouded in mystery. Neither the chapel's riotous carvings nor its dark mysteries disturbed Saint Clair, who relished his sanctuary until his death in 1484.

Whether you wish to find a place of solace or to see this curious sanctuary, you can visit Rosslyn Chapel, south of Roslin. From Edinburgh Airport, travel by bus, rail, taxi, or rental car. No photography or video is allowed inside the chapel.

Soothe Your Spirit

Tour the chapel, making note of images that comfort and unsettle you. Later, use those impressions to create your own sanctuary.

A Deeper Look

Rosslyn Chapel has fueled the imaginations of many artists and writers, including Dan Brown, in whose novel, *The Da Vinci Code*, the chapel figures largely.

171. Le Mont-St-Michel (Mont Saint-Michel)

NORMANDY, FRANCE

God is absence; God is the solitude of man.
—Jean-Paul Sartre (1905–1980), French existentialist philosopher, writer, and
Nobel laureate

ont Saint-Michel, a granite islet rising 260 feet above the Bay of Mont St-Michel and separated from the mainland by a channel of turbulent water, is virtually impenetrable, and during the sixth and seventh centuries A.D., it served as a Romano-Breton stronghold. Yet, the site has stood as a sacred sanctuary for more than a century, since the first monastery was built there in the eighth century. Today, the Romanesque abbey and church built in the eleventh century to replace the Gothic monastery provides a place of refuge and safety for both the Benedictine monks who live and worship there and the pilgrims who journey there.

Whether you seek respite from turbulence in your life or are fascinated with French pilgrimage destinations, come to Mont Saint-Michel, a World Heritage Site. From Paris, take the TGV to Rennes; then catch the regional bus. The nearest rail station is in Pontorson. Alternatively, you can rent a car or take a coach tour from Avranches or Saint-Malo.

Be prepared for the steep stairway to the abbey—the only access. The best time to visit is winter when there are fewer tourists.

Soothe Your Spirit

Soak in the serenity and sense of security emanating from these sacred walls. Pray for the release of trouble or protection from turbulence.

A Deeper Look

Visit the adjoining cloisters, where hermitic monks live in secluded devotion, reading scripture, praying, meditating, and tending their gardens.

172. The Sacred Garden

LUMBINI, NEPAL

On life's journey faith is nourishment, virtuous deeds are a shelter, wisdom is the light by day and right mindedness is the protection by night. If a man lives a pure life, nothing can destroy him.
—Siddhartha Gautama, the Buddha (563–483 B.C.), father of Buddhism

As a small boy, Buddha likely played in the shade of the beautiful sal trees (*Shorea robusta*), which grew in the tranquil gardens of the Kolias and Shakya clans of Lumbini. His father, King Suddhodana, belonged to the Shakya clan. Situated near the Sacred Garden is the famous Ashoka pillar, which bears the inscription identifying this sacred site as the birthplace of Buddha.

If you seek the spiritual protection of the Buddha in the way that he sought spiritual shelter through introspection and meditation, come to the Sacred Garden. Even if you don't, visit Lumbini to experience his enlightening presence; the Buddha dictated that the four holy places of Buddhism would include his birthplace. Lumbini is located roughly 15.5 miles east of Kapilavastu.

Soothe Your Spirit

Sit under the sal tree that, according to legend, gave support and protection to Maya Devi, the Buddha's mother, who is said to have reached up and clutched its branch while in labor with her son.

A Deeper Look

Recent excavation in the Sacred Garden uncovered a stone with the imprint of a foot that is believed to mark the exact spot of the Buddha's birth.

173. Plaza Uta el-Hammam

CHEFCHAOUEN, MOROCCO

I have spent my days stringing and unstringing my instrument while the song I came to sing remains unsung.
—Rabindranath Tagore (1861–1941), Indian writer and Nobel laureate

With fortified walls to protect against medieval invaders, Chefchaouen is tucked safely into the majestic Rif Mountains not far from Tangier. Here, away from the hustle and bustle of the modern world, a pilgrim can take respite in the refuge of the seventeenth-century mosque, sit under the mulberry trees sipping mint tea, or wander beneath the cypress in the castle garden.

If you are ready to put away your Blackberry and enjoy some peace and quiet, let your senses be calmed by the sanctuary of Chefchaouen. Daily CTM buses run from Tangier, Fez, Casablanca, Tetouen, Cueta, and Meknes.

Soothe Your Spirit

Notice the sacredness of each moment as you walk along the cobblestone streets and marvel at the soft hues of the sky, horn-shaped mountain peaks, houses awash in shades of blue, and flocks of sheep dotting the landscape. Breathe the mountain air.

A Deeper Look

Despite the bustling trade in marijuana that openly goes on in Chefchaouen, there is practically no crime, and it is one of the safest cities in Morocco. Spanish language is widely spoken here because of the community's proximity to the border with Spain.

174. Temple of Isis

DELOS, GREECE

If virtue precede us, every step will be safe.
—Seneca (5 B.C.–A.D. 65), Roman dramatist, philosopher, and politician

*R*uins are all that remain of the gorgeous Doric-style temple built in Isis's honor by the people of Delos so that fishermen, seafarers, and locals could pray to her for safe passage, protection, good health, and fortune. The temple is flanked by a craggy outcropping and perched stalwartly on a hill that overlooks the harbor of Delos, which is said to be the birthplace of the sun god Apollo and his twin sister, Artemis.

If you have been feeling lost, buffeted by the winds of uncertainty, and you long for a feeling of safe harbor and security, head to Delos and the Temple of Isis. Since there are no overnight accommodations for tourists on Delos, book a day trip on one of the many boats leaving Venezia on Mykonos.

Soothe Your Spirit

Soak up the light and the subtle energy of the ruins, contemplating your life and how you might achieve a sense of stability and security in the ever-changing world. Consider the possibility of establishing more routines or finding ways to ground yourself through yoga or some other discipline.

A Deeper Look

This small, sacred, desolate island was once the holiest island in all of Greece, and it was even forbidden for anyone to be born or die on the island as it was the birthplace of gods.

175. Saint Catherine's Monastery

SINAI, EGYPT

*Now the priest of Midian had seven daughters: and they came and drew water
. . . And Moses was content to dwell with the man: and he gave Moses Zipporah
his daughter.*
—Bible, Exodus 2:16–21

Saint Catherine's Monastery (also Katherine, in the Orthodox tradition) is home to one of the world's largest and most precious collections of sacred manuscripts. Built in A.D. 527, it is one of the oldest Eastern Orthodox religious communities. Its library holds magnificent paintings, Byzantine icons, sacerdotal ornaments, illuminated manuscripts, and reliquaries. The monastery is situated on the holy site believed to have been where Moses saw the burning bush, heard God's voice, and (on the mountain above the monastery) received the Ten Commandments. The fortified compound is named for Saint Catherine, the Alexandrian Christian martyr whose body, according to legend, was carried away by angels and discovered five centuries later on a nearby mountain peak (today, a reliquary next to the main altar holds the saint's relics).

If you seek spiritual uplifting in a sacred sanctuary protected in a fortified compound, visit the ancient pilgrimage site of St. Catherine's. Fly from Cairo to Sharm el-Sheik, but plan on a three-hour trip to the monastery.

Soothe Your Spirit

Embrace the feeling of protection provided by the 9-foot-thick walls that rise 60 feet to protect the sanctuary and the natural spring where Moses met his future wife, Zipporah.

A Deeper Look

Some say the library of Saint Catherine's Monastery rivals that of the Vatican.

176. Thian Hock Keng Temple (Temple of Heavenly Bliss)

SINGAPORE, REPUBLIC OF SINGAPORE

Being deeply loved by someone gives you strength, while loving someone gives you courage.
—Lao Tzu (600–531 B.C.), Chinese philosopher and father of Taoism

The Thian Hock Keng Temple honors both Matsu, Taoist goddess of the sailors and fishermen, and Kuan Yin, the Buddhist bodhisattva of mercy and compassion. The temple serves as a reminder to visitors of the Chinese immigrants who prayed to Matsu for safe passage. Built in 1839 on the site of a joss house, it reflects the ornate Chinese-temple style with its square shape, crenulated roof, and stone threshold.

If you seek divine protection for a journey, visit the Thian Hock Keng Temple at 158 Telok Ayer Street. Walk from Raffles Place or the Tanjong Pagar metro station. The nearest airport offering international service is the Singapore Changi International Airport.

Soothe Your Spirit

Write a prayer on a piece of paper to burn in the red kiln in the courtyard for good luck.

A Deeper Look

The statue of Confucius sits inside one pagoda and sacred ancestral tablets of the temple's founders are in the other pagoda.

177. Ronchamp Chapel (Chapelle-Notre-Dame-du-Haut)

RONCHAMP, FRANCE

One thing have I desired . . . to behold the beauty of the Lord, and to enquire in his temple. For in the time of trouble he shall hide me in his pavilion: in the secret of his tabernacle shall he hide me; he shall set me up upon a rock.
—Bible, Psalm 27:4–5

The Ronchamp Chapel has long been a place of ritual worship by pagans, Romans, and followers of the cult of the Virgin. Situated in the Haute-Saône department of Franche-Comté region, the chapel was designed by Le Corbusier and has protective, overly thick, delicately curved white walls that support a brown concrete veil of a roof, which has been compared to a nun's cap.

If you want to hide away in a sanctified and safe pilgrimage site, come to the Ronchamp Chapel in the French countryside. It is a day trip from Paris, and slightly more than an hour from the nearest airport at Basel-Mulhouse near the border of France, Switzerland, and Germany.

Soothe Your Spirit
Retreat to the chapel to renew your spiritual self-enrichment, perhaps utilizing Christian meditation, prayer, and mental calisthenics that were compiled and practiced by the sixteenth-century saint Ignatius Loyola in his *Spiritual Exercises*.

A Deeper Look
Le Corbusier, the French architect, said of Ronchamp Chapel that the walls were absurdly but practically thick . . . and the light through the horizontal slit in the wall created as a narrow entrance for light will amaze.

178. Cathedral Church of Saint Canice

KILKENNY CITY, COUNTY KILKENNY, IRELAND

The Lord is good, a strong hold in the day of trouble; and he knoweth them that trust in him.
—Hebrew Bible, Nahum 1:7

When Saint Columba and his fellow monks flailed in a storm at sea, the monks beseeched Columba to pray for their safety. He calmly replied that he would leave that to Saint Canice (who was eating his supper at the time on dry land). According to legend, Canice bolted upright, darted out of his house with one foot shoeless, dashed into the church to pray for the brothers at sea, and soon the storm ended. Dedicated to Saint Canice, the medieval cathedral church in Kilkenny City is a Gothic jewel in a close (complex) that includes a lovely old cemetery, a seventeenth-century cottage, a library, a round tower dating to A.D. 800 with 167 steps, and several other buildings.

If you long for safe passage, shelter from a storm, or protection of any kind, come to the Cathedral Church of Saint Canice in the lovely hill country of Ireland.

Soothe Your Spirit

While in the cathedral, ask Saint Canice to carry your prayer for your safety and security to God. Purchase a Saint Canice medal or locket to keep or wear to remind you of the power of prayer.

A Deeper Look

Saint Canice's cathedral houses an important historical document that is relevant to the twentieth century: Ireland's Memorial Records, seven volumes filled with the names of the Irish soldiers who fell during the Great European War 1914–1918.

179. Buddha Tooth Relic Temple

REPUBLIC OF SINGAPORE

When the mind is pure, joy follows like a shadow that never leaves.
—Siddhartha Gautama, the Buddha (563–483 B.C.), father of Buddhism

*B*efore the passing of his physical body, the Buddha mentioned in the Mahaparinirvana Sutra that viewing his relics was as good as visiting him while he was alive because the subtle energy of his relics upon cremation would become crystallized and remain ever-serene without further tainting by nature. In the relic chamber of the Buddha Tooth Relic Temple, the Buddha's relics of blood, bone, intestine, brain, and tongue are enshrined and showcased.

If you believe your sense of safe passage through levels of spiritual evolution might improve from viewing the Buddha's relics and feeling the sacred subtle energy that surrounds them, visit the Buddha Tooth Relic Temple. The temple is located at 288 South Bridge Road in Singapore and is easily accessible with public transportation.

No photography, no pets, or eating of meat is allowed on temple grounds. Dress appropriately; no bare skin should show, such as low-cut or backless tops or sleeveless blouses/dresses.

Soothe Your Spirit

Purchase incense or flowers in the Offering Shop after crossing the temple courtyard. Light a stick of incense or place flowers in the temple in front of the various Buddhas and bodhisattvas. Say a prayer with your offering and then visit the relic chamber.

A Deeper Look

The multistoried temple has many rooms and shrines, including a Buddhist cultural museum with many artifacts.

180. Il Gesù

ROME, ITALY

Him that overcometh will I make a pillar in the temple of my God . . .
—Bible, Revelation 3:12

After Saint Ignatius Loyola founded the Society of Jesus (the Jesuits) in 1540 (as the Reformation revolt was raging in Europe), the pope gave Ignatius a small church, Santa Maria della Estrada (Mary/or Our Lady of the Wayside). Although Ignatius accepted the church, he believed it was too small for the Jesuits' headquarters. Today on the site of the smaller church stands the magnificent Il Gesù (Church of the Holy Name of Jesus) whose exquisite sacred art includes a fresco symbolizing a spiritual passage that is the pillared gateway to eternal life.

If you believe that time on Earth spent in spiritual endeavor provides safe passage into eternal life or you would like to see the chapel enshrining Ignatius's tomb, come to Il Gesù. The church is at Via degli Astalli, 16, in the Piazza del Gesù (central Rome).

Soothe Your Spirit

Light a candle and pray before Saint Ignatius's chapel-tomb, the first on the left aisle. Pray for spiritual advancement and safety as you progress in this life, and thereafter.

A Deeper Look

Michelangelo offered to design the church gratis, but Cardinal Alessandro Farnese, the grandson of Pope Paul III, funded the project, and architect Giacomo Barozzi da Vignola drew the design.

181. Ise Jingu

ISE, MIE PREFECTURE, JAPAN

Be charitable to all beings, love is the representative of God.
—Ko-ji-ki, Hachiman Kasuga, Shinto tradition, ca. A.D. 500

*I*se Jingu, built in the third century B.C., is the most sacred shrine in the Mie Prefecture, Japan's area of sacred Shinto shrines. In ancient times, only the emperor, the empress, and the crown prince were allowed to step into "heaven" or the inner shrine, Naiku, dedicated to the worship of Ameratsu Omikami, Shinto goddess of the sun and spiritual ancestress of the Japanese royal family. Here, the emperor would pray for the protection and safety of his people. In medieval times, however, the samurai visited, and since the 1600s, ordinary citizens have worshiped there.

If you seek spiritual safeguarding, undertake a pilgrimage to venerate Ameratsu. Take the train from Nagoya, Kyoto, or Osaka. Or, catch the bus at Uji-Yamada Station; it takes fifteen minutes to reach Naiku. By car, take the Ise Expressway and exit at the Ise-Nishi exit.

Soothe Your Spirit

Adopt an attitude of reverence as you step onto the Uji Bridge to cross the Isuzu River; the river is sacred. When you reach the water ablution station, wash your hands and mouth. Then wash your hands again in the river before passing through the forest and ascending the stone steps to the main shrine to pray for divine protection and good fortune. Taking pictures is forbidden.

A Deeper Look

The outer shrine, Geku, safeguards the sanctuary of the goddess of the harvest.

182. Mother Cathedral of Holy Etchmiadzin

VAGHARSHAPAT, ARMENIA

But Noah found grace in the eyes of the Lord.
—Bible, Genesis 6:8

The Etchmiadzin Cathedral, world headquarters of the Holy Armenian Apostolic Church, is the most visited pilgrimage destination in Armenia by Orthodox Christians. The fourth-century A.D. buff-colored, angular church has three towers capped with crosses, a fifth-century dome, and a softly lit Byzantine interior adorned with sacred art. This ancient holy site was once home to a Zoroastrian fire temple and then a temple of Venus under the Romans. In the early fourth century, a Christian church was built by Saint Gregory the Illuminator, after he experienced a numinous vision of the Holy Spirit, in which Christ descended with a golden hammer to show him where to build a church that would shelter the Armenian faithful for centuries to come. The cathedral safeguards holy relics such as the sword that pierced Jesus's side and a piece of wood that has been carbon-dated to 6,000 years and is believed to be from Noah's Ark.

If you are seeking God's safekeeping, visit Etchmiadzin Cathedral to be reminded that even in the Great Flood, God protected Noah, his family, and the animals in the Ark. The cathedral is located about 15 miles from Yerevan in the town of Vagharshapat.

Soothe Your Spirit

Light a candle and pray that just as the Holy Spirit descended upon Saint Gregory, you, too, might be sheltered and safeguarded in your passage through life.

A Deeper Look

Frescoes from biblical scenes and saintly figures adorn the interior of this magnificent World Heritage Site, believed to be the oldest cathedral in the world.

183. Mount Tai Shan

TAI'AN SHANDONG PROVINCE, CHINA

When you realize there is nothing lacking; the whole world belongs to you.
—Lao Tzu (600–531 B.C.), Chinese philosopher and father of Taoism

Tai Shan, holiest of China's five sacred mountain peaks, offers views of majestic peaks, shimmering waterfalls, deep gorges, ancient groves of pine and cypress, and verdant valleys. The four routes to the top of Tai Shan abound with cultural relics and majestic scenery whose names speak to a long relationship with deity: Jade Emperor Summit, Eight Immortals Cave, and Heaven and Earth Square. Humans have left their traces on this holy mountain since the Paleolithic period, 400,000 years ago.

If you seek a fertile mind or body, offer prayers to Songzi Niangniang, goddess of fertility, one of several deities venerated in the Azure Cloud Temple. Walk there on the Peach Blossom Ravine Route in springtime, when breezes carrying blossoms impart an even deeper spiritual ambiance. Take 104 National Highway to the shuttle bus area, and then continue on the bus to the cable car station at Midway Gate to Heaven. The cable car takes you to the top in a few minutes.

Soothe Your Spirit

Improvise on an ancient tradition: take a small shot glass and place it in the sun, add water, place your hands over the glass, and pray for fertility (thus imbuing the water with spirit before drinking it). Light a stick of incense so the curling tendril of smoke carries your prayer into heaven. Leave the glass in the sun when you've finished; the sun's rays energize the water.

A Deeper Look

Tai Shan's main peak rises 5,068 feet (1,545 meters) above sea level.

184. Saint Catherine's Chapel

ABBOTSBURY, DORSET, ENGLAND

A husband, Saint Catherine, / A handsome one, Saint Catherine, / A rich one, Saint Catherine, / A nice one, Saint Catherine, / And soon, Saint Catherine.
—Old English prayer

When sailors had to cross Lyme Bay at night to Abbotsbury or worshipers set off to church, they only had to look toward the beacon of the medieval chapel perched on the hill behind the village to find their way. Dedicated to Saint Catherine, the stone chapel has served as a house of worship, a navigational beacon, and a place for women to pray for a husband (to get one or for the safe passage and enduring love of the one they had).

If you would like to pray for the safety and protection of a loved one, come to Saint Catherine's Chapel some summer morning. Abbotsbury sits in southern England, near the west end of the English Channel. Two rail lines connect Dorset County to London, or you can take the B3157 to Abbotsbury, approximately 9 miles west of Weymouth.

Soothe Your Spirit

Walk up the hill from the village to the chapel to pray and then enjoy the views over Lyme Bay, the Fleet (the inlet of water), and Chesil Beach.

A Deeper Look

Saint Catherine's Chapel, according to local lore, may have been spared destruction during the Dissolution of Monasteries between 1536 and 1541 by King Henry VIII because of its value as a navigational tool.

185. Saint Michael's Cathedral

SHIMLA, HIMACHAL PRADESH, INDIA

And at that time shall Michael stand up, the great prince which standeth for the children of thy people . . . .
—Bible, Daniel 12:1

The first Catholic church to be built in the British Hill station of Shimla in India in 1885 was dedicated to Saints Michael and Joseph during the era of the British Raj, when Lord Ripon, an Englishman and a Catholic, served as viceroy. Architect Henry Irwin's restraint in the church design is obvious: its interior is unassuming, but the sanctity and protection here is implicit by the dedication to Archangel Michael, invoked by the church as patron and protector, and Saint Joseph, protector of Mary and Jesus.

If you seek to feel sheltered in sacred sanctuary, visit Shimla. It is situated 48 miles north of Delhi. The church sits just off the Shimla Mall, reached by a passenger lift that walkers take from Cart Road.

Soothe Your Spirit

Put on your walking shoes. Go to Saint Michael's for prayers of protection and safety and enjoy the peace and security of this church. Then, find a chaat house and enjoy some chai (tea) and samosas before hiking this little town, once the summer capital of the Raj.

A Deeper Look

The church is made of dressed stone, French Gothic style, with a cluster of chiming bells in the belfry.

186. Leshan Buddha

SICHUAN PROVENCE, LESHAN, CHINA

When the river is deepest, it makes least noise.
—Proverb

When Chinese Buddhist monk Hai Tong wanted to still the treacherous, turbulent waters near Leshan (an extremely holy area of Sichuan Provence) at the convergence of three rivers, which were the bane of local fishermen and their vessels, he decided to build a giant statue of Buddha into the cliffs. He started the project in A.D. 713 and his disciples finished it in 803. Because of the massive amounts of earth and stone removed, the course of the confluence shifted, the waters became calmer, and fishermen felt safer.

If feelings of safety are important for your spiritual life, come and see the Leshan Buddha. The Buddha is lodged against Mount Emei. Fly to Chengdu Shuangliu International Airport and drive to Leshan (about 93 miles). The cities of Emei and Leshan are also connected by freeway, train, and bus, and there is ferry service to Mount Emei Park.

Soothe Your Spirit

Take a ferry to approach the Buddha by water. Try to imagine how turbulent the river must have been in the eighth century before the construction of the giant Buddha calmed the turbulence. Allow feelings of safety and security to arise and offer thanks to the Buddha and his servant Hai Tong.

A Deeper Look

The Leshan Buddha is the world's tallest stone-seated Buddha and is a World Heritage Site.

187. The National Shrine of Saint Maximilian Kolbe

LIBERTYVILLE, ILLINOIS, UNITED STATES

The glory of God is the human person fully alive.
—Irenaeus (ca. A.D. 202), Church father

In Auschwitz, the dark Nazi reign of terror was interrupted in late July 1941 by the blinding light of love, exhibited by a Catholic priest named Maximilian Kolbe. Father Kolbe offered to exchange his life for that of fellow prisoner Francis Gajowniczek, who was among ten men the Nazis selected to die in retaliation for the earlier escape of a prisoner. When Gajowniczek cried out that he had a family and children, Father Kolbe stepped forward and offered his life instead.

If you feel that giving selflessly for the protection and safety of another (especially children) is important spiritual work, visit the national shrine of Maximilian Kolbe to honor someone who gave his life so another could live. The shrine is located at 1600 West Park Avenue, in Libertyville, Illinois.

Soothe Your Spirit

Undertake a pilgrimage to this shrine and exhibit on Saint Kolbe's feast day, August 14. Pray for the spiritual strength to help those who need it.

A Deeper Look

In 1982, Pope John Paul II canonized Maximilian Kolbe, calling him a "patron for our difficult century." Saint Kolbe is the patron of families, unborn children, and prisoners.

188. Temple Church

LONDON, ENGLAND

I will lift up mine eyes unto the hills, from whence cometh my help.
—Bible, Psalm 121:1

ounded by the Knights Templar, the order of monks who provided safe passage to pilgrims during the Crusades as they traveled to and from the Holy Land, the Temple Church's round nave finds resonance with the Crusaders' holiest shrine, the Church of the Holy Sepulchre in Jerusalem. Nine marble effigies of medieval knights are placed on the floor of the round nave. The church's spectacular stained-glass windows, exquisite altar inscribed with the Ten Commandments, and interior gargoyles made it a stunning setting for scenes from *The Da Vinci Code*.

If you want to pray for your safety or that of someone you love, visit Temple Church, located at Inner Temple Lane, King's Bench Walk. The church is located in a historical area of London between the River Thames and Fleet Street.

Soothe Your Spirit

Read Psalm 121 from the Old Testament about the safety that comes from the Divine in time of human need. Ask God for what you need and give thanks.

A Deeper Look

In 1185, the patriarch of Jerusalem consecrated the round church, designed to symbolize Jerusalem's Church of the Holy Sepulchre.

189. Shrine of Our Lady of Good Help

CHAMPION, BROWN COUNTY, WISCONSIN, UNITED STATES

Hail Mary, full of grace. The Lord is with thee.
—Portion of the Hail Mary, a prayer for the intercession of the Virgin Mary

When Adele Brise, the daughter of Belgian immigrants who'd settled in a farming community in northeast Wisconsin, saw a blinding light emanating between a hemlock and a maple tree in a rural wooded area, she stopped and prayed before the apparition. The apparition identified herself as the Queen of Heaven and, during subsequent visitations, instructed Adele to establish a religious school for the farm children, which she did.

If you seek protection or answers, visit the Shrine of Our Lady of Good Help. The chapel is located at 4047 Chapel Drive off County Road K, between N. Sugarbush Road and Oakleaf Drive/County Line Road in Champion (16 miles northeast of Green Bay and roughly 4 miles from New Franken).

Soothe Your Spirit

Light a candle and say the Hail Mary with the intention of asking her to assist you in your prayers to God for protection from peril or to receive guidance.

A Deeper Look

This is the first apparition of the Blessed Virgin Mary in the United States recognized by the Roman Catholic Church, which recently gave approval after more than 150 years of investigation. The chapel is a pilgrimage site of many miracles.

190. Saint Ives Church

CORNWALL, ENGLAND

I am sailing into the wind and the dark. I'm doing my best to keep my boat steady and my sails full.
—Arthur Ashe (1943–1993), American athlete

Saint Ives Church, in the picturesque seaside town of Saint Ives, Cornwall, on the southwest English coast, is dedicated to three saints: Ia (who legend has it, crossed the Irish Sea on a cabbage leaf), Andrew (patron of fishermen), and Peter (the Rock). The medieval church of Cornish granite has an 80-foot tower that stands as a spiritual beacon to seamen and parishioners alike, guiding them safely and steadily to the place where heaven, Earth, and the sea meet.

To feel the energy that continuous worship for more than 600 years has created, visit this sacred sanctuary. The church is located on Saint Andrews Street near the intersection of Highways B3306 and A3074.

Soothe Your Spirit

Feed your spirit by reading stories about the journeys of safe passage by Saint Ia or the apostles Andrew and Peter and enjoy a worship service in this Anglican church.

A Deeper Look

The church was consecrated in 1434. The region of Cornwall is recognized by the Cornish people as one of the Celtic nations, with a cultural identity distinct and different from the rest of England.

CHAPTER 8

FORGIVENESS, REDEMPTION, RECONCILIATION

*Forgiveness is the fragrance the violet sheds
on the heel that has crushed it.*

*—Mark Twain (1835–1910),
American writer and humorist*

191. Mount Croagh Patrick

COUNTY MAYO, IRELAND

Before I was humiliated I was like a stone that lies in deep mud, and he who is mighty came and in his compassion raised me up and exalted me very high and placed me on the top of the wall.
—Saint Patrick (ca. A.D. 387–493)

When English missionary Patrick desired to fast and pray in solitude during the season of Lent in preparation for Easter, he climbed the cone-shaped mountain that rises from the verdant plain of County Mayo and stayed up there for forty days and nights. Legend says he banished the snakes from Ireland while on that mountain and, before descending, threw down a silver cup that turned black, symbolically gathering all the blackness from Ireland into that vessel.

If you feel the urge for penance and seek spiritual redemption and wholeness, walk Mount Croagh Patrick, Ireland's most important holy site of pilgrimage. Take a train from Dublin to Westport or drive down the N5 or the N59 and follow the signs. Westport is 5 miles from the mountain.

Soothe Your Spirit

Stop at each of the three marked stations on your ascent and pray, make declarations, or perform spiritual rituals as suggested on the signs. If your beliefs differ from Judeo-Christian, take time to honor your beliefs. At the summit, enter the small white chapel to reflect. Then ask forgiveness for any unkind thoughts and actions and forgive others to make things right with the Higher Power in your life.

A Deeper Look

Roughly a million people reach the top of Mount Croagh Patrick each year, with close to half that number climbing the mountain the last Sunday in July, some on their knees.

192. Chartres Cathedral

CHARTRES, FRANCE

And it was then that in the depths of sleep / Someone breathed to me: "You alone can do it, / Come immediately."
—from "The Call" (tr. Geoffrey Gardiner), by Jules Supervielle (1884–1960), French poet born in Uruguay

When French pilgrims could not travel to Jerusalem during the Middle Ages to do penance or to pray for forgiveness of their sins, they sought closer sanctuary in local places of worship such as Chartres, perhaps the most magnificent of the French Gothic cathedrals. With its flying buttresses, exquisite carvings, the two towers soaring over its pale green roof, and the effulgent light and vertical space in the nave, the church provided a beatific sanctuary for worshipers, especially those who venerated Mother Mary. The cathedral safeguards the Sancta Camisia, or cloak of the Blessed Virgin.

Whether your goal is to pay homage to the Mother of Christ and venerate the relic of the Sancta Camisia, which was given to the cathedral by Charles the Bald, or to spend time in self-introspection and prayer, Chartres Cathedral, about 50 miles from Paris, provides a stunning setting, on a grand scale, and spiritual tools (such as its labyrinth) for you to further those spiritual goals.

Soothe Your Spirit

Feel the vibe of the sanctuary as you enter the nave and notice light through the beautiful 176 stained-glass windows that reflects on everything. Proceed to the 42-foot labyrinth; walk it with your mind and heart united in prayer.

A Deeper Look

The four-quadrant labyrinth was laid into the floor in the thirteenth century to help the spiritual seeker draw closer to God while following the labyrinth to its center. The walk ends on the rose, a sacred symbol in Judaism, Islam, and Christianity of the human heart unfolding to transcendent Truth that is God. If the goal was penance, medieval pilgrims would move along the labyrinth on their knees.

193. Via Dolorosa "Way of Sorrows," Jerusalem

ISRAEL

And when they were come to the place, which is called Calvary, there they crucified him and the malefactors . . . Then said Jesus, Father, forgive them; for they know not what they do.
—Bible, Luke 23: 33–34

The Via Dolorosa (Way of Grief or Way of Suffering) in the Old City of Jerusalem links the Madrasa al-Omariya (or, nearby the Lion's Gate) to the Church of the Holy Sepulchre. It is the path Jesus walked in agony carrying his cross, from Pilate's judgment / death sentence to Golgotha (site of his Crucifixion) and his entombment in the sepulcher or cave. Through many centuries the ancient road has changed, but the greatest significance of Christendom's most sacred route is in the reflection by pilgrims on the events that happened on that fateful day in Jesus's life and the religious and spiritual meaning and significance that it had then and has now for the faithful.

Whether you struggle with forgiveness or release of anger, walking the Via Dolorosa can help you begin to shift your feelings and to expand your understanding of the process of forgiving and letting go. From Jerusalem, you can get around pretty easily using public transportation, cars, taxi, bus, and also local tours, as well as walking.

Soothe Your Spirit

Join the weekly Friday walk along the Via Dolorosa that is orchestrated by the Franciscans, with re-enactments. Take time before each station to reflect and pray, forgive and release.

A Deeper Look

Along the Via Dolorosa are the nine Stations of the Cross, marked by plaques, indicating each of the places where there was a significant occurrence during Jesus's walk to his Crucifixion. There are another five stations inside the Church of the Holy Sepulchre.

194. Pashupatinath Temple

KATHMANDU, NEPAL

Om namah Shivaya.
—Ancient Sanskrit mantra dedicated to Shiva

The square pagoda-style Pashupatinath Temple, built over an older temple dating to the ninth century A.D., has been erected and razed several times. Still it remains the holiest pilgrimage site for Nepalese Hindus; devotees descend the temple's ancient stone steps daily to immerse themselves in the sacred Bagmati River. Dedicated to Lord Shiva (Hindu god of destruction), every inch of the temple astonishes visitors with its beauty: carved lattice windows from Bhutanese monasteries, a gold-plated roof, jewel-embellished doors, spectacular floral motifs carved in wood, and an inner sanctum where the four-sided 3-foot-tall lingam (phallus) of Lord Shiva is venerated.

If you have experienced the end of a relationship, desire reconciliation, or feel as though your life needs a major shift in a new direction, go to the incomparable Pashupatinath Temple that honors Shiva, who oversees the breaking down of old structures so that new ones can be created (Shiva's lingam or phallus symbolizes generative power). Access to the temple interior is for Hindus only, but there are areas open to tourists and visitors.

Soothe Your Spirit

Travel to this World Heritage Site on the "rooftop of the world," and find a quiet place to say a prayer for forgiveness or reconciliation.

A Deeper Look

Thousands of Hindu pilgrims visit the temple daily, but during festivals dedicated to Shiva, the crowds grow large. During the annual Maha Shivaratri, the temple remains open all night to accommodate ochre-clad *sadhus* (or mystics), devotees, pilgrims, and tourists from Nepal and elsewhere in the world.

195. Coventry Cathedral

COVENTRY, MIDLANDS, ENGLAND

You will know that forgiveness has begun when you recall those who hurt you and feel the power to wish them well.
—Lewis B. Smedes (1921–2002), American ethicist and theologian

The morning after the Luftwaffe bombed their cathedral on November 14, 1940, the people of Coventry, led by the vision of their spiritual leader Provost Dick Howard, decided to rebuild in the spirit of forgiveness and reconciliation. The new Coventry Cathedral, dedicated to Saint Michael, rises in glorious splendor next to the decimated ruins of the blitzed medieval cathedral, and linking them are two sacred works: the Cross of Nails, from nails found in the ruins, and *Reconciliation*, a beautiful bronze sculpture.

If you want to work on forgiveness and also learn more about reconciliation and peace, visit Coventry Cathedral, located in the West Midlands District of England at 1 Hill Top, Coventry. The nearest airport is in Birmingham and the nearest train station is in Coventry, a ten-minute walk to the cathedral. If you go by rental car, there is parking a short distance away at Pool Meadow public car park. There is a small fee to tour the site unless you are visiting to worship.

Soothe Your Spirit

Visit the new cathedral as well as the ruins of the medieval church next door and reflect upon the destruction as well as the new construction as departure points into your prayer for reconciliation and world peace.

A Deeper Look

Both the wooden cross, made of charred beams from the ruins, and the cross of nails, made from the nails found in the rubble, were created after the bombing and have become symbols for peace and reconciliation around the world.

196. Church of the Pater Noster

JERUSALEM, ISRAEL

Our Father, who art in heaven, hallowed be thy name . . . forgive us our debts as we forgive our debtors.
—Bible, Matthew 6:9–12; Luke 11:1–4

Under the ruins of a fourth-century A.D. basilica built by Roman emperor Constantine I, evidence of the holy cave long associated with the Ascension of Jesus was discovered in 1910. At that sacred location where Jesus taught his followers to pray the "Our Father" and to forgive those who trespassed against them, Constantine's Church of the Disciples basilica was constructed. The church was destroyed in A.D. 614, rebuilt in 1152, abandoned during the Crusades, and finally became the site of a nineteenth-century Carmelite Convent that moved nearby after evidence of the ancient cave was rediscovered.

If you would like to immerse yourself in the atmosphere of the holy site where the Lord taught his followers the most famous prayer in Christendom, visit the partially reconstructed Church of the Pater Noster and see the sacred prayer inscribed in many languages on colorful plaques lining the nearby convent walls.

Soothe Your Spirit

When you visit the cloister of the convent, chant the "Our Father" and meditate on forgiveness. Breathe in, breathe out, and let go. Don't probe the wound anymore.

A Deeper Look

The partially restored Byzantine church closely follows the fourth-century church's dimensions. When the church was rebuilt in 1152, the funds were provided by the bishop of Denmark who, according to tradition and legend, was subsequently buried there.

197. Cathedral of the Madeleine

SALT LAKE CITY, UTAH, UNITED STATES

Thou has turned for me my mourning into dancing: thou has put off my sackcloth, and girded me with gladness.
—Bible, Psalm 30:11

The stunning Gothic interior of the Cathedral of the Madeleine is a visual feast: white-marble altar with gold veining situated on a three-step marble riser, scrubbed and shined hardwood floors, a plethora of exquisite stained-glass windows, delicately carved wooden screens and pews, sweeping arches, and colorful embellished columns combine to create a breathtaking sacred interior. Through its sacred art, this Utah treasure reminds those who step inside that Jesus stood at the heart of Mary Magdalene's personal transformation story.

Whether you would like to venerate Saint Mary Magdalene or see the awe-inspiring cathedral under her patronage in Utah, take time to visit this sacred place honoring the woman Jesus trusted and loved, as he did all his disciples. The cathedral is located at 331 East South Temple in Salt Lake City, not far from Temple Square and the Mormon Tabernacle. There is an international airport and good metropolitan transportation, including buses and taxis.

Soothe Your Spirit

Make a silent confession and pray for forgiveness for a thought, word, or deed that you regret. Reflect on the special relationship that Mary Magdalene, who was not perfect, had with Jesus, some say as his closest friend, most loyal disciple, and trusted confidante.

A Deeper Look

The Cathedral of the Madeleine (the French spelling of Magdalene) was dedicated in 1909 and rededicated after renovations in 1993. It serves as the mother church for Roman Catholics in Utah.

198. The U.S. Memorial Holocaust Museum

WASHINGTON, D.C., UNITED STATES

In Italy, the country where fascism was born, we have a particular relation with the Holocaust, but as a turning point in history, it belongs to everybody in the world. It is a part of humanity.
—Roberto Benigni (1952–), Academy award–winning Italian actor, comedian, and filmmaker

*D*esigned by Holocaust survivor and architect James Ingo Freed, the interior spaces of this structure and exhibits are created to be a "resonator of memory," meaning that careful thought has been given so that the interior spaces allude to some aspect of the Holocaust, as uncomfortable, terrifying, and solemn as that is for visitors. This is not a sacred sanctuary in the usual sense, but rather a haunting place that can deeply touch the spiritual core of those who visit. The museum optimizes the use of hard, cold, impersonal surfaces, spaces, and exhibits to unfold a narrative about our inhumanity to fellow human beings.

Whether you carry some darkness in your heart that blocks your spiritual light or vision, take time to visit the U.S. Memorial Holocaust Museum for it has lessons for all of us on forgiveness, reconciliation, and redemption. Use the blue and orange metro lines to get to the museum located at 100 Raoul Wallenberg Place. Walk west after getting off at the Smithsonian's Independence Avenue exit.

Soothe Your Spirit

Give yourself time to process your feelings as you work your way through the exhibits. Be cognizant of the opposites of dark and light, despair and hope, for this double-sided Janus face is present throughout. Pray for the elimination of those things that cause division and aggression and intolerance in humanity. Pray for healing.

A Deeper Look

The priceless collections of Holocaust-related materials housed in the museum have been amassed from all over the world and organized into eight groupings.

199. Church of Saint Peter in Gallicantu

JERUSALEM, ISRAEL

And the second time the cock crew. And Peter called to mind the word that Jesus said unto him, Before the cock crows twice, thou shalt deny me thrice. And when he thought thereon, he wept.
—Bible, Mark 14:72

*O*n the site that Catholic tradition holds was the castle of the High Priest Caiaphus, the Crusaders built the Church of Saint Peter in Gallicantu. Since *Galli-cantu* means "cock-crow," the church is a reference to the scriptural accounts of Peter's denial of Jesus. They erected a golden rooster to crown their sanctuary roof. Inside, a stunning glass-enclosed chapel features a viewing hole to the caves below.

If you would like resolution or redemption for something you have finally forgiven yourself for or if you are working on forgiving, visit the Church of Saint Peter, Gallicantu on the eastern slope of Mount Zion. From the Old City, walk through the Zion Gate, up the hill to the right, and follow the signs to the church.

Visit the church daily from 8:30 A.M. to 12:00 P.M. It's closed Sundays. There is an entrance fee.

Soothe Your Spirit
Go to the lower room and the sacred pit where Jesus was purportedly held prisoner; stand and pray.

A Deeper Look
The prison cells under the Church of Saint Peter are dug out of bedrock. In custody, Jesus would have been placed in one of the dank, claustrophobic cells.

200. Boa Island

COUNTY FERMANAGH, NORTHERN IRELAND

Death leaves a heartache no one can heal / Love leaves a memory no one can steal.
—Inscription on a headstone in Ireland

*I*n Caldragh Cemetery on Boa Island, named for Badhbha, Celtic goddess of battle, stands a thousand-year-old stone figure of a male torso facing east and its opposite female side facing west. The megalith's purpose remains unknown, but what's certain is that on the vernal equinox (March 20/21 when day and night are equal), the sun rises and sets precisely over the center of this enigmatic stone figure, possibly symbolizing a balance between opposites.

If you believe seeing this ancient figure would help you see both sides of an issue and move from opposition to understanding and a truce, come to Caldragh Cemetery. Located 15.5 miles from Enniskillentown (the nearest community), take A47, the main road around the island, and turn off when you see the sign.

Soothe Your Spirit

Vow to reconcile with someone, strive for balance, and establish peace. Drop a coin in the cleft of the statue's head to symbolize your resolve.

A Deeper Look

The Boa Island Figure (the two-headed stone) and another one called the Lustymore Island Figure, which was found on Lustymore Island and moved to the Boa Island cemetery in 1939 and is believed to be older than the other figure, are both situated close in the Caldragh Cemetery on pillars and under a canopy to protect them from the weather.

201. Bara Synagogue

EASTERN UPPER GALILEE, ISRAEL

. . . Hope needs to be like barbed wire to keep out despair, hope must be a mine field.
—Yehuda Amichai (1925–2000), "Ein Yahav," German-born Israeli poet and novelist

Lying along the border between Israel and Lebanon in Baram are the ruins of an old synagogue. According to legend, the tombs of the Old Testament's Queen Esther and prophet Obadiah are nearby. The ancient synagogue is one of the best preserved of the fourth century A.D. Its decorative twining vines, symbolizing holy sacraments, are intricately carved into the small edifice over the intact window of the façade—still quite visible, lovely, and suggestive of redemption and renewal.

If your mind keeps turning over the memories of a loss or a period when you felt spiritually blunted or a lack of hope thwarts your moving on, visit the ruins of this fourth-century synagogue (now a national park), so rich in cultural and religious symbolism of another time. It is a place where the faithful read the Torah, prayed, and perhaps found a daily renewal through their faith. By car, take Route 886 north from Meron, turn right on Route 899 and follow the signs.

Soothe Your Spirit
Let your mind go back in time to when this beautiful old synagogue was actively used. Perhaps Queen Esther even knew of it. Reread the story of Esther and let her courage inspire you to do what your spiritual core is guiding you to do.

A Deeper Look
The large synagogue is believed to have belonged to Simeon bar Yochaim, who lived during the Second Jewish War in 13 B.C.; however, the synagogue, according to scholars, most likely dates to a later century.

202. Dilwara Temples

MOUNT ABU, RAJASTHAN, INDIA

God, our Creator, has stored within our minds and personalities, great potential strength and ability. Prayer helps us tap and develop these powers.
—Abdul Kalam (1931–), eleventh president of India

The Dilwara Temples are a cluster of five white-marble, intricately carved temples sacred to the Jains, a religious sect in India whose principles embrace nonviolence, forgiveness, and self-effort as the path to self-realization and enlightenment. These astonishing temples sit in a complex among mango trees and wooded hills and are unique because each temple is dedicated to a different Jain saint and named for the village to which it belongs.

Whether you need to forgive yourself or another or accept forgiveness, visit the Dilwara complex. If you are a Jain, you are welcome to bathe and perform the ritual puja; otherwise, enjoy a guided tour. Mount Abu is located 4,000 feet above sea level and easily reached by bus, automobile, or train (the nearest station at Abu Road links the Golden Triangle of cities: Delhi-Jaipur-Agra).

Soothe Your Spirit
Soak up the sacred ambiance of the beautiful temples within the Dilwara complex while reflecting on forgiveness, even self-forgiveness because it injures your spirit to hold onto psychological wounds, anger, and resentment.

A Deeper Look
The temples are located about 1 mile from Mount Abu and are a sacred pilgrimage site for Jains.

203. Elijah's Cave

HAIFA, ISRAEL

And Elijah the Tishbite, who was of the inhabitants of Gilead, said unto Ahab, As the Lord God of Israel liveth, before whom I stand, there shall not be dew or rain these years, but according to my word.
—Bible, 1 Kings 17:1

The cave in which the Hebrew Prophet Elijah (also known as Elijah the Tishbite) lived and meditated in the ninth century B.C. is located on Mount Carmel and is sacred to Jews, Christians, and Muslims. Characterized by the Qur'an as a great prophet for his denunciation of the pagan worship of Ba'al, and compared with John the Baptist and Jesus in Christian writing, the Jewish prophet Elijah's popularity has remained strong through the centuries. His longevity may be thanks to a legend asserting that in troubled times Elijah will appear for relief, reconciliation, and redemption. Elijah's Cave is located at 230 Allenby Road and is easily accessible by public transportation such as buses and taxis.

The entrance splits into a right side for men, a left side for women, with a central area for private prayers. Head coverings are required. Entrance is free, but donations are welcomed.

Soothe Your Spirit

Read about the prophet Elijah in 1 Kings of the Old Testament and visit the cave. With the faith of Elijah, believe that the power of God forgives and reconciles and pray for what you seek.

A Deeper Look

A chapel stands over the entire cave. The chapel has two altars: the main one and a smaller altar just for the cave.

204. Church of Ágios Dionysios

ZANTE, ZAKYNTHOS ISLAND, GREECE

Who is a God like unto thee, that pardoneth inquity, and passeth by the
transgression of the remnant of his heritage? . . . retaineth not his anger . . .
delighteth in mercy and . . . wilt cast all their sins into the depths of the sea.
—Bible, Micah 7:18–19

*N*amed for Saint Dionysios, born on Zakynthos in 1547, the
Venetian-style church has an illuminated bell tower, replicating
the one in Saint Marcos Square that serves as a lighted beacon to sailors
navigating dark seas. The church sits adjacent to the monastery and
a museum. Known as the "Forgiveness Saint" because he forgave and
protected his brother's murderer when the murderer asked for help,
Dionysios is honored twice yearly with processionals of his relics in a silver
reliquary.

If you are having trouble forgiving someone or yourself, consider a
pilgrimage to the Church of Saint Dionysios to start the process of
forgiveness. The church sits at water's edge in the heart of Zante and is
easy to locate.

Soothe Your Spirit

Embark on a pilgrimage for the saint's feast day or Day of Dormition. Light
a candle in the sanctuary and pray for mercy, turning to Saint Dionysios to
assist you with the process of forgiveness and to pray with you and for you
to God.

A Deeper Look

The Greek Orthodox Church marks December 17 as the Dormition of
Dionysios.

205. Church of the Primacy of Peter

TABGHA, GALILEE, ISRAEL

So when they had dined, Jesus saith to Simon Peter, Simon, son of Jonas, lovest thou me more than these? He saith unto him, Yea, Lord; thou knowest that I love thee. He saith unto him, Feed my lambs.
—Bible, John 21:15

There have been several iterations of churches upon the holy site that commemorates the place where the resurrected Jesus gave Peter charge of his flock of followers. When Peter came ashore from fishing with other disciples, his nets were full, thanks to Jesus telling him to fish on the right side of the boat. Three times Jesus asked Peter whether he loved him, and Peter replied yes (in contrast to his previous three denials of Jesus, Luke 22:54–62).

If you have doubted your love for God or the Divine's love for you, reaffirm your love as Peter did, redeeming himself. Visit the Franciscan Church of the Primacy of Peter in Tabgha. To get to the site, take a taxi from Tiberius. The church opens daily 8:00 A.M. to noon, and then from 2:00 to 5:00 P.M. Entrance is free.

Soothe Your Spirit
Pray for divine love as sustenance to feed your soul.

A Deeper Look
The plain stone church is located at the edge of the northwestern corner of the Sea of Galilee and a part of its altar is a piece of the stone table (*Mensa Christi*) where Christ laid out the bread when appearing to his disciples after the Resurrection.

206. Old Ship Church
(also Old Ship Meetinghouse)

HINGHAM, MASSACHUSETTS, UNITED STATES

Some rise by sin, and some by virtue fall.
—William Shakespeare (1564–1616), English playwright and poet

When the Puritans built the Old Ship Meetinghouse in 1681 amid rolling verdant hills on the easternmost flank of coastal Massachusetts, they created in their sacred sanctuary a Gothic timber ceiling that resembles the inverted hull of a ship. Now a Unitarian Universalist church, the site showcases a framed 1680s seating chart and The First Settlers Cemetery, a colonial graveyard filled with centuries-old markers and headstones of upstanding pilgrims and the less notable who surely took secrets and sins to the grave as humans always have.

Whether you have a grudge, a secret, or a sin you'd like to bury, begin the process by attending a worship service in Old Ship Church. It's located at 107 Main Street. Hingham is located between Cohasset and Weymouth off of Highway 3A, just inland from Massachusetts Bay.

Soothe Your Spirit

Ask divine forgiveness for yourself or others involved in the burden you carry. Write on paper a sentence forgiving yourself and others. Visit the cemetery with a vow not to take the burden with you to the grave. When you are alone, burn the paper; do not mentally revisit what your conscience has cleared.

A Deeper Look

Old Ship Church is considered the oldest surviving Puritan meetinghouse in North America and the only continuous ecclesiastical house of worship with regular services still offered.

207. Ágios Gerásimos Monastery

VALSAMATA, KEFALONIA, GREECE

All that spirits desire, spirits attain.
—Kahlil Gibran (1883–1931), Lebanese-born American poet

When Saint Gerásimos, a sixteenth-century monk, arrived on Kefalonia, he lived in a cave for five years, spiritually absorbed because of his deep devotion to the Divine despite the temptation of sensual pleasure beckoning everywhere—swaths of white sandy beaches, warm and sparkling emerald waters, and dark forests of Kefalonian fir, all sheltered under an endless Mediterranean sky. The uncorrupted body of Saint Gerásimos is enshrined in the monastery near the Valsamata area, in the fertile Omala Valley dotted with vineyards and patchwork fields.

If you desire spiritual redemption or forgiveness, consider visiting Kefalonia to ask for assistance from Saint Gerásimos whose intercession is believed to be efficacious for healing body, mind, and spirit. The best way to get around the island is by car, which you can rent at the airport in Athens on mainland Greece and drive onto a ferry to the deck for cars. Fly to Argostóli; or cross on the ferry and find transportation to the main port of Sami or Argostóli.

Soothe Your Spirit

Venerate Saint Gerásimos and ask him to help you find forgiveness, redemption, or reconciliation. Let your healing begin on this beautiful island.

A Deeper Look

October 20 is a special processional day when the faithful pay their respects to their island's patron saint, who many believe makes possible miracles in their lives.

208. Shrine of Our Lady of Montserrat

BASILICA OF MONTSERRAT MONASTERY, CATALONIA, SPAIN

Draw nigh to God and he will draw nigh to you.
—Bible, James 4:8

*T*he *Black Madonna (La Moreneta) and Child* is a sacred sculpture in the Monastery of Montserrat that, according to a legend, was carved by Saint Luke and brought to Spain where it was hidden from the Moors until the ninth century A.D. when it was discovered on the mountain of Montserrat. A monastery was established there, and today a magnificent basilica enshrines the miracle-producing icon that draws millions of pilgrims each year.

If you have felt spiritually estranged from the faith (in which you were raised or once embraced), start the process of reconciliation with a visit to the monastery to see the Black Madonna. The monks welcome visitors to their sacred sanctuary located near the summit of the 4,000-foot mountain. The best way to get there is to fly to Barcelona and take a taxi to Plaça d'Espanya. Once there, catch one of a dozen trains to Montserrat that connect with an aerial lift to reach the monastery.

Soothe Your Spirit

Participate in a Mass or recitation of the Liturgy of the Hours and start reconnecting your heart with the Divine within who has never left you.

A Deeper Look

The Black Madonna's color is probably due to the passage of time and smoke from devotional candles and varnishes.

209. Mariazell Basilica
(Basilica of the Birth of Virgin Mary)

MARIAZELL, AUSTRIA

God pardons like a mother, who kisses the offence into everlasting forgiveness.
—Henry Ward Beecher (1813–1887), Protestant minister and author

The Alpine basilica is easily recognized in the Austrian hamlet of Mariazell because of its Gothic central steeple and twin baroque spires. It has an ornate high altar and a sacred shrine that holds the holy Madonna and Child wooden sculpture, which is said to be miraculous. The church has been a popular pilgrimage site from the twelfth century but especially after a fourteenth-century secular court ordered criminals to make the Mariazell pilgrimage to atone for their crimes.

If you feel the need to atone for something, visit the Mariazell Basilica. The basilica is open from 6:00 A.M. to 8:00 P.M. with a two-hour break at noon. Fly into Vienna and take the train to St. Polten and then to Mariazell; a bus will take you into the heart of town. Then, walk the short distance remaining. Or, take Route 20 from Vienna southwest to Mariazell, roughly 80 miles.

Soothe Your Spirit

Confess your sin. Attend the celebration of the Mass and receive the sacrament of penance at this center of Austrian pilgrimage. Let spiritual inspiration further guide you to a method of atonement.

A Deeper Look

The Mariazell Basilica is central Europe's most visited Marion shrine. Our Lady of Mariazell is known by many names, including the "Great Mother of the Slavic People" and the "Great Mother of Austria."

210. Konarak Sun Temple

KONARAK, ORISSA, INDIA

I believe in the fundamental truth of all the great religions.
—Mohandas K. Gandhi (1869–1948), Indian political leader and father of India

The Konarak Sun Temple, a stunning carved stone sanctuary dating from 1250, is dedicated to Surya, Hindu sun god. Built in the shape of a chariot with twenty-four wheels and seven horses to pull it, the temple enshrines the green stone statue of Surya astride his steed, accompanied by dancers and musicians and surrounded by beautiful carvings of men and women engaged in various erotic positions.

If you are interested in reconciling conflicting ideas about sacred sexuality and would like to explore the subject using different spiritual traditions as a lens, begin by visiting the Konarak Sun Temple. The nearest airport is in Bhubaneswar, the capital of Orissa, about 22 miles away. Puri, 20 miles away, has a railroad station. Alternatively, you can take a bus, jeep, or auto rickshaw from Puri to Konarak.

Soothe Your Spirit

Read the *Kama Sutra* and Tantric texts about the divine energy of Shakti and about how the universe exists as the divine play of Shakti and Shiva.

A Deeper Look

The temple has endured decline through the centuries but still visible are carvings of military scenes, flowers, animals, and men and curvaceous women engaged in erotic positions, perhaps suggesting the soul's bliss in union with the Divine.

211. Canterbury Cathedral

CANTERBURY, KENT, ENGLAND

I will lay thy stones with fair colours, and lay thy foundations with sapphires. And I will make thy windows of agates . . .
—Isaiah 54:11–12

Canterbury Cathedral, the Anglican Gothic-style cathedral in England, has been a site of worship since its founding in A.D. 602 by Saint Augustine. In 1170, while praying in the cathedral, Thomas Beckett, the archbishop of Canterbury, was murdered by knights loyal to King Henry II. Within three days, miracles began to take place; their stories are depicted in a series of stained-glass windows in the Trinity Chapel. For centuries, pilgrims have meditated on these windows as they seek a miracle, pray, or repent.

If you feel sorry for some infraction and would like to offer your remorse to God, do so, and consider a pilgrimage to the church where the Holy Spirit is still felt and the windows still reflect light through Thomas Beckett's story. Fly to Kent or from London, take the Southeastern Railway from London Pancras to Canterbury West Station. Walk the remaining short distance. Alternatively, drive the M2 or M20 motorway into Canterbury.

Soothe Your Spirit

Take time to feel the deep spiritual energy of countless pilgrims who undertook soulful travel to pray here. Express the sorrow held by your spirit and feel your burden lift.

A Deeper Look

The Trinity Chapel enshrines the martyred Saint Thomas's relics. Canterbury Cathedral is designated a World Heritage Site.

212. Sangam

ALLAHABAD, UTTAR PRADESH, INDIA

Aum. I release all troubling thoughts. I open myself to feelings of peace. My surroundings are peaceful. The external forces acting upon me are peaceful. I am diving deeply into the pool of divine nectar. In the peace of the temple of my heart, I recognize my real Self as the Imperishable soul.
—Anonymous, prayer based on the *Amrita Bindu Upanishad*

According to Hindu mythology, the peaceful surreal confluence (Sangam) at the city of Allahabad where the Ganges, the Yamuna, and the invisible, mythical Saraswati Rivers merge is one of the holiest places on Earth and an important pilgrimage center. Sangam is believed to be the site where drops of *Amrit Bindhu* (nectar of the gods) fell, energetically charging the site with a sacred energy vibration.

If your mind is troubled and an act of forgiving and releasing would give you peace, embark on a pilgrimage to the Sangam. Fly to Delhi and then to Allahabad. From there, take a bus, automobile, rickshaw, or horse or camel cart to Sangam.

Soothe Your Spirit

Read the *Amrita Bindu Upanishad* before hiring a boat to take you on the river. Fill a small container with river water, hold it, and reflect on all you want to release. Pour the water charged by your thoughts into the Sangam. Imagine holy atoms of energy recharging your body, mind, and spirit. Then meditate on the imperishable soul.

A Deeper Look

Every twelve years, the world's largest ablution event, the Maha Kumbh Mela, takes place at the Sangam.

213. Lateran Baptistery

ROME, ITALY

That which is born of the flesh is flesh; and that which is born of the Spirit is spirit.
—Bible, John 3:6

*L*ong before baptismal fonts became an integral part of every Christian church, Constantine the Great, the Roman emperor who converted to Christianity, built a baptistery over a first-century villa and a second-century bathhouse in A.D. 315 and dedicated it to Saint John the Baptist. The baptistery's exterior brick walls date to Constantine's time, however, popes of the fifth and seventh centuries, remodeled, restored, and added chapels and a large entry to this building that holds a green basalt font depicting the baptisms of Christ and Constantine.

If you are considering a baptism or reconciliation and a rebaptism, spend an afternoon at the Lateran Baptistery where countless Christians have been baptized since the fourth century. Located at the heart of the Piazza di San Giovanni in Laterano, the baptistery is easily accessible by the San Giovanni A Line metro. Alternatively, take a taxi or bus from other areas of Rome.

Soothe Your Spirit

Feel the magic energy of the ancient holy place where faith moved thousands to take the step of baptism. Then visit the baptistery adjacent to the Cathedral of Saint John Lateran to examine your heart, recite a psalm or prayer, and infuse your spirit with hope and certainty.

A Deeper Look

At the baptistery, there is a chapel dedicated to the Christian martyr Cyprian, a magician from Antioch who used spells to win the heart of a pious Christian girl, Justina. He repented and was baptized; they married and, later, were martyred.

214. Chapel of Our Lady at Rocamadour

ROCAMADOUR, FRANCE

The word of God hidden in the heart is a stubborn voice to suppress.
—Billy Graham (1918–), Southern Baptist evangelical minister

According to legend, when Zaccheus, the husband of Veronica (who purportedly wiped the brow of Christ en route to Calvary), left the Holy Land, he came to Rocamadour with an icon of the Black Virgin. A small chapel was built to enshrine it and was dedicated to Mary. Thousands of faithful pilgrims have since climbed the 216 steps to this small chapel on a rocky plateau to venerate the shrine of Zaccheus, who touched the Redeemer, and to see the holy statue (in part, perhaps, because of the disputed date of the chapel's origins and the legend surrounding it that the oral traditions keep alive).

If you seek redemption and would like to pray about it in a pilgrimage church charged with devotional energy from centuries of continual worship, visit Rocamadour in southern France. The church is at Place St. Amadour in Rocamadour, 110 miles north of Toulouse. From Paris, you can take the train at the Austerlitz station, but you'll have to change trains at Brive-la-Gaillarde. By auto, proceed from Toulouse north on N-20 to Payrac and turn right onto D673 to Rocamadour.

Soothe Your Spirit
Light a candle and venerate the holy beings whose pious spirits graced this chapel/shrine. Express and then release any negative thoughts and emotions. Open yourself to Divine guidance.

A Deeper Look
In 1166, the Benedictine monks caring for the chapel discovered a grave containing the body of Saint Amadour, a Christian hermit now enshrined at the chapel.

215. Oyu Stone Circle

KAZUNO-SHI (KAZUNO CITY), AKITA PREFECTURE, HONSHU, JAPAN

The pebble in the brook secretly thinks itself a precious stone.
—Japanese proverb

Japan's "Stonehenge" is a sacred 4,000-year-old prehistoric site. Two large stone circles are set in a sundial shape (along with other stone structures and artifacts) a few miles from the Akuya River, the source of many of the stones. Some people believe that the subtle energy around these stone monuments constructed by prehistoric people still remains offering a spiritual benefit, although scientists speculate about the purpose of ancient stone circles. It is a mystery, but they may have been used for rituals, sacrifices, or burials.

If you desire to release negative energy to achieve a natural and positive state of being, visit the Oyu Stone Circle. The address is Aza, Manza 45, Oyu, Towada, Kazuno-shi, Akita (on Japan's largest island, Honshu). Admission is free and the site is open daily throughout the year. Take the Shuhoku bus from J.R. Kazuno-Hanawa Station bound for Oyu Onsen, a twenty-minute trip, and get off at Kanjo-Resseki-Mae bus stop.

Soothe Your Spirit

Walk the site, breathing out to release energy and inhaling to refresh and nourish. Reflect on the spiritual yearning of the ancients and what might have inspired them to create such rock shrines for religious rites, possibly using astro-calendrical reckonings to align earthly sites with stars or planets to measure the passage of time or for some other purpose.

A Deeper Look

The Oyu Stone Circle Hall displays many artifacts found at the site and provides an opportunity for visitors to create their own piece of earthenware.

216. Bourges Cathedral

BOURGES, FRANCE

And he kneeled down, and cried with a loud voice, Lord, lay not this sin to their charge. And when he had said this, they fell asleep [died].
—Bible, Acts 7:60

*T*his glorious Roman Catholic cathedral with some of the finest medieval stained-glass windows of any church in France rises above the fertile Loire Valley in all its medieval Gothic grandeur with a long nave and flying buttresses. This cathedral is dedicated to Christianity's first martyr Saint Stephen, stoned to death for blasphemy in A.D. 35.

If you would like to ask Saint Stephen to assist you in praying for forgiveness for an infraction or to lift your spirit closer to the Divine, then come to Bourges Cathedral, located at Place Étienne-Dolet in Bourges. Admission to the cathedral is free, but there is a small fee for entering the crypt of this World Heritage Site. Bourges is about 156 miles from Paris by automobile; take the A10 and then the A71 highway. The nearest airport is Auvergne (96 miles away). Or, take the train from the Austerlitz station in Paris; the trip lasts an hour and three-quarters.

Soothe Your Spirit

Notice the beautiful stained-glass windows (nearly two dozen date to the thirteenth century) of saints. In this sanctified shelter, pray for what you want to release and to call into your heart.

A Deeper Look

Elaborately carved sculptures (one reveals scenes from the life of Stephen) cover sections of the west façade.

CHAPTER 9

MOURNING, LOSS, DEPARTED SOULS

*Death is not extinguishing the light; it is only
putting out the lamp because the dawn has come.*

—Rabindranath Tagore (1861–1941),
Indian writer and Nobel laureate

217. Cathedral of Christ the Light

OAKLAND, CALIFORNIA, UNITED STATES

When two texts, or two assertions, or perhaps, two ideas are in contradiction, be ready to reconcile them rather than cancel one by the other . . .
—Marguerite Yourcenar (1903–1987), American writer

The Christ the Light Cathedral replaced the Cathedral of Saint Francis de Sales in Oakland, destroyed in the 1989 Loma Prieta earthquake. The cathedral's ultramodern look is nothing short of astonishing—the wood, glass, and steel structure resembles a bishop's miter; the worship space is shaped like a *vesica piscis* (womb-shape); and walls of wood louvers and glass flood the sanctuary with natural light.

If you want to find a place of hope and renewal to fill a void left by a devastating loss, visit the Cathedral of Christ the Light, located at 2121 Harrison Street and Grand Avenue, across from Lake Merritt. The nearest airport is Oakland International. To get to the cathedral, take Bay Area Rapid Transit (BART) as the Nineteenth Avenue station is 6 blocks from the church. If you drive, several nearby parking garages are available.

Soothe Your Spirit

Sit in the cathedral on a bright day to feel wrapped in a cocoon of loving, protective light while praying about your loss. Talk to a priest or spiritual adviser about relief, renewal, and regeneration.

A Deeper Look

The cathedral complex includes the chancery offices of the bishop's curia, a conference center, a café and bookstore, a crypt, a mausoleum, and a health services center.

218. Taj Mahal

AGRA, INDIA

Only let this one teardrop, this Taj Mahal, glisten spotlessly bright on the cheek of time, forever and ever.
—Rabindranath Tagore 1861–1941), Indian writer and Nobel laureate

When his beloved wife died giving birth to their fourteenth child in 1631, Shah Jahan spent the next twenty-two years building a suitable resting place for her: the incomparable Taj Mahal (Crown Palace). Often called the most graceful structure on Earth, this shrine to enduring love towers above the banks of the Yamuna River; its white-marble dome and twin minarets shimmer in symmetrical perfection, as its mirror image reflects in the gazing pool below.

Whether you are mourning a lost love, celebrating a new one, or still searching, visit the Taj Mahal. Catch an early train from New Delhi, or arrive in Agra the night before. Sunrise at this World Heritage Site is spectacular.

Remove your shoes to enter the central chamber of the mausoleum, where the light streams through the intricate latticework. Mumtaz's cenotaph, bearing ninety-nine names of Allah, sits in the center of the semiprecious stone-encrusted interior; her husband's modest cenotaph is nearby.

Soothe Your Spirit

Sit by the gazing pool of the Taj Mahal, or find another peaceful body of water closer to home. Offer a prayer of love for a loss in your life. Give yourself permission to mourn but also to feel peace.

A Deeper Look

The cenotaphs are only decorative representations of the actual coffins of the shah and his wife, contained in the lower crypt, where the humid air is heavily scented with incense and rose petals.

219. Mount Olympus

THESSALONIKI, GREECE

[Odysseus weeps] *as a woman weeps when she throws her arms round the body of her beloved husband, fallen in battle before his city and his comrades, fighting to save his home-town and his children from disaster.*
—Homer (800–700 B.C.), *The Iliad*, Greek epic poet

Spectacular Mount Olympus rises regally above the clouds in central Greece, silently blessing those seeking the treasure of its peace. In the classical Greek and Hellenistic worlds, the mountain was known as "the home of the Gods," where Zeus, king of Olympus and the supreme deity, resided with his divine family.

If you seek serenity and strength, visit the sanctuary of Zeus and let the breathtaking beauty of the mountain permeate your being with restorative healing. Catch a bus or train from Athens or Thessaloniki to Litochoro at the base of Mount Olympus, and rise early to see the mountain blaze awake with the fiery colors of crimson and ginger.

Soothe Your Spirit

Hike to the summit to feel the breath of those ancient gods caressing you as the breezes blow. Affirm the richness of life. Pray for someone you have lost or for strength and serenity to deal with the loss.

A Deeper Look

Mount Olympus rises a spectacular 9,577 feet near the Thermaic Gulf on the Aegean Sea bordering Thessaly and Macedonia. Often snowcapped, the mountain, with its fifty-two peaks, frequently has cloud cover despite Homer's observation, in his epic poem *The Odyssey*, that it never has storms but basks in cloudless ether.

220. Shrine of Sayyidda Zeinab

DAMASCUS, SYRIA

Cast away the burdens of the earth and fly upward toward heaven!
—Jalal al-Din Rumi (1207–1273), Persian poet and mystic

In the Iraqi quarter of the city, the magnificent mausoleum of Sayyidda Zeinab, granddaughter of the Prophet Muhammad, features a glistening, golden onion-shaped dome flanked by two graceful, intricately decorated blue minarets stretching upward like hands in a prayerful entreaty for peace and strength. After the murders of her two brothers, Sayyidda Zeinab was kidnapped by soldiers of Yazid I, and subsequently died of shock and grief.

At this shrine, pilgrims wail their tearful laments, beat their chests, kiss the bars around the tomb, or kneel to pray. You can take a taxi to the mosque, which is about 6 miles from the city center behind bustling shops and hotels.

Remove your shoes. The mosque is divided into separate sections for men and women. Women must wear a burqa, a long cloak (available at the entrance kiosk at the mausoleum). Men must wear long-sleeve shirts and trousers. Non-Muslims are welcome to stroll around the courtyard and, although not allowed into the mausoleum, are permitted to glimpse the glittering mirrored-tile interior with its shimmering chandeliers.

Soothe Your Spirit

Slowly stroll around the courtyard and imagine your grief as a weight that can be moved. As you walk, release that weight and feel the lightness of your spirit. Say prayers for the loss in your life. Remember, too, the souls from all faiths who have died for their beliefs and left behind loved ones who mourn their loss.

A Deeper Look

The martyrdom of the Ali family was a defining moment in the history of the Shiites, members of the Shia sect of Islam; thus, the Shrine of Sayyidda Zeinab is especially sacred.

221. Church of the Holy Sepulchre

JERUSALEM, ISRAEL

And when the Sabbath was past, Mary Magdalene, and Mary the [mother] of James, and Salome, had bought sweet spices, that they might come and anoint him. And very early in the morning of the first [day] of the week, they came unto the sepulcher at the rising of the sun. And they said among themselves, Who shall roll us away the stone from the door of the sepulcher?
—Bible, Mark 16:1–3

Illuminated by candles and shimmering lamps, the golden sculpted images of Christ on the cross and his mother sparkle inside the Church of the Holy Sepulchre located in Jerusalem's walled Old City. Also known as the Church of the Resurrection by Orthodox Christians, it stands on the hallowed sites where Jesus was crucified and his body was taken for burial.

If you seek solace through a heartfelt connection to Christ's death and Resurrection this site offers you a place for deep reflection and prayer. Step through the south transept's single door where a Roman-style façade with foliate moldings and pointed arches visually announce a holy place. Pause to consider the symbolism of the raised slab of stone where Jesus's body was readied for burial.

Soothe Your Spirit

Walk slowly through the church, tune into the spiritual energies of centuries of pilgrims. Light a candle and pray for a departed soul or for someone who is distant or in distress. If you cannot travel to Jerusalem, take a virtual tour: www.3disrael.com/jerusalem/Church_of_the_Holy_Sepulcher.cfm.

A Deeper Look

The Roman Catholic, Armenian Apostolic, and Greek Orthodox churches share this holy site and are responsible for its safekeeping.

222. Vietnam Veterans Memorial

WASHINGTON, D.C., UNITED STATES

War is a poor chisel to carve out tomorrow.
—Martin Luther King, Jr. (1929–1968), Baptist minister and Civil Rights leader

On a grassy area of Constitution Gardens, stretches a long, smooth V-shaped slab of black granite that reveals the names of 58,249 men and women who served and perished in the Vietnam War, as well as 1,200 more who are missing. With one wing pointing toward the Washington Monument and the other toward the Lincoln Memorial, this serenely positioned monument is more than a memorial to the loss of life; it highlights the valiant efforts of servicemen and women whose patriotism will never be forgotten.

Whether you lost someone during the conflict, feel conflicted about it, or would like to offer a moment of silence, visit this national landmark, designed by artist Maya Lin. The memorial, located at the intersection of Constitution Avenue and Henry Bacon Drive, is easiest to reach by car. There is a parking lot near Constitution Gardens.

Soothe Your Spirit

Find the name(s) of your loved one and spend a moment in silence. Some families bring flowers or leave letters, poems, and photographs. Others trace the name with a finger and whisper a prayer. Do what feels right to you.

A Deeper Look

Faith, Hope, and Charity are the names of the three nurses in the Vietnam Women's Memorial, located north of the Reflecting Pool and south of the memorial, which honors the women, mostly nurses, who died in the war. The memorial park receives 3 million visitors each year.

223. Mount Kailash

WESTERN TIBET

This is my simple religion. There is no need for temples; no need for complicated philosophy. Our own brain, our own heart is our temple; the philosophy is kindness.
—Dalai Lama (1935–), Tibetan spiritual leader

Sacred to four faiths—Hindu, Buddhist, Jain, and Bon—the incomparable Mount Kailash juts 22,028 feet out of the Himalayas in western Tibet as a spectacular jewel. Its snowcapped peak glistens in the light at the rooftop of the world, beckoning the faithful to come, walk, reflect, pray, and find peace. Annually, thousands of pilgrims answer that call, believing that circumambulating the mountain bestows blessings and abolishes sin.

If you feel a spiritual connection to mountains and believe that time spent in a meditative walk would nurture your spirit, and you are physically able to do the arduous walking and tent camping, make a pilgrimage to Mount Kailash. The easiest way is to book an all-inclusive tour from Kathmandu or Lhasa; however, the trek begins and ends in the city of Darchen. The best time to go is May through September when the weather is more hospitable.

Soothe Your Spirit
Make your pilgrimage a devotional walk, focus on engaging the mind in prayer, recitation of a mantra, or reflection, or, quietly hum or sing of spiritual chants or sacred songs.

A Deeper Look
The Kailash pilgrim's circuit will take about three days to walk; it stretches 32 miles. Hindus and Buddhists circumambulate the mountain in a clockwise direction, while followers of the Bon and Jain trek it in a counterclockwise direction.

224. Our Lady of the Spasm Church

JERUSALEM, ISRAEL

And there followed him a great company of people, and of women, which also bewailed and lamented him.
—Bible, Luke 23:27

After falling under the weight of the heavy wooden cross (Station 3 on the Via Dolorosa), Jesus met his mother (Station 4) at the site of Our Lady of the Spasm, just behind the walls lining a short section of the Via Dolorosa. This modest Armenian Orthodox church was built in the sixteenth century, and its chapel, located in the crypt, displays several evocative paintings of Jesus. A fifth-century floor mosaic survives in which the Holy Mother's footprints are represented as sandals.

Coming to terms with loss is a process that could begin at this site. Getting around Jerusalem is fairly easy using local transportation. You could also take a local tour and walk.

Soothe Your Spirit

Read the passage about Jesus's counsel to his mother and his women followers. Reflect on why he told them not to weep, and consider the possibility that belief in a higher power in times of darkness may bring comfort when nothing else can and help you embrace life.

A Deeper Look

Although the New Testament is silent about Jesus and Mary meeting along the Via Dolorosa, popular tradition supports the story, and a lunette (a half-moon-shaped space) over the church doorway commemorates the meeting in a bas-relief.

225. Tomb of Lazarus

AL-ELZARIYA, ISRAEL

And when he thus had spoken, he cried with a loud voice, Lazarus, come forth. And he that was dead came forth, bound hand and foot with grave-clothes: and his face was bound about with a napkin.
—Bible, John 11:43–44

In the fourth century A.D., the cave and its antechamber where Jesus called his friend Lazarus from death became a holy pilgrimage site upon which several churches were built, although today the Mosque al-Uzair occupies that hallowed place. The burial chamber's original entrance once used by Christian pilgrims was bricked over after the mosque was built; however, the faithful can still enter from a side entrance cut for access by Franciscan monks in the sixteenth century. In the 1950s, a modern Franciscan Church of Saint Lazarus was erected nearby.

If you are pondering ideas of death and resurrection or the demise of something in your life that you desire to revive, spend time at the Tomb of Lazarus, 6 miles from Jerusalem in the West Bank town of Al-Elzariya. Reach the site by bus, taxi, coach tour, or rented car.

Soothe Your Spirit

Walk down the two dozen rock-hewn steps to see the vestibule where Jesus is believed to have called out to Lazarus. The burial chamber was, according to one tradition, on the right. After viewing the tomb, visit the Church of Saint Lazarus; reflect on the ancient miracle, and pray that your thoughts might be illumined and sanctified as you use Lazarus's rising from the dead as a point of departure to write about death and resurrection in a personal context.

A Deeper Look

The nearby Franciscan Church of Saint Lazarus was designed by Antonio Barluzzi in 1954.

226. Normandy American Cemetery

COLLEVILLE-SUR-MER, FRANCE

I give unto them eternal life and they shall never perish.
—Chapel inscription, Normandy American Cemetery

When the fighting was over in Normandy at the end of World War II, the battlefield there had hundreds of small burial grounds, more than ten American cemeteries, and numerous isolated graves of Americans who had fallen on French soil. Roughly 60 percent of the burials were repatriated to the United States; the remaining casualties were divided between the Brittany cemetery and the 172.5-acre Normandy cemetery. In this cemetery rest four women, three Medal of Honor recipients, and thirty-three pairs of brothers buried side by side, including the two who inspired the movie *Saving Private Ryan*.

Whether you are a veteran interested in military history, lost a loved one in this war, or would like to say a prayer for the 9,387 soldiers who fell here, visit the Normandy American Cemetery. It is located at 14710 Colleville-sur-Mer, France and is regularly open until 5:00 P.M. Visit the website: *www.abmc.gov.* If your loved one is buried in this cemetery, this website will also help you find the location of the grave.

Soothe Your Spirit

Pass the memorial, the Garden of Missing, and follow the path to the chapel. Reflect on the service given to our country by those young men and women, perhaps your relative among them. Pray for eternal peace for their souls and for the safety of all the men and women serving the cause of freedom today.

A Deeper Look

The cemetery paths are laid out in a Latin cross and there is a viewing platform of Omaha Beach where the 1st Division landed on D-Day.

227. Basilica of the Dormition (also Hagia Maria Scion Abbey)

MOUNT ZION, JERUSALEM

The quieter the mind, the more powerful, the worthier, the deeper, the more telling and more perfect the prayer is.
—Meister Eckhart (1260–1328), German philosopher, theologian, and mystic

On top of Mount Zion, just beyond Zion Gate, sits an organic-looking German Benedictine abbey with a blue conical roof punctuated with four turrets and a domed clock tower that safeguards the traditional site of the last "falling asleep" of the Blessed Virgin Mary when her soul was taken to heaven. The event is also known as the Assumption of Mary. Above the main altar, a gold Byzantine-style mosaic of the Madonna with Child shimmers with light and finds resonance in other sacred art that adorns the basilica.

If you are searching for spiritual meaning from sacred feminine images, are connecting with your higher self or soul in sleep, or want to see the traditional place of Mary's death (another tradition cites Ephesus), visit the Basilica of the Dormition. You can walk to the church from Mount Zion. Otherwise, take a taxi, rental car, or local buses 1, 2, or 38. There is no admission fee.

Soothe Your Spirit
Study the beauty of the sacred art, noticing the imagery of Mary in the icons and mosaics. Pray in the nave. In the crypt a sculpture of the Holy Mother lays in repose, while in the dome above her, Christ receives her soul. Reflect on death as the final "falling asleep."

A Deeper Look
Architect Heinrich Renard used the cathedral of Aix-la-Chapelle as his model for the basilica. The Room of the Last Supper is located beside the abbey.

228. Tomb of King David

JERUSALEM, ISRAEL

The Lord is my light and my salvation; whom shall I fear? The Lord is the strength of my life; of whom shall I be afraid?
—Bible, Psalm 27, composed by David, the second Israelite king

Tradition supports the burial site of David, the beloved second king of the ancient Israelites, in a corner of the ground-level floor of what used to be a Byzantine church. The holy tomb attracts pilgrims who recite the psalms King David composed, pore over Scripture in the anteroom, or recite prayers. David faced many losses in his life, including the death of his newborn son and rejection by his favorite son Absalom.

Perhaps you face spiritual challenges, setbacks, and losses. Visit the Tomb of King David, a man whose love for God inspired him to live a God-centered life despite errors in judgment. Get to the site located near the Dormition Abbey on Mount Zion by taxi, or local buses 1, 2, and 38.

Men should wear a hat or yarmulke, or cover their heads. Admission is free, and the tomb is open Saturday through Thursday 8:00 A.M. to 5:00 P.M., and Friday 8:00 A.M. to 1:00 P.M.

Soothe Your Spirit

Pay your respects to this great king of the ancient Israelites. Read Psalm 23, in which David professes his faith in God, or Psalm 43, in which David encourages his soul to trust in God; let King David's words lift your heart to embrace the divine love and guidance that is always available to you.

A Deeper Look

The sacramental velvet cloth covering King David's cenotaph is embroidered with the words: *David Melech Israel Hai Vekayam* (David King of Israel Is Alive).

229. Tomba di Coddu Vecchiu di Giganti

ARZACHENA, SARDINIA

Great griefs are mute.
—Italian proverb

The people of the ancient Nuragic civilization on Sardinia during the Bronze Age produced sacred megalithic tombs of astonishing size, including the giant tomb of Coddu Vecchiu, with its 33-foot-long burial chamber and a semicircular area in front where sacred ceremonies for the dead were performed. The later addition of the giant stele (large, upright carved stone) connects this tomb with other megalithic tombs found across Europe.

If you are having difficulty finding closure over a personal loss and would like to feel rejuvenated, visit the Tomb of Coddu Vecchiu to gain perspective about the cycles of birth and death and the rise and fall of civilizations. The main airport is Olbia Costa Smeralda Airport. There are daily passenger ferries from Italy to Olbia as well as two rail networks that will get you from cities on Sardinia to Olbia. From Olbia, take a local bus to Arzachena or take the main road (S.S. 125) to Arzachena. The gigantic tomb sits in the southwestern area of Arzachena known as Capichera.

Soothe Your Spirit

Pay your respects to the ancient spirits. Sit near the tomb, breathe deeply, and relax before intuitively attuning to the energy of this sacred place. According to a prevailing belief, this site rejuvenates those who come in contact with it. Let it revitalize you, help you gain perspective, and find closure.

A Deeper Look

There are 321 megalithic monuments across Sardinia, including the Tomba di Coddu Vecchiu di Giganti, which archaeologists suggest was most likely a community burial chamber.

230. Saint Michael's Chapel

KOŠICE, SLOVAKIA

One joy shatters a hundred griefs.
—Chinese proverb

When the Saint Michael's cemetery chapel, adjacent to the beautiful high Gothic–style Saint Elizabeth's Cathedral in Košice, was undergoing renovation, seventeen gravestones from the fourteenth through the seventeenth centuries were discovered in the chapel's lower level. The headstones were removed and bricked into the exterior. Today, Saint Michael's altar bears the image of the patron saint of the dead—Archangel Michael as well as the archangels Gabriel and Raphael.

If your spiritual goal is to work through a grieving process because of a catastrophic loss, embark on a trip to Saint Michael's. The nearest airport is Košice International Airport with daily service to Prague and Bratislava. Highway E50 links Košice with Presov. The train station has daily connections to many cities in Slovakia, Poland, and Hungary, including Prague, Bratislava, and Budapest.

Soothe Your Spirit

Reflect on the five stages of grief outlined in the Kübler-Ross model: denial, anger, bargaining, depression, and acceptance. Understand that there is no need to hurry the process. Let this cemetery chapel, now classified as a church, be a loving reminder that death and birth are bookends to a life; this has been true since the birth of humanity.

A Deeper Look

Saint Michael's was built in the center of a cemetery in the heart of the city and the lower level served as an ossarium (to house bones) while the upper level was used for requiems or services to offer prayers for the deceased.

231. The Valley of the Kings

LUXOR, EGYPT

He who cannot change the very fabric of his thought will never be able to change reality . . .
—Anwar Sadat (1918–1981), third president of Egypt

When the ancient Egyptians said goodbye to a king, he was sent into the afterlife with jewels, ritual sacred objects, statues of deities, furniture, and scrolls; that is why tomb robbing was such a lucrative practice. Ramses XI, who reigned from 1124 B.C. until his death in 1106 B.C., was the last king to build a tomb in the valley. His simple tomb is vibrantly colored with scenes from the *Book of the Dead* and other ancient texts.

If you are facing the end of a karmic cycle and must say goodbye to someone or something, it might help to see how the ancient Egyptians handled death. The Valley of the Kings is on the west bank of the Nile; from Luxor, take a taxi or a rental car approximately 4 miles upriver. Alternatively, cross the river on a ferry. The coolest months to visit are December through March. Otherwise, daytime temperatures reach triple digits.

Buy your tickets at the West Bank ticket office since you cannot purchase tickets at the site. Women must cover bare shoulders and knees.

Soothe Your Spirit

Formulate a ritual for achieving closure (when you return home); for example, write a note saying goodbye. Cut it into pieces and plant it in a pot with some forget-me-nots. Or, if you want a permanent ending, write the note and burn it.

A Deeper Look

The tomb has been open since antiquity; more than a dozen messages of graffiti were left in the tomb by ancient tourists.

232. Père Lachaise

PARIS, FRANCE

Have courage for the great sorrows of life and patience for the small ones; and when you have laboriously accomplished your daily task, go to sleep in peace. God is awake.
—Victor Hugo (1802–1885), French poet, dramatist, and novelist

A walk through the beautiful and serene Père Lachaise, amid broad, leafy trees, moss-encrusted headstones, gleaming marble busts, stoic stone cherubs, columned temples, ornate crosses, marble statues of children, legions of angels, and red roses everywhere, can be a soul-soothing and spiritually moving experience. This special cemetery that Parisians call the "City of the Dead" is notable for the famous people interred in its hallowed ground, including the tragic lovers Abelard and Heloise, Chopin, Edith Piaf, Colette, Marcel Proust, Honoré de Balzac, Alice B. Toklas, Yves Montand, and Jim Morrison. Père Lachaise has served as the model for the gardens found in rural cemeteries of the United States since about 1831.

If you feel that cemeteries serve as a spiritual link to the past or you would like to venerate a departed soul buried in Père Lachaise, embark on a trip to Paris. The main entrance is located at Rue de Repos.

Soothe Your Spirit
Walk through the cemetery and feel the peace in your heart. If there is someone with whom you would like to commune, invite that person's spirit to be present with you, inspiring you as you explore. Offer a prayer for that departed soul.

A Deeper Look
For a partial listing of notable people buried in Père Lachaise, see the website: *www.paris.org/Expos/PereLachaise/pl.index.html*.

233. The Catacombs of Saint Callixtus

ROME, ITALY

Precious in the sight of the Lord is the death of his saints.
—Bible, Psalm 116:15

*F*irst established for Rome's early Christian community, the Catacombs of Saint Callixtus hold almost a half-million sepulchers and tombs spanning 12 miles and five levels. Saint Cecilia was martyred with three ax chops to her neck in the third century and is entombed where a statue marks the place of her burial. Her relics were moved to a basilica dedicated to her in the Trastevere, along with forty-six other martyrs; and the Crypt of the Popes is the oldest.

If holy burial sites depicting ancient Christians' spiritual beliefs and their sacred art and symbols inspire you to create a rich spiritual life for yourself, visit the Catacombs of Saint Callixtus. The catacomb address is Via Appia Antica (Old Appian Way), 110/126, Rome; the entrance is located near the small church of Quo Vadis and the Basilica of Saint Sebastian, with parking off Via Ardeatina. To reach the catacombs, take the metro, your rental car, taxi, coach tour, or any of various city buses that depart from central Rome.

Photography is not permitted inside the catacombs.

Soothe Your Spirit

Tap into your artistic self and draw the beautiful symbols you see. Later, your images will carry you back to what you saw and felt in the catacombs. Use the emotion to lead you into prayer, meditation, and absorption on the Divine.

A Deeper Look

The catacombs bear the name of early Christian deacon Callixtus, administrator of the cemeteries of the Church of Rome through appointment by Pope Zephyrinus early in the third century.

234. The Saadian Tombs

MARRAKESH, MOROCCO

There is no God but God. Muhammad is God's messenger.
—Qur'an

*P*erhaps the most beautiful burial sites in North Africa are the tombs of the Saadian sultans and their families, who ruled in the sixteenth and seventeenth centuries. The tombs, buried for centuries, were rediscovered and restored in 1917 by the Beaux-arts service. The sacred site (next door to the Mosque of the Kasbah) continues to be a place of veneration. Some tombs are embellished in gorgeous mosaics and epitaphs while others are housed inside two mausoleums with richly decorated rooms, pillared arches, stunning patterned floors and domed ceilings, Arabic script, and amazing plaster work.

If funerary art provides solace to you during your time of loss or is spiritually evocative, visit the tombs. Located on Rue de la Kasbah Marrakesh, the site is easily accessible via the international airport and through regular bus and train service from other Moroccan cities. Arrive early to avoid long lines of tourists. Entrance fee is 10 dirham (about $1.25). Hours are 9:00 A.M. to noon and 2:30 to 6:00 P.M.

Soothe Your Spirit

Allow the art and subtle spiritual energy of this tranquil, sacred site to magnify the longing in your heart for God's love.

A Deeper Look

The Saadian Tombs lie in an enclosed garden of roses in Marrakesh's old Medina. Sultan Ahmed al-Mansur (1578–1603), who oversaw the design and construction of the tombs, is buried here, along with 166 to 200 others.

235. Brahma Temple

PUSHKAR, RAJASTHAN, INDIA

The realm where eternal luster glows, in which the light divine is set
—place me, Purifier, in that deathless, imperishable world.
—Rig-Veda, Book 9, Hymn 113:7

This sacred fourteenth-century temple dedicated to Lord Brahma, Hindu god of creation, rests on a raised platform at the edge of holy Pushkar Lake. Thousands of pilgrims from all over India descend on Pushkar each year in October and November. This is a holy time when the faithful ritually purify body and soul by immersing in the lake water before praying before Brahma and perhaps leaving a silver coin engraved with the names of loved ones who have been born or have passed away during the year.

Whether you have lost someone dear to you or you want to focus on creation (birth of a new project) and seek blessings, visit the Brahma Temple. The nearest airport is located in Jaipur, roughly 90 miles away and has regular service to Pushkar from major cities in India.

Soothe Your Spirit

Have a coin engraved with the name of your loved one or with your name or the name of your project. Leave the coin in the temple and expect Divine blessings to flow to you from the Hindu "Creator of the Universe."

A Deeper Look

The temple is constructed of marble, features a red spire and the image of a *hans* or goose, and shelters a silver turtle that holds engraved coins. Inside, there is a life-size image of Brahma and a small cave dedicated to Lord Shiva and marked by a silver door.

236. Hill of Tara

NAVEN, COUNTY MEATH, IRELAND

The Irish forgive their great men when they are safely buried.
—Irish proverb

Near Newgrange in County Meath lies an emerald-green, grassy hillock named the Hill of Tara. This ancient ritual site of coronation and seat of power for as many as 142 Celtic high kings is also the dwelling place for the gods and entrance to the otherworld. The ancient Celtic earthmovers created structures on Tara such as the Mound of Hostages and the Stone of Destiny, a megalithic stone that would render a sound when struck by the true high king.

If your spiritual beliefs are enhanced or informed by seeing sacred places of the ancients and their spiritual constructions, visit the Hill of Tara. But do so soon; the government of Ireland plans to build a four-lane toll road that preservationists say will damage the site. From Dublin, drive the M3 to the site's car park. Go early to avoid crowds and wear good walking shoes or boots with traction as wet field grass is slippery.

Soothe Your Soul

View the audio-visual presentation at the visitor's center first so you'll understand what you are seeing, then walk around the site and let the 4,000-year-old landscape work its magic on you. Use your imagination and feel the energy of ancient spirits.

A Deeper Look

The views from Tara Hill, where archaeologists say human activity dates to the Neolithic period, provide spectacular views of a quarter of Ireland's coast and mainland.

237. Crypt of Yogananda

GLENDALE, CALIFORNIA, UNITED STATES

*I give my love to all thirsty hearts, both to those who love me and those who
do not love me.*
—Paramahansa Yogananda (1893–1952), enlightened spiritual leader and founder
of the Self-Realization Fellowship

$\mathcal{C}$alled the Incarnation of Divine Love by both his successor and
his own guru Sri Yukteswar, the enlightened Kryia Yoga master
Paramahansa Yogananda passed from death to eternal life and was interred
in Forest Lawn Cemetery in the stately Great Mausoleum, Sanctuary of
Golden Slumber. Some people mark special dates of the saint's life and
passing through a personal pilgrimage to places associated with his life and
his passing.

If you are a devotee, love this great teacher and support his work, or
want to pay your respects, consider visiting the mausoleum at 1712 South
Glendale Avenue. Hours are 8:00 A.M. to 5:00 P.M. daily, seven days a
week.

Soothe Your Soul

Ring the bell for entry into the mausoleum and inform the security guard you
desire to visit Yogananda's crypt to pray. Find the marble entombment site
with the plaque that reads, "Paramahansa Yogananda March 7, 1952," and
offer your prayer. Enjoy the holy energy believed to emanate from there.

A Deeper Look

Modeled on Campo Santo in Genoa, Italy, the Great Mausoleum is the
largest building at Forest Lawn. Access to the Mausoleum is restricted and
security cameras monitor activity; however, in the public area, there is a
stunning stained-glass reproduction of Leonardo Da Vinci's *Last Supper*,
and in another area, there is a labyrinth modeled on the one at Chartres
Cathedral in France.

238. The Great Mound

KNOWTH, COUNTY MEATH, IRELAND

On earth there is no heaven, but there are pieces of it.
—Jules Renard (1864–1910), French novelist and dramatist

*O*f the three famous passage tombs of Ireland (Newgrange, Dowth, and Knowth), the Great Mound, or Knowth, is singularly impressive, having, by some estimates, a quarter of Europe's megalithic art. Important as a ritual site for the ancient Neolithic people and honored by modern pagans, Wiccans, and New Age followers, the Great Mound is encompassed by seventeen smaller mounds and is adorned with 127 carved kerbstones. Inside the structure (with its main chamber and two passageways), archaeologists have found a stone phallus, a mace (a clublike weapon of metal or stone), and a large basin known as Dagda's cauldron.

If ancient Irish history stirs your spiritual yearnings to see the mounds created by the Neolithic earthmovers, visit the Great Mound with its eastern and western passages of the portal tomb. Visitation is by guided tour only from Meath's Brú na Bóinne visitor's center. Knowth and Newgrange together is a three-hour tour. Take the M1 roadway from Dublin to the village of Donore to the visitor's center; or, take the Eireann Bus from Drogheda to the visitor's center gate. Dublin, thirty minutes from County Meath, is the nearest international airport.

Soothe Your Soul
Follow the path winding between the mounds, view the kerbstone area, and reflect on the ancient Neolithic people, what spiritual meaning they might have attributed to their rituals, and what relevance that holds for your beliefs.

A Deeper Look
Knowth and other Boyne Valley megalithic sites are designated World Heritage Sites; their artifacts are in the National Museum of Ireland.

239. Cathedral Basilica of Saint Louis King of France

NEW ORLEANS, LOUISIANA, UNITED STATES

Louisianan brave men, this bell whose name is Victoire was molten in glorious memory of this day of January 8, 1815.
—Inscription in French on the cathedral's bell

*T*he Saint Louis Cathedral, the oldest cathedral in continuous use in America, was built over the remains of churches dating back to 1727. Located in the heart of New Orleans, the cathedral holds the crypts of notables of the city, members of the clergy, and the Capuchin Père Antoine, who spent his life laboring on behalf of the people of New Orleans. Wives, husbands, and children of early Louisiana colonists, settlers, and slaves were married, baptized, and mourned in the cathedral. Today, Masses may be requested, reserved, and said for a loved one. See the website at *www.stlouiscathedral.org*.

If you would like to see this New Orleans landmark and honor the families who pioneered and built the great city, visit the Saint Louis Cathedral at 615 Père Antoine Alley. Located near famous Bourbon Street within the French Quarter, and facing Jackson Square, the cathedral is easily accessible using public transportation or rental car.

Soothe Your Spirit

Attend a service in this lovely church with its gorgeous mosaics and other sacred art and let the holiness of the sanctuary speak directly to your spirit. Light a candle for the people of New Orleans.

A Deeper Look

When the cathedral collapsed around 1849 after a remodeling attempt, new construction began on the neo-Byzantine cathedral in 1907 using granite and marble as well as beautiful mosaics in the interior.

240. La Recoleta Cemetery

BUENOS AIRES, ARGENTINA

You leave old habits behind by starting out with the thought, "I release the need for this in my life."
—Wayne Dwyer (1940–), motivational speaker and bestselling author

*L*a Recoleta Cemetery, built by the Order of the Recoletos in 1822 on donated land, encompasses 6 hectares in a highly desirable Buenos Aires neighborhood of mansions and estates enclosed by expansive gardens (many gardens were built in the late 1800s as a barrier against the raging yellow fever epidemic). Neoclassic doors and high Greek columns mark the entrance to the necropolis of crypts, mausoleums, statues, and graves with astonishing sculptures, many unique and beautiful motifs and artistic elements, and architectural styles including the art deco crypt of the family of Eva Perón, also known as Evita in the center of La Recoleta (perhaps the lovely art accounts for comparisons between La Recoleta and Père Lachaise in France).

If you are ready to embrace a loss that you choose—for example, to release a bad habit, a relationship, a dead-end job, a negative pattern of behavior, or something else that may be holding back your spiritual progress—consider visiting La Recoleta as a destination for release.

Soothe Your Spirit

Stroll the grounds of La Recoleta, mentally burying whatever limits your spiritual progress and then imagine replacing the loss with something new. For example, start forming a positive new habit to replace a bad one that you release. Give yourself about three weeks to ensure the new habit has formed.

A Deeper Look

La Recoleta is a necropolis of the elite and safeguards the tombs of several Argentinean presidents, governors, soldiers, writers, diplomats, the grandchild of Napoleon Bonaparte, a Nobel laureate in chemistry, musicians, composers, and writers.

241. Bardsey Island (*Ynys Enlli*)

GWYNEDD, WALES

The Lord is nigh unto them that are of a broken heart; and saveth such as be of a
contrite spirit.
—Bible, Psalm 34:18

At the tip of the Llyn Peninsula in North Wales lies a desolate, wind-swept island a mile long and 0.6 miles across that becomes virtually unreachable in treacherous sea currents. Nevertheless, it served as a sacred haven for devoutly religious monks and persecuted Christians during the fifth century. Legend holds that the island is also the burial site of King Arthur. All that remains of the thirteenth-century monastery and gardens built by Saint Cadfan are the ruins, a tower, and a knobby old Bardsey apple tree that some say the monks planted.

If you are brokenhearted and want to keep a memory alive or see new beginnings from loss or departure, visit Bardsey Island. Summer is best. Catch a ferry or a boat from Porth Meudwy or the main market town Pwllheli (market day is Wednesday) on mainland Wales, where the Cambrian Railway from Shrewsbury in Shropshire, England, clacks past the scenic Cambrian Mountains and the coast to its terminus. You can't bring your dogs or other pets, swimming in the sea in not allowed, nor is disturbing the wildlife.

Soothe Your Spirit
Stay in a farmhouse and give the site time to reinvigorate your spirit as you pray and reflect on how death and destruction can give rise to regeneration and renewal in the cycles of nature and also in human civilization.

A Deeper Look
The *Book of Llandaff*, assembled in the mid-1200s, noted Bardsey Island as a burial site for 20,000 "holy confessors and martyrs" and called it the "Rome of Britain" for its sanctity and dignity.

242. Anne Frank House

AMSTERDAM, NETHERLANDS

How wonderful it is that nobody need wait a single moment before starting to improve the world.
—Anne Frank (1929–1945), German Jewish diarist

When Anne Frank and her family hid to escape Nazi persecution in 1942 in a house at Prinsengracht 267, Anne detailed the isolation and fears of discovery in her diary until her family was betrayed. Anne and her sister, Margot, were sent to the Bergen-Belsen concentration camp, but her father survived and drew spiritual strength from his daughter's diary (now published in fifty-five languages).

If you feel a spiritual calling to improve the world, visit the Anne Frank House. It is open year-round, except on December 31 and January 1 when it is opened for half the day and closed on Yom Kippur. Take streetcar 13, 14, or 17, and get off at the Westermarkt stop or, take the bus 21, 170, 171, or 172 to the Westermarkt stop. Also the Museum Boat stops on the canal directly in front of the house. No photography is allowed.

Soothe Your Spirit

Take your time walking through this house, see the original diary, and use what you learn as a lens for gaining a larger perspective about how one person might make a difference to those who have no voice.

A Deeper Look

The house that hid the Frank family dates to 1635, built by Dirk van Delft with the canal-facing façade renovated in 1739.

243. The House of Peter

CAPERNAUM, GALILEE, ISRAEL

*And Jesus walking by the sea of Galilee, saw two brethren, Simon called Peter, and
Andrew his brother, casting a net into the sea: for they were fishers. And he saith unto
them, Follow me, and I will make you fishers of men.*
—Bible, Matthew 4:18–19

Capernaum, a small fishing village on the coast of the Sea of Galilee,
was home to brothers Peter and Andrew who worked in their
father's fishing business until called by Jesus to become fishers of men. In
modern times, Franciscans built an octagonal church with a glass viewing
platform over Peter's house, which is said to be the place where Jesus
healed Peter's mother-in-law of a fever, cured a paralytic lowered through
the roof, and stayed when in the area.

If seeing this holy site would help you release something or give you
hope, come to the House of Peter. Capernaum is about 9 miles from
Tiberius, capitol of Galilee, and is easily reachable by car or bus from
Tiberius. Visit the site as a self-guided day trip, or with a guide or as part
of a bus tour.

Soothe Your Spirit
Make a vow at the holy site affirming what you want to release. Later, put
some grains of salt into your palm and mentally repeat the statement of
release before tossing the salt away.

A Deeper Look
Peter's house is situated near an ancient home church with writing about
Jesus in Aramaic, Latin, Greek, and Syriac on the wall, as well as references
to Peter in graffiti.

244. Memorial to the Murdered Jews of Europe

BERLIN, GERMANY

I can feel the sufferings of millions and yet, if I look up into the heavens, I think that it will all come right, that this cruelty too will end, and that peace and tranquility will return again.
—Anne Frank (1929–1945), German Jewish diarist

This touching memorial, designed by Peter Eisenman, consists of 2,711 gray stone slabs of different sizes and shapes without any markings of names, dates, or places. Eisenman wanted the design to create a sense of disorientation, instability, and groundlessness. It took ten years for Germans to approve a fitting memorial to the Jews who died before and during World War II as part of Hitler's extermination plan, but when construction on the memorial was completed in 2004, it covered an astonishing 205,000 square feet (4.7 acres).

If honoring those who died because of their spiritual and cultural heritage would have a special spiritual meaning to you, visit the Holocaust Memorial in Berlin. It can be found at Cora-Berliner-Strasse 1, in the heart of the city, between Potsdamer Platz and Brandenburg Gate.

Soothe Your Spirit

As you walk through the memorial and museum, take pictures, let fresh impressions and feelings sink in, and use them as departure points in a journal to write about ideas of religious tolerance.

A Deeper Look

Below the field of concrete pillars is an underground museum.

245. National Cathedral

WASHINGTON, D.C., UNITED STATES

Death is not the greatest loss in life; the greatest loss is what dies inside us while we live.
—Norman Cousins (1912–1990), American essayist

America's Episcopalian National Cathedral with its lofty vaulted ceiling, exquisite stained-glass windows, exhibit of state flags, exterior flying buttresses, elegant carvings, and statuary, fulfilled Pierre L'Enfant's vision to create a grand house of prayer for national purposes. The cathedral has served as the sanctuary for the nation's final goodbyes to four U.S. presidents.

If you want to say a final goodbye to a friend, a leader of our nation, someone in service, or someone working for a community's greater good, visit the National Cathedral. Located at 3101 Wisconsin Avenue, N.W., in Washington D.C., the easiest way to get there is by car from downtown. Take Massachusetts Avenue north to Wisconsin and turn right. The cathedral sits on the right.

Soothe Your Spirit

Sink into the peace of this national house of worship that welcomes people of all faiths. Let your heart mourn its loss and say a final prayer of goodbye. Go home and plant some forget-me-nots in a pot with some soil in honor of your loved one. The flowers come back year after year.

A Deeper Look

In keeping with the medieval belief that only God is perfect, the cathedral was built with flaws of intentional asymmetry.

246. San Fernando Cathedral

SAN ANTONIO, TEXAS, UNITED STATES

For death is no more than a turning of us over from time to eternity.
—William Penn (1644–1718), Quaker and visionary

The gorgeous focal point of this old Texas cathedral, built in 1738, is an ornate gold tabernacle of the Crucified Christ and the Holy Spirit, surrounded by heart-stopping retablos (devotional paintings based on church art) of saints, believed to have been created in Seville, Spain. A majestic statue of King Ferdinand III of Spain, namesake of the cathedral, appears to stand as guardian and protector of the sanctuary's beautiful treasures: shrines to Our Lady of Candlemas, patroness of the Canary Islands, and Our Lady of Guadalupe, a reliquary containing the relics of the "Heroes of the Alamo," and a coffin engraved with the Lone Star that holds remains of the fallen soldiers.

If your heart is heavy over the loss of a soldier and praying would lighten your spirit, come pray in the San Fernando Cathedral. It is located at 115 Main Plaza, in the downtown area between Highways 10 and 37.

Soothe Your Spirit

Let the grief wash over you. Pray to the Lord and his Holy Mother to help you bear the burden of loss. Give thanks when you feel your heart growing lighter and the weight of grief shifting.

A Deeper Look

It was from the tower of San Fernando that General Antonio Lopez de Santa Ana ordered the dropping of the red flag to start the battle of the Alamo.

247. Peace Memorial

HIROSHIMA PEACE MEMORIAL PARK, HIROSHIMA-SHI, HIROSHIMA PREFECTURE, JAPAN

Rest in peace, for the error shall not be repeated.
—Inscription on the Hiroshima Peace Memorial Park cenotaph

The Hiroshima Prefectural Industrial Promotion Hall, a four-tiered building with a wire dome crown, escaped the atomic bombs dropped in 1945 even though it was only a few yards from ground zero. The building's dome (referred to by some as the "Atomic Dome") is a bookend for the other memorial on the opposite side of the park—an inverted U-shaped cenotaph bearing the names of the dead.

Whether your ancestry is Japanese or you would like to pray at this site, come to Hiroshima Peace Memorial Park located at 1–2 Nakajima-cho, Naka-ku, Hiroshima-shi (Hiroshima City), Hiroshima-ken, Japan. It is open daily, except December 29 through January 1. The Hiroshima International Airport is about 31 miles east of the city. Hiring a taxi is the easiest way to get to the site.

Soothe Your Spirit

Visit the park on the anniversary of the bombing. On August 6th at 8:15 A.M., the moment of detonation, join others in the observed moment of silence to honor those who lost their lives, those who are maimed, and those whose lives will never be the same. Pray for peace.

A Deeper Look

The Hiroshima Memorial Museum was established in 1955 and also includes a memorial for the children who died in the bombing. Despite objections by China and the United States, the Hiroshima Peace Memorial was listed in 1996 on the World Heritage List.

CHAPTER 10

DEEPENING FAITH, TRANSFORMATION, ENLIGHTENMENT

You are here to realize your inner divinity and manifest your innate enlightenment.

—Morihei Ueshiba, (1883–1969),
Japanese founder of aikido martial art

248. The Golden Temple

AMRITSAR, PUNJAB, INDIA

Give up your selfishness, and you shall find peace; like water mingling with water, you shall merge in absorption.
—*Shri Guru Granth Sahib*

The Harmandir Sahib, or Golden Temple, is the holiest, most exquisite shrine in the Sikh religion with elaborate gold gilding and white-marble walls, precious-stone floral inlay, and richly patterned floors. Its atmosphere of reverence and devotion befits a sacred sanctuary whose name means "abode of God." Sitting on an island surrounded by the Amrit Sarovar (Pool of Immortal Holy Nectar), the temple houses the eternal spirit of the Sikh founder, Guru Nanak, who preached that spiritual enlightenment could be achieved through meditation on God's name.

To appease your spiritual hunger or to find deeper meaning in your spiritual life, visit the Temple. Take a flight into Amritsar International Airport, and then a bus, a taxi, or a cycle-rickshaw to the temple. Allow several hours to explore the compound and the Temple of God (Hari Mandir), beautifully adorned with verses from the Sikh's holiest book, the *Granth Sahib*.

Remove your shoes and wash your feet in the wading pool before entering the temple. Dress respectfully and cover your head (scarves are provided). Do not consume alcohol, cigarettes, or meat while on the premises. Photography is not permitted inside the shrine.

Soothe Your Spirit

Read a sacred verse at random from the *Granth Sahib*, considered the living embodiment of the Sikh gurus and their sacred teachings. Contemplate the deeper meaning of the verse and let it guide you through your day.

A Deeper Look

Construction of the temple began in 1574 and was completed in 1604 when the holy book was installed. The temple was designed with four entrances to symbolize Sikh's welcome and acceptance of all who enter.

249. Glastonbury Tor

GLASTONBURY, SOMERSET, ENGLAND

The only words that ever satisfied me as describing Nature are the terms used in fairy books, charm, spell, enchantment. They express the arbitrariness of the fact and its mystery.
—G. K. Chesterton (1874–1936), English essayist, novelist, and poet

*R*ising above the wispy fog like a delicate prayer veil that covers the face of the English market town that is its namesake, Glastonbury Tor soars 557.6 feet above Somerset and has been a holy site, perhaps since the Neolithic era, according to anthropologists. At the top are the ruins of two old churches of Saint Michael and a fifteenth-century tower so tall you can view three English counties—Somerset, Dorset, and Wiltshire.

Whether you are interested in self-discovery or want to feel the powerful transformational energies of Glastonbury Tor, visit England's smallest city and its environs, which include an abbey long associated with Arthurian legend, the relics of Saint Patrick who ended his days at the abbey, and Joseph of Arimathea, who purportedly took his nephew Jesus there on pilgrimage.

Soothe Your Spirit

Walk in silence along the steep path or follow the complex labyrinthine course to the summit of Glastonbury Tor. Sit and listen to your breathing as it slows. When you are completely calm, feel the subtle vibration of energy around the site and pray to the ancients for close attunement with the infinite and progress toward self-realization.

A Deeper Look

The discovery of two bodies in coffins dated to 1191, supposedly those of King Arthur and Queen Guinevere, has spurred the belief that the legendary court of King Arthur and the Knights of the Round Table may have been here, but the site is also associated with the religion of the Iron Age Celtic people.

250. Mahabodhi Temple of Bodh Gaya

BIHAR, INDIA

The greatest gift is to give people your enlightenment, to share it.
—Siddhartha Gautama, the Buddha (563–483 B.C.), father of Buddhism

The *stupa* (bell-shaped tower) of the red-brick Mahabodhi Temple, Buddhism's most sacred shrine, finds resonance in four small towers thrust upward as if to pull the ancient Indian sky to Earth made holy when the Buddha achieved enlightenment under a *Bodhi* tree. A massive gold statue of Buddha in the Earth-touching *mudra* (symbolic gesture) occupies the temple's inner sanctum as if it had been sitting in that *asana* (yoga position) for the last 2,500 years since Siddhartha Gautama achieved self-realization and became known as the "Awakened One."

If you desire enlightenment, visit the temple in the village of Bodh Gaya where you can sit, pray, even walk in meditation. The trip from Gaya to Bodh Gaya is 13 miles, easily traveled by a daily deluxe bus service, with time to gather your thoughts before entering the Buddhist sanctuary, visiting the tree, or studying the exquisite images of Buddha carved in the walls.

Soothe Your Spirit

Walk alongside the Cankamana (Cloister Walk) where the footsteps of the Buddha are marked with rounds of carved lotuses to indicate where he walked back and forth in meditation. Inside, study the silk-draped gilded Buddha seated serenely before a turquoise background. In this holy sanctuary, before the altar and ghee lamps, offer heartfelt prayers to develop the compassion of a bodhisattva for those who suffer. Pray for the blessings of the Buddha to guide you in your quest for enlightenment.

A Deeper Look

A section of stone railing from the first century B.C. was added as an enclosure of the small, simple shrine that Emperor Ashoka had built in the third century. You can still make out images of imaginary beasts on the railing medallions.

251. Bete Giyorgis Church of Lalibela

ETHIOPIA, AFRICA

All loves should simply be stepping stones to the love of God.
—Plato (429–347 B.C.), Greek philosopher and mathematician

When Ethiopian king Lalibela envisioned building a New Jerusalem in the twelfth century, he created a complex of rock-hewn churches in Roja. The eleventh church, the incomparable Bete Giyorgis (Saint George's), was built as a beautiful memorial to him by his widow from a single slab 40 feet down and shaped into a Greek cross with a large access trench encircling it.

If you are in a spiritual slump or rut, shake things up with a visit to Lalibela. Visit this World Heritage Site for Christmas or Timkat (the Orthodox celebration of Epiphany). Travel from Addis-Ababa by air to Lalibela's new airport. Or, take the bus (it's a two-day trip with a stopover). Outside the airport, take a minibus or horse-drawn cart.

Women are not allowed in the room where the saint/king's relics are kept, and only the priests are allowed in the inner sanctums of the churches where the rituals take place. Wear comfortable walking shoes with traction to avoid slipping in the passageways.

Soothe Your Soul

Explore these Orthodox churches on your own, or with a guide who can ask questions for you. Soak up the ambiance of this religiously oriented community with more than a thousand priests and unusual sanctuaries dating to the twelfth century, and you might just feel a shift in your spiritual perspective. Pray for deepening faith and transformation at each church, or at one that draws you more than the others.

A Deeper Look

To strengthen his power against his adversaries, King Lalibela may have built his monolithic churches in part to garner the support of the medieval Ethiopian Orthodox Church.

252. Yamunotri Temple

YAMUNOTRI (LOWER HIMALAYAS), INDIA

The Vedas teach that the soul is divine, only held in the bondage of matter; perfection will be reached when this bond is burst and the word they use for it, therefore, Mukti —freedom; freedom from the bonds of imperfection, freedom from death and misery.
—Swami Vivekananda (1863–1902), Indian spiritual leader

The Yamunotri Temple, honoring the Hindu goddess Yamuna, sits buttressed against the massive rock of the lower Himalayas at an altitude of 10,614 feet. The temple is a daylong trip from the cities of Haridwar, Rishikesh, or Dehra Dun and another 8.1 miles from Hanuman Chatti (where the road ends). With its simple pitched roof construction supported by stone columns, the temple houses the black stone *murthi* or, image representing the goddess associated with sanctity, purity, and the holy Yamuna River, whose promise to those who bathe in her glacial waters is to be spared a painful death.

If you want to undertake a spiritual purification pilgrimage to deepen your meditation practice, come to the Yamunotri Temple to pay your respects. From Hanuman Chatti, take a jeep to Janki Chatti and then rent horse, a palanquin (covered sedan chair), or walk to Yamunotri.

The temple is closed to the outside world from November to May.

Soothe Your Soul

Enjoy a dip in a glacial pool or a soak in the hot springs near the temple. Bring along a small bag of rice to dip into the boiling hot spring and take as an offering to the goddess for blessing. Make the customary bow before the rock pillar before entering the temple. Sit absorbed in meditation.

A Deeper Look

The source or birthplace of the Yamuna River and seat of the Goddess Yamuna is the Champasar Glacier, stretching out below the Banderpoonch Mountain.

253. Church of Our Lady

BRUGES, BELGIUM

Listen to your life . . . Touch, taste, smell your way to the holy and hidden heart of it because in the last analysis all moments are sacred moments and life itself is grace.
—Frederick Beuchner (1926–), American writer and theologian

The art inside the Church of Our Lady in Bruges speaks to the soul. While Michelangelo's *Madonna and Child* beckons worshipers to remember the humanity of his subjects, the painting of the crucified Christ by Van Dyck evokes the suffering of Jesus, and the cenotaphs of Charles the Bold and his daughter who died at age twenty-five demonstrate that life can end in an instant and induce contemplation of life's moments as sacred.

If you want to discover your spiritual core or to see sacred art, visit this site. The church is located at Onze-Lieve-Vrouwekerkhof Zuid. Take the train from Brussels to Bruges (60 minutes). The E40 connects Calais and Ostend to Bruges, as does the train. Autocars l'Elan provides shuttle-bus service four times daily to Bruges from Charleroi airport.

Soothe Your Spirit

Use your senses to see the potential for transformation or deepening faith in your life. Make this your prayer: "Holy One: Teach me to listen to my life. Bless my vision that I may see all moments of my life as sacred. Let me live in gratitude and appreciation for this blessed gift of grace."

A Deeper Look

Michelangelo created the *Madonna and Child* for the Cathedral of Siena, but when the cathedral couldn't pay for it, Bruges merchants Jan and Alexander Moscroen purchased it in 1506.

254. Tsuglag Khang Temple

DHARMASALA, HIMACHAL PRADESH, INDIA

Do not dwell on the past, do not dream of the future, concentrate the mind on the present moment.
—Siddhartha Gautama, the Buddha (563–483 B.C.), father of Buddhism

When the Dalai Lama and his government were forced to flee Tibet after the Chinese annexation in 1959, His Holiness established his headquarters in Dharmasala, a former British summer retreat in a lush pine and deodar forest in India. The Tsuglag Khang Temple, the most important outside Tibet, enshrines three magnificent statues: a gilded Shakyamuni Buddha, Avalokiteśwara (Buddha of Compassion), and a statue of Padmasambhava, long venerated as Tibet's great Tantric leader. These three statues link the Tibetan refugees with their great religious and cultural past as they transform their lives in India.

If you desire to experience a transformative shift in your thinking through Tibetan Buddhist practices and meditation, come to Dharmasala where the Dalai Lama and thousands of Tibetan refugees have constructed cultural, religious, and educational institutions. From Delhi, there is a direct bus to Dharmasala or take the train from Delhi to Pathankot and then take a bus, car, or taxi to Dharmasala.

The best times to visit are during the dry months, March to June or September to October.

Soothe Your Spirit

Enter the new prayer hall that displays the Kalachakra tantra cycle in stunning frescoes. Turn the prayer wheels as you circumambulate the hall with fellow Buddhists, pilgrims, and tourists. Find a quiet corner for meditation and prayer and indulge yourself. Experience the peace within, fully present in the moment.

A Deeper Look

The Dalai Lama's compound is located in an area of McLeod Ganj, or Upper Dharmasala, which is actually 5.5 miles up from the town center.

255. The Cave of the Apocalypse

PÁTMOS, GREECE

Write the things which thou hast seen, and the things which are, and the things which shall be hereafter . . .
—Bible, Revelation 1:19

When Roman emperor Domitian exiled Saint John the Divine in A.D. 95 to Pátmos, an arid Greek island sandwiched between Fourni, Leros, and Ikaria in the Dodecanese chain, the saint took refuge in a cave on a rocky hill and began to dictate his astonishing dreams and apocalyptic visions to his disciple Prohoros. The cave became the Cave of the Apocalypse and the words became the Revelation of Saint John the Divine, the last book of the New Testament.

Whether you desire a rejuvenation of your spiritual life or a total spiritual transformation, come to Pátmos and sit in the cave. Take a hydrofoil plane from the airports on Samos, Kos, or Leros or catch the ferry from Piraeus—a nine- to ten-hour trip to Pátmos. It is possible to take the ferry from other islands of the eastern Aegean or Dodecanese chains. Reach the cave on foot from Skala (a bit of walk), catch one of the buses that follow regular routes through the villages, or drive your rental car.

Soothe Your Spirit

Sit on a bench inside the cave, close your eyes, and open your heart. Let the energy of this holy place transform you, rejuvenating your spirit and filling your heart with Divine love.

A Deeper Look

Guides will tell you about what to see in the cave: icons, rock formations, niches, droplets of ancient water sealed inside volcanic rock. However, tourists and pilgrims are welcome to sit, pray, and meditate.

256. Bathing Ghats

VARANASI, UTTAR PRADESH, INDIA

The Ganges front is the supreme showplace of Benares . . . soaring stairways, sculptured temples, majestic palaces . . . human life everywhere, and brilliantly costumed . . .
—Mark Twain (1835–1910), American writer and humorist

*H*alfway between Delhi and Calcutta, the city of Varanasi (or Benares) bears witness to the throngs of pilgrims from all over India whose daily ritual or sacred pilgrimage is to dip their bodies into the holy Ganges for purification and divine blessings. For over 3,500 years, this vibrant city has been a spiritual heart and religious and cultural capital of India.

If you would like to see this ancient Indian spiritual tradition of ritual purification for healing and absolution, visit the Bathing Ghats of Varanasi at dawn. You can reach the city by air from Delhi or other major Indian cities, or by rail; there are two railway stations, Varanasi Junction and Kashi. Remove your shoes at the Ghats out of respect for the sacred rites performed here. No photography, especially of the Indian women bathing, is allowed.

Soothe Your Spirit

Hire a boat to take you out into the river to observe this ancient tradition: purification of body, mind, and spirit in water and light. As the *jyoti* or light of a new day breaks, look toward the sun and intone the sacred sound of A-U-M, the sound of the subtle vibration that eternally exists in the cosmos, according to Hindu belief.

A Deeper Look

Cremations are also performed in certain areas of the Ghats. Tradition holds that when the ashes of the departed are put into the Ganges, their soul attains eternal peace.

257. Pyramid of the Sun-Teotihuacán

MEXICO CITY, MEXICO

The conscious mind may be compared to a fountain, playing in the sun and falling back into the great subterranean pool of the subconscious from which it rises.
—Sigmund Freud (1856–1939), Austrian psychologist

The Pyramid of the Sun, one of the three largest pyramids in the world, towers 215 feet over the Mexican landscape. A sacred stone monument, according to some theories, it is dedicated to the Great Goddess, one of two main Teotihuacán deities. The cave beneath the pyramid may have been associated with the human emergence (from the "womb") and the clover leaf–shaped chambers off the cave may have been the sacred site of water and fire rituals.

If you want to visit an ancient site to feel its energy, this is it. The nearest airport is in Mexico City. Take a bus from Mexico City's north bus terminal; Autobuses Teotihuacán travel between the site and the town every thirty to sixty minutes, or purchase a coach tour from various tour businesses or hotels in Mexico City.

Soothe Your Spirit

Meditate on top of the pyramid. Imagine warm energy running from your tailbone to the top of your head on the right side of your spine and cool energy returning from the top of your head to your tailbone on the left side. Do several cycles.

A Deeper Look

A second pyramid, the Pyramid of the Moon, is connected to the Pyramid of the Sun by the roughly mile-long Avenue of the Dead. The most visited archaeological sites in Mexico, both were once plastered and painted red and covered in magnificent murals; today only the natural color of the stone remains.

258. Ales Stenar (Ale's Stones)

KÅSEBERGA, SWEDEN

We should build with the stones we have.
—Swedish proverb

*T*his Swedish megalithic monument, an enigma similar to Stonehenge, consists of fifty-nine stones that form the shape of a boat on the green plains of southern Sweden near the fishing village of Kåseberga. Scholars have determined the approximate creation date of the monument was at the end of the Nordic Iron Age or roughly 2,700 years ago. They speculate that the stone formation could have been an ancient burial site, a monument to the Vikings (who believed death was a journey into the unknown), or possibly the earthly stone ship of the sun-god Heimdall of the ancient Scandinavians. The position of this ship on Earth in relation to celestial bodies in heaven has implications for measuring the transit of the sun, cycles of the seasons, and winter and summer solstices.

If you are curious about the spiritual beliefs of the ancient peoples who constructed the megalithic monuments or would value time in quiet reflection in the serene, cool climate of southern Sweden, visit Ales Stenar. There are bed-and-breakfast establishments in Kåseberga and hotels in nearby Ystad. Take bus 322 (June 17 to August 20) or drive from Ystad to Kåseberga and then walk from the parking lot uphill to the stones.

Soothe Your Spirit

Read about Ales Stenar in preparation for seeing the monument. As you walk around the monument, reflect on the ancient builders of the megalithic monuments (there are many in Sweden), as well as the Vikings, and what relevance their spiritual beliefs might have for you.

A Deeper Look

The Ales Stenar monument is over 219 feet long. At the solstices, the ship's bow and stern are aligned to the position of the sun.

259. Chapel of the Ascension

JERUSALEM, ISRAEL

And he led them out as far as to Bethany, and he lifted up his hands, and blessed them.
And it came to pass, while he blessed them, he was parted from them, and carried up
into heaven.
—Bible, Luke 24:50–51

A brick octagonal chapel with a dome marks the sacred site on the Mount of Olives where, according to tradition, Christ ascended into heaven forty days after the Resurrection. The chapel was built over the ruins of Byzantine and Crusader structures in a brick-wall enclosure dotted with hooks that once secured the tents of pilgrims, who gathered to commemorate the Ascension, and safeguards an imprint of Jesus's foot in stone.

If you have been thinking about the "footprint" one human life leaves in the lives of others or want to contemplate the meaning of Jesus's human body ascending into heaven, start the process in this chapel. It lies east of the main road that runs along the top of the Mount of Olives in the suburb of al-Tur and is easily reachable from Jerusalem by bus 37 and the Mount of Olives' bus 75, taxi, or car (there is parking near the entrance).

Soothe Your Spirit

Light a candle next to the sacred foot imprint, and read Mark 16:19 and Acts 1:9–12 from the New Testament. Reflect on the metaphorical "footprint" that Jesus left behind in the lives of those who remained and consider the idea of ascension of the soul, using the spiritual or religious discipline that most appeals to you.

A Deeper Look

The Ascension of Christ has been celebrated since the fourth century. The Chapel of the Ascension is both a Christian and Muslim holy site; in fact, the Islamic-style dome reflects that in the thirteenth century, the shrine was a mosque.

260. Puerta de Hayu Marca

OR AMARU MERU'S DOORWAY (GATE OF THE GODS), PUNO, PERU

The forest is not a resource for us; it is life itself . . . the only place for us to live.
—Rigoberta Menchú Tum (1959–), Guatemalan rights activist for indigenous people and Nobel laureate

Thirty-five miles from Puno, on the shores of sacred Lake Titicaca, juts a mysterious landscape of rock formations that resemble buildings and other structures; sometimes unexplained balls of light appear. But the most puzzling feature of this amazing landscape, known as the "City of the Gods," is the door cut into a massive block of bedrock with a smaller doorway carved into the bottom; local Indians call it a "gateway to the lands of the gods."

Whether you want to experience higher consciousness through contact with the magnetic energies of ancient holy places or are intrigued by the mysterious sites of ancient civilizations, visit Puerta de Hayu Marca. The nearest airport is Manco Càpac in nearby Juliaca, but many visitors arrange their trip through Lima. Trains run three times a week from Cuzco or Arequipa to Puno and buses travel daily among the three cities. Contact tour agencies in Puno for a local guide.

Out of respect for the local people, do not take their pictures; they believe photographs pull out their souls.

Soothe Your Spirit

Some people who have knelt in prayer in the ancient doorway feel dizzy or as if they were flying (sensations similar to meditation or a dream), suggestive of transitioning into higher consciousness. If you experience these sensations, declare your intention to manifest larger-than-life dreams of transformation and enlightenment, drawing upon the Inca's sacred wisdom.

A Deeper Look

According to local legends, the great heroes passed through Puerta de Hayu Marca to meet their gods and embrace immortality; in rare instances, they returned with the gods to revisit their kingdom on Earth. This is also called "Spirit Forest" for the strange rock formations that archaeologists believe were carved by an ancient civilization.

261. Mount Shasta

SHASTA CITY, CALIFORNIA, UNITED STATES

Doubt makes the mountain which faith can move.
—Proverb

○♪acred to numerous Native American tribes, more than 100 New
Age sects, the Rosicrucian Order, and a Buddhist monastery, this
holy mountain at the southern end of the Cascades straddles the California-
Oregon border and has been continually inhabited for 9,000 years. Today,
more than a New Age mecca, it might be more appropriately described as
a holy New Age epicenter following the Harmonic Convergence of 1987
when more than 5,000 spiritual people from around the world gathered to
pray and meditate on world peace.

If you want to transform yourself or the world, visit Mount Shasta to
jump-start the process. Take Highway 5 to Shasta City and pick up Everitt
Memorial Highway to Bunny Flat Trailhead. There, at 6,860 feet, enter
onto trails to the summit, or enjoy the verdant meadows (in summer) and
the shimmering waterfalls.

To enter the wilderness areas, you will need a permit; contact the
Ranger District office at (530) 926-4511 for information on getting a
permit.

Soothe Your Spirit

Hike the mountain trails until you find a place where you'd like to meditate
upon the mountain that New Age practitioners believe is a sacred energy
vortex. Tune into Earth's energy and dive deeply into meditation, opening
your heart to messages, inspiration, or changes.

A Deeper Look

Mount Shasta supports more than 400 species of wildlife.

262. Prambanan Temple

CENTRAL JAVA, INDONESIA

Enlightenment is not imagining figures of light, but making the darkness conscious.
—Carl Gustav Jung (1875–1961), Swiss psychiatrist

*C*alled the most beautiful Hindu temple in Indonesia, the Prambanan Temple complex actually contains many temples, including three dedicated to the Hindu trinity of Brahma, Vishnu, and Shiva, the Creator, Sustainer, and Destroyer, respectively. With its various lovely temples, astonishing panels of relief depicting the story of the Ramayana, and a magnificent tree of life, the Prambanan Temple stands as a masterpiece of tenth-century sacred Hindu architecture.

If you want to deepen your faith or experience the centuries-old holy temple art, visit Java's Prambanan Temple. The temple is located approximately 11 miles from Yogyakarta.

Allow for a full day to see this temple and arrive early as crowds of tourists are already arriving at 9:00 A.M. (the temple opens at 6:00 A.M.). The nearest airport, Yogyakarta, is about 6 miles from Prambanan and serves Jakarta, Bali, and Singapore. There is also direct bus service to the temple complex through Transjogja, running about every twenty minutes from Malioboro Street in Yogyakarta. Taxis will also take you to the complex. Once you are at the temple, there is a miniature train to take you around if you find the walking too strenuous.

Soothe Your Spirit

Choose a place to meditate, possibly the serene and sheltering temple garden, and, using a one-two-three count for three breaths, intensify and lift your consciousness with each inward breath, attaching to it a Divine name as you breathe out.

A Deeper Look

The complex once held 237 temples in three zones: outer, middle, and inner; the latter is considered the most holy of the three.

263. Yosemite Chapel

YOSEMITE NATIONAL PARK, NORTHERN CALIFORNIA, UNITED STATES

The clearest way into the universe is through a forested wilderness.
—John Muir (1838–1914), Scottish-born American naturalist

After the National Sunday School Assembly raised enough funds in donations, mostly from schoolchildren, construction began on a small, New England–style church with a single spire in 1879. Although it has been moved from its original location near the Four Mile Trail, Yosemite Chapel, the oldest constructed structure in Yosemite National Park, sits in a picturesque area of Yosemite Valley with awe-inspiring views of gorgeous wilderness. Spectacular waterfalls, verdant forests, astonishing cliffs, giant sequoias, and breathtakingly beautiful mountain peaks stir the spirit beyond comprehension.

If you long for renewal by communing with the Divine in the beauty of nature or in an exquisite natural setting, visit the chapel in Yosemite. By car or coach, take Highway 120 or California State Highways 41 or 140 to Yosemite National Park. Learn more at *www.yosemitevalleychapel.org/*.

Highway 120 is subject to closure in the winter when Tioga Pass is impassable (usually November though late May).

Soothe Your Spirit

In this chapel, vow to make your worship regular, joyous, and intimate, and then commune with the Divine often throughout the day(s) as you roam, hike, camp, and relax in this stunning natural setting.

A Deeper Look

Yosemite became a U.S. national park in 1890 and receives 4 million visitors each year (mainly during the summer). Half Dome, one of the peaks, rises 4,000 feet above the valley floor, making it a world-renowned landmark that visitors love to photograph.

264. San Miguel de Huejotzingo

HUEJOTZINGO, PUEBLA, MEXICO

Certain thoughts are prayers. There are moments when, whatever be the attitude of the body, the soul is on its knees.
—Victor Hugo (1802–1855), French poet, playwright, and novelist

*P*rior to the Spanish conquest of Mexico, Augustinian, Dominican, and Franciscan clerics arrived in Mexico from Spain in the early sixteenth century to convert the indigenous people and to establish fortress monasteries on Popocatepetl, Mexico's second-highest mountain peak and an active volcano. The medieval church of San Miguel de Huejotzingo (dedicated to the Archangel Michael) features magnificent murals and carved niches for statues. The most astonishing piece is the sixteenth-century altarpiece depicting numerous scenes of Christ's life by Flemish painter Simon Pereyns.

Whether you would enjoy a spiritual retreat in colonial Mexico to deepen your faith or want to view some astonishing monuments, churches, and sacred art, visit San Miguel de Huejotzingo. The nearest international airport, Hermanos Serdán, is just outside Huejotzingo; the next closest is Benito Juárez in Mexico City. You can take the federal highway MEX 190 (16 miles from Puebla, 66 miles from Mexico City) or a coach tour. Additionally, there are buses and taxis from Puebla City to the town of Huejotzingo.

Soothe Your Spirit

Permit the exquisite, centuries-old sacred art to work its magic on your heart and spirit. Draw closer to the sacred images, reflecting on the symbolism and meaning of each lovely piece and let your thoughts turn to prayer.

A Deeper Look

This group of World Heritage Site monasteries, southeast of Mexico City and including San Miguel de Huejotzingo, cover 150 miles; three are in the state of Puebla and eleven are in the state of Morelos.

265. Duomo di San Martino (Cathedral of Saint Martin)

LUCCA, ITALY

Gloria in excelsis Deo ("Glory to God in the highest," from the Latin)
—Bible, Luke 2:14

The Lucca Cathedral of Saint Martin houses a unique sacred treasure: the miraculous *Volto Santo* (Holy Face), a carved wooden crucifix purportedly carved by Nicodemus, (who accompanied Joseph of Arimathea to ask Pilate for the body of Jesus); unable to carve the face, Nicodemus fell asleep and an angel finished the work. The richly decorated medieval cathedral in the heart of Lucca's old town also has a finger labyrinth, its grooves worn deep though centuries of tracings.

If the veneration of holy icons or relics deepens your devotion or you would like to work with your dreams for revelations, come to the Cathedral of Saint Martin, but plan on arriving for the *Luminara*, or candlelight procession, on September 13, honoring the carving of the *Volto Santo* (perhaps done by miraculous holy light and the hands of angels).

Soothe Your Spirit

Incubate a dream: eat lightly, take a bath before bed, and meditate with your head against the pillow, asking for spiritual elucidation or guidance in your dream, affirming that you will remember the dream upon awakening.

A Deeper Look

Hidden in a cave in the Holy Land for centuries, the *Volto Santo* was discovered by a bishop who had a revelatory dream. This carving displayed today is a thirteenth-century copy of the original that was splintered away by pilgrims desiring pieces of it.

266. Aradhana Gala (Meditation Rock)

MIHINTALE, SRI LANKA

You cannot travel the path until you have become the path itself.
—Siddhartha Gautama, the Buddha, (563–483 B.C.), father of Buddhism

When Indian Emperor Ashoka wanted to spread Buddhism, he sent his son Mahinda with yellow-robed Buddhist monks to the island of Sri Lanka on the full moon of June 247 B.C. While camping on the sacred mountain of Minhintale, they encountered King Devanampiya Tissa and gave him a sapling from the *Bodhi* tree of the Buddha's enlightenment. Today, Minhintale is considered the cradle of Sri Lankan Buddhism and meditation on the holy peak under the full moon in June is a popular pilgrimage.

If climbing a sacred mountain with a meditation rock on its peak and amazing panoramic views is the kind of pilgrimage that speaks to your spiritual yearning, come to Aradhana Gala in Mihintale. Get there early and give yourself plenty of time to walk the site and climb the 1,840 granite steps.

The mountain is about 5 miles from the bus depot of Anuradhapura, the nearest city.

Soothe Your Spirit

Carry the words of Buddha in your heart as you explore the upper terrace; then remove your shoes and climb to the white Mahaseya Dagoba (said to house a single hair and some ashes of the Buddha) before venturing up to the meditation rock and even beyond to the seated Buddha. Find a place to meditate, if only for a few moments—there are a couple of stone meditation slabs near where the eight or so monks live overlooking a pond and the mountains.

A Deeper Look

When Mahinda first introduced Buddhism to Sri Lanka, Buddhist monks at Mihintale would take refuge and meditate in caves during the rainy season.

267. Staronová (Old-New) Synagogue

JOSEFOV, PRAGUE, CZECH REPUBLIC

I marvel at the resilience of the Jewish people. Their best characteristic is their desire to remember. No other people have such an obsession with memory.
—Elie Wiesel (1928–), Romanian-born Jewish-American writer, Holocaust survivor and Nobel laureate

When the medieval Orthodox Alt-neu Schul (Old New Synagogue) was built in 1275, the Holy Roman Empire controlled Bohemia and Jews were not allowed to be architects, so the Franciscans executed the Gothic design of the one-story brick building with saw-toothed gabling. A red flag displaying the Star of David, given to the Jews of Prague by Charles IV, hangs above the wrought-iron *bimah*, or dais, in the center hall where men gather for services; women view services through wall slits in the corridor in keeping with Orthodox tradition.

If you desire to reconnect with your cultural and religious heritage or to see the oldest-surviving, still-active synagogue in Prague's Jewish Quarter (*Josefov*), visit this site. Open to visitors every day except Saturday and Jewish holidays, the synagogue is located at Cervená 2. The nearest international airport is Prague-Ruzynê Airport, located roughly 10 miles from the center of the city. Take the metro Green A Line to Staroměstská, or take Tram 17, and then walk toward the Law Faculty (Právnická Faculta).

Men must wear a yarmulke or hat (disposable hats are available); women need no head covering but must dress appropriately. No photography is allowed inside.

Soothe Your Spirit

Take note of the east wall where the Ark containing the holy Torah scrolls, holy words that have served the Jews attending services in this church since medieval times except when the Nazis occupied Prague. Reflect on your spiritual heritage and the rich legacy of your spiritual ancestors.

A Deeper Look

Writer Franz Kafka attended services at this synagogue and was barmitzvahed here.

268. Sri Ranganathaswamy Temple

SRIRANGAM, TRICHY, TAMIL NADU, INDIA

Lead me from the unreal to the Real . . . from darkness unto Light . . . from death to Immortality.
—"Gayatri Mantra"

One of the largest Hindu temple complexes in the world is dedicated to Lord Ranganatha, a reclining form of the Hindu deity Vishnu, sustainer of the universe. The stone carvings, bas-reliefs (or carved images that are slightly raised from the surface from which they are carved), and friezes, the horizontal bands that run across doorways and windows, adorn, embellish, and dramatize this colorful temple.

Whether you seek a spiritual awakening or transcendental states of consciousness, or love sacred Indian temple architecture, visit this 2,000-year-old temple where devotees believe that the Lord is ever-present. It is situated on Sri Rangam Island in the Kavery River, roughly 10.5 miles north of Trichy, and less than a mile from the Rangam railway station. The nearest airport is in Bangalore. Buses are available from major Indian cities, take a taxi or rental car, purchase a coach tour, or hire a car and driver from one of the hotels.

Come during the dry season (October through May), but start by 7:00 A.M. to avoid the crowds and the heat. Guides are available at the shoe depository. Photography is prohibited.

Soothe Your Spirit

Buy a flower, remove your shoes, and perform a *namaskar* (bow with hands folded in prayer) before the deity. Sit in meditation, inviting Divine inspiration to fill and sustain you. If you are a non-Hindu, visit the temple as a tourist; incorporate regular periods of silence in your spiritual practice; meditate on God as the Sustainer of All.

A Deeper Look

Millions of Hindus visit each year. The complex encompasses 156 acres and is the holy site of the enlightenment of Ramanujacharya, a pre-eminent Vaishnavi scholar.

269. Newgrange Passage Tomb

COUNTY MEATH, SLANE, IRELAND

When we quit thinking primarily about ourselves and our self-preservation, we undergo a truly heroic transformation of consciousness.
—Joseph Campbell (1904–1987), American mythologist, writer, and lecturer

About 3100 B.C., prehistoric inhabitants of Ireland created the Newgrange Passage Tomb, a sacred stone circle with a passage leading to a burial chamber similar to other ancient stone circles that align the circle's axis to the solstices. Here, a roof box allows the winter solstice's sunlight to align precisely with the center of the tomb's passageway. This sacred site might have been an ancient temple with ceremonial importance, but it has upright stones that are richly decorated in triple spirals and outside the tomb, twelve of thirty-five stones that once may have encircled the massive turf-covered mound remain with a solitary carved kerbstone at the entrance.

If you feel a connection to Celtic beliefs or a reverence for Earth, come to see the Newgrange Passage Tomb. Visits to Newgrange are by guided tour only (6 euros for adults, 3 euros for children) from Brú na Bóinne Visitor's Center, located on the south side of the River Boyne 1.2 miles west of Donore. To get to Donore, take the M1 heading north and exit at Donore, near Drogheda, and follow the signs.

Soothe Your Spirit

Find a stone that you feel attracted to; use it as a talisman to remind you that transformation can take millennia or it can happen in an instant.

A Deeper Look

Archaeologists say it probably took hundreds of people working twenty years or more to build Newgrange. The site is older than the Pyramid of Giza and approximately 1,000 years older than Stonehenge.

270. Dwarkanath Temple (Trilok Sunda)

DWARKA, GUJARAT, INDIA

The power of God is with you at all times; through the activities of mind, senses, breathing, and emotions; and is constantly doing all the work using you as a mere instrument.

—Bhagavad Gita

*A*ccording to legend, when the great-grandson of the Hindu god Lord Krishna desired to build a temple for the Lord, work on the five-story limestone-and-sand Dwarkanath Temple was completed in one night through divine intervention. This holy temple, punctuated by its sixty soaring columns and ornately carved spire, has long been a place of pilgrimage for the veneration of Lord Krishna, especially on the god's birthday: August 22 in 2011. Krishna's birthday (Krishna Janmashtami) occurs on the eighth day of the Sravana month on the Hindu calendar and although the date changes from year to year, Janmashtami usually falls between mid-August to mid-September.

The sanctuary is 90 miles from Jamnagar (the nearest city with an airport). Excellent roads, rail, and bus service link Jamnagar with Dwarka.

Soothe Your Spirit

Undertake a one-day fast (if it does not pose a health risk). According to the *Bhavishya Purana* (Hindu scriptures), pious people who fast during Janmashtami become free from the sins of seven births (Hindus believe in reincarnation) and reap the rewards of prosperity and their hearts' desires. Fold your hands in prayer, bow, and offer a flower before meditating in the temple.

A Deeper Look

Janmashtami is the celebration of Krishna's birthday when thousands of Hindu pilgrims descend on Dwarka. In some Indian cities, pots of butter and curds are hung between buildings, and human pyramids are formed to get at the pots, symbolizing Krishna's childhood pranks.

271. Jubilee Church
(La Chiesa del Dio Padre Misericordioso)

ROME, ITALY

And God said, Let there be lights in the firmament of the heaven to divide the day from the night . . .
—Bible, Genesis 1:14

*L*a Chiesa del Dio Padre Misericordioso (Church of God Our Merciful Father), also known as the Jubilee Church is an ultramodern, holy sanctuary constructed of white concrete-covered shells with three curvilinear "sails" that represent the Holy Trinity. Inside, a clerestory, or row of windows, on the ground floor and glass skylights between the shells bathe worshipers in natural, yet seemingly, mystical light intended to define the sacred space and impart an emotional link between worshipers and the Divine Source of All Light. This graceful, sleek church constructed in 2003 is a new paradigm for sacred space and yet has traditional elements such as a churchyard that serves as a piazza or gathering place for locals. Located at Via Francesco Tovaglieri in Tor Tre Teste (6 miles east from central Rome), the church is accessible by bus, taxi, or car.

Soothe Your Spirit

Adore God as light, seeing the natural light of the sanctuary as a metaphor for the Divine presence. Close your eyes to focus your inner gaze at the point between your eyebrows. Use your cycles of breath to lead you into meditation, dissolving the duality of *I* and *Thou* to merge the light of your soul into the all-pervasive light of the Divine.

A Deeper Look

The Jubilee Church was one of fifty new churches built in honor of the Vatican's Millennium project. It was the first church designed by Richard Meier, an American architect. The church cost $10 million and took five years to complete.

272. Mahaparinirvana Temple

KUSHINAGAR, KASIA, UTTAR PRADESH, INDIA

It is better to conquer yourself than to win a thousand battles.
—Siddhartha Gautama, the Buddha (563–483 B.C.), father of Buddhism

*I*n the temple, a massive bronze statue of Buddha lies on his side as if in the great sleep of *parinirvana* (passing away), draped in shimmering golden ochre (the color of renunciation). Pilgrims from around the world offer prayers of homage and veneration to the Enlightened One at Kushinagar—one of the four sacred sites of pilgrimage specified by the Buddha, along with Lumbini (his birthplace), Bodh Gaya (place of enlightenment), and Sarnath (site of the Buddha's first teaching). If you love the Buddha and his teachings about love, compassion, and liberation (enlightenment), visit the sacred site of his *parinirvana*. Take Highway 81 or 72.

Soothe Your Spirit

Take as much time as you need to absorb the ambiance and subtle sacred energy of the place where Buddha discarded the body he no longer needed. Be open to the inspiration that comes when you pray to the Buddha to help you in your spiritual quest.

A Deeper Look

The ruins of many ancient monasteries are located around the Buddha's Parinirvana Temple at Kushinagar near the border of Nepal.

273. The Church of Our Lord in the Attic (now Museum Amstelkring)

AMSTERDAM, NETHERLANDS

Certain thoughts are prayers. There are moments when, whatever be the attitude of the body, the soul is on its knees.
—Victor Hugo (1802–1885), French playwright, poet, and novelist

In 1661, wealthy merchant Jan Hartman purchased property in Amsterdam and created, in his home, a sacred sanctuary that included a magnificent altarpiece, *Baptism of Christ* (1716), by Jacob de Wit, marble columns, and sculptures of angels. Even though Catholicism was banned in Amsterdam in 1578, Hartman's love for his faith compelled him to allocate the top story of his dignified home as a Catholic church, hidden from view.

If you desire to deepen your religious beliefs, visit the church that one man's love for his faith built during a time of religious persecution, but know that the stairs to reach the church are quite steep.

The Church of Our Lord in the Attic, now a museum, is located at Oude Zijde Voorburgwal 40. Fly to Amsterdam's Schiphol International Airport and take a taxi, bus, or rental car to the church. It is also a short walk from Central Station / Damrak.

Soothe Your Spirit

Take at least an hour to see everything. Answer the question: What can I do, inwardly and outwardly, to deepen my love for my faith and to put my love into actions that will benefit others? Follow your answers with an action list.

A Deeper Look

The Church of Our Lord in the Attic served Amsterdam's Catholic community for 200 years before other churches were built.

274. The Golden Temple at Bylakuppe

KUSHALNAGAR, COORG DISTRICT, KARNATAKA, INDIA

Established in Self Realization, one is not moved even by the greatest calamity.
—Bhagavad Gita

*W*hen relations between the Dalai Lama and the Chinese government became strained in the 1950s, His Holiness fled to India and thousands of Tibetan Buddhists followed him. The oldest resettlement of Tibetan Buddhist refugees was in Bylakuppe, near the south Indian town of Kushalnagar; nunneries, monasteries, schools, and temples soon dotted the Indian landscape. But perhaps the most magnificent is the Golden Temple in the sprawling Namdroling Nyingmapa Monastery complex.

To follow the Nyingma tradition and deepen your faith through contact with Tibetan Buddhists, visit the Golden Temple and surrounding community. Buses connect Karnataka's second-largest city, Mysore, to Madikeri (18 miles from Kushalnagar). Then you must take a car, taxi, or auto rickshaw to Kushalnagar. From there, the auto rickshaw is the best way to get to Bylakuppe. If you drive, take State Highway 88 from Mysore to Madikeri, and follow the signs.

Soothe Your Spirit

Sit on one of the blue cushions inside this temple where the splendid Tibetan architecture pulls all but the most oblivious visitors into silence. Enjoy the visual peace imparted by gazing upon the three massive gilded Buddha and the altar adorned with flowers, incense, and ghee lamps. Meditate on transcendence.

A Deeper Look

Tibetan culture has taken root in Bylakuppe. Around the Golden Temple, Tibetan shops sell handcrafts, art, and food.

275. The Cathedral of Our Lady of Peace

HONOLULU, OAHU, HAWAII, UNITED STATES

First keep thyself in peace, and then shalt thy be able to be peacemaker toward others.
—Thomas à Kempis (1380–1471), medieval Catholic monk

The white-painted, unassuming Romanesque revival–style cathedral is a rare gem inside, with a beautiful marble altar and statue of Joseph (gifts from the Italian government). Built during a period of intense missionary work in Hawaii, the cathedral courtyard has a gorgeous gilded statue of Our Lady of Peace holding the Christ Child in her left arm, close to her heart.

If you seek a deepening of your faith and find sacred sanctuaries help you dive ever deeper into the ocean of divine peace, visit the Cathedral of Our Lady of Peace in Honolulu. Located at 1184 Bishop Street, the church is at the north end of Fort Street in the downtown business district. Park on the street or in the Century Square Building garage as parking is limited.

Soothe Your Spirit

Attend Mass and permit the sacred song of ancient hymns and Hawaiian prayers to soothe your cares, bathe your heart, mind, and spirit in peace, and intensify and deepen your faith.

A Deeper Look

The Cathedral of Our Lady of Peace is the oldest cathedral of continuous worship in the United States. In 1972, it was listed on the National Register of Historic Places.

INDEX

ABOUT THE AUTHOR

*M*eera Lester is an internationally published author of articles, columns, and books on a variety of topics ranging from history, health, and lifestyle to religion, travel, and culture. An avid traveler, she has visited twenty-nine countries and four continents in a quest to find inspiration and better understand the spiritual and cultural traditions of people of other nations. A recent transplant from Miami, Meera lives on a farmette in the San Francisco Bay Area city of Concord. Read more at *www.meeralester .com; www.mysacredworld.com,* or find her on Facebook.

jane
ON TOP

Getting Where Women Really Belong

- Trying to lose the losers you've been dating?
- Striving to find the time to be a doting mother, dedicated employee, and still be a hot piece of you-know-what in the bedroom?
- Been in a comfortable relationship that's becoming, well, too comfortable?

Don't despair! Visit the Jane on Top blog—your new source for information (and commiseration) on all things relationships, sex, and the juggling act that is being a modern gal.

Sign up for our newsletter at
www.adamsmedia.com/blog/relationships
and download a **Month-ful of Happiness!**
That's 30 days of free tips guaranteed to lift your mood!

ML   1/12